TO  UPHOLD  THE  WORLD

# To Uphold
# the World

A Call for a New Global Ethic

from Ancient India

BRUCE RICH

Beacon Press
BOSTON

Beacon Press
25 Beacon Street
Boston, Massachusetts 02108-2892
www.beacon.org

Beacon Press books
are published under the auspices of
the Unitarian Universalist Association of Congregations.

13   12   11   10      8   7   6   5   4   3   2   1

This book is printed on acid-free paper that meets the uncoated paper ANSI/NISO
specifications for permanence as revised in 1992.

Text composition by Wilsted & Taylor Publishing Services

Library of Congress Cataloging-in-Publication Data

Rich, Bruce.
    To uphold the world: a call for a new global ethic from ancient India / Bruce
Rich.
        p. cm.
    Reprint. Originally published in New Delhi by Viking in 2008 as: To uphold the
world: the message of Ashoka and Kautilya for the 21st century.
    Includes bibliographical references and index.
    ISBN 978-0-8070-0613-9 (alk. paper)
    1. Ashoka, King of Magadha, fl. 259 B.C.  2. Kautalya. Arthasastra.  3. Globaliza-
tion—Social aspects.  4. International cooperation.  5. Social ethics.  I. Title.
    DS451.5.R53 2009
    172'.4—dc22                                                        2009019503

IN MEMORIAM

DORIS MILLER RICH (1911−1998)

# CONTENTS

Talking about Emperor Ashoka, who was born more than 2,300 years ago (in 304 BC), H.G. Wells remarked: "Among the tens of thousands names of monarchs that crowd the columns of history, their majesties and graciousnesses and serenities and royal highnesses and the like, the name of Ashoka shines, and shines almost alone, a star."[1] The important question to explore is why the name of Ashoka "shines almost alone." He was, of course, a mighty ruler, the third Mauryan emperor of India. His territory was larger than that of any of his predecessors, stretching from Afghanistan to Bengal and beyond.[2] However, if Ashoka's name is still honored not just in India, but also, as Wells noted, "from Volga to Japan," and if "more living men cherish his memory to-day than ever have heard the names of Constantine or Charlemagne," this is not because of the size of Ashoka's empire or the powerful armed forces he once commanded. Rather, it is for the ideas that he championed and that formed the basis of his rule as well as his well-remembered deeds, like building hospitals and placing inscriptions written on stone across the country and abroad about the nature of good behavior and the regard we should have for each other. Ashoka's critically important role in spreading Buddhism abroad—to the east and the west and also down south to Sri Lanka—was related to this basic commitment.

Ashoka's transformation from a tough tyrant in the traditional mould into a ceaseless advocate of kindness and benevolence and into a public promoter of the social good was not only a decisive moment in Indian history, it was also accompanied by his reasoned reflections that were momentous at his time and remain very relevant to the problem-ridden world of today. The ambitiously grand title of Bruce Rich's book, *To Uphold the World*, relates to Ashoka's diagnosis of what was needed to make the world a good place. Ashoka's focus was primarily on good human behavior, and on the mutual respect and sensitive deliberation that can generate it.

The author tells the historical story with concision, highlighting interesting events in the lives of Ashoka and his ancestors. The reader is drawn powerfully into a long-gone world in which an extraordinary human being dramatically changed his own life and the world around him, led mainly by moral and political deliberation. Where Bruce Rich goes much beyond history is in his brief but pointed discussion of the contemporary relevance of Ashoka's ideas on how "to uphold the world." With ingenious political analysis at a very broad but clearly tractable level, Rich examines the relevance of Ashoka's approach to subduing the persistent violence and wars of our time, and also to remedying the deep inequalities and injuries that make our globalized world so badly in need of betterment. He discusses how Ashoka's particular ideas on social responsibility and his general diagnosis of the power and reach of behavioral improvement can help overcome a significant lacuna in contemporary thinking. If, as H. G. Wells noted, Ashoka's name continues to shine even after more than two thousand years, this is at least partly because Ashoka's ideas remain critically pertinent to the problems of our time.

Bruce Rich argues that the core of Ashoka's "essential doctrine" lies in the "reverence for life." "It is a principle," he argues, "that goes beyond the role of just treatment by human beings of one another: reverence for life means upholding the world." The underlying concept of fairness is based on Ashoka's basic belief, influenced by his conversion to Buddhism, in the fundamental value of all life. It is a shared reverence for life that can, according to this approach, make everyone behave spontaneously in a responsible and considerate way, without the compulsion of forced good behavior.

However, Bruce Rich also discusses how Ashoka's pointer to the potency of good behavior based on reverence for life is in fact an incomplete guide to what the world needs. In contrast with Ashoka's focus on human behavior, Kautilya, who was the principal adviser to Ashoka's grandfather Chandragupta, the first Mauryan emperor, and also the author of the celebrated fourth-century-BC book *Arthasastra* (translatable as "Economics," or as "the discipline of material wealth"), put his emphasis on building up and making use of social institutions. This was based evidently on Kautilya's conviction that people could be made to behave well only through the force of restraint, punishment, and well-devised incentives.

Kautilya's political economy was based on his understanding of the role of institutions in successful politics and the limits they can helpfully impose on behavioral license. It is an approach that, Bruce Rich argues, can importantly supplement Ashoka's vision, which concentrates on reflective behavior, rather than on an institution-based behavioral straitjacket. Ashoka's desire to transcend the institutional limits may have been in some tension with his realism, so that something of the "fierce Ashoka" had to remain, as Rich notes, in the later Ashoka as well. This "imperfection" in Ashoka's practical reason has an element of a "tragedy," as Bruce Rich notes, pointing out that "Ashoka's success and his failure were very much tied up with the Kautilyan system of administration in the Mauryan Empire." Indeed Ashoka did rely substantially "on the Kautilyan system, while in important respects trying to go beyond and infuse it with a different ethic" (see chapter 7).

This is a subject on which much more work can be fruitfully done, following up and scrutinizing the points that emanate from Rich's book. Ashoka was an early advocate of the need for everyone to follow good rules for discussion and debates. His inscriptions included a kind of a beginning of an ancient version of the nineteenth-century "Robert's Rules of Order." Ashoka argued, for example, for "restraint in regard to speech, so that there should be no extolment of one's own sect or disparagement of other sects on inappropriate occasions, and it should be moderate even in appropriate occasions." Even when engaged in debating, other points of view "should be duly honored in every way on all occasions."

Robert's rules are, of course, requirements that are meant to be forcibly imposed on the participants, whereas Ashoka's general approach is one of convincing the participants to behave in certain ways. Could Ashoka escape the need for enforced rules? Did he try it in practice, rather than just advocating it in theory? We do not know enough about what happened in Ashoka's own arrangements for debating encounters to be quite sure. For example, how was order kept in the apparently highly fruitful deliberations in the huge Buddhist council—it was the third since Buddha's death—that Ashoka hosted in his capital city of Pataliputra (now called Patna), where participants from different regions argued with each other on social as well as religious points of view? Ashoka's support for public reasoning is rightly celebrated (it can be seen even as a part of the gradual evolution across the world of the traditions of deliberative democracy), but there are issues of interest about the mechanisms behind the practice of public reasoning on which we know, as yet, too little.

If there are interesting historical questions that we can ask in following up Bruce Rich's work, there are some philosophical questions of importance that can also be raised. This includes the appropriateness of the formulations standardly used in theories of justice in modern political philosophy. Inspired by Hobbes and Kant, and led in our time by John Rawls, the typical understanding of the demands of justice in contemporary Western philosophy tends to take the form of focusing primarily on social institutions. Indeed, in the Rawlsian "theory of justice as fairness," the demands of justice are defined overwhelmingly in terms of "just institutions."[3] Kautilya would have seen this institutional approach to be on the right lines (even though his own substantive theories were quite different), but Ashoka placed his focus instead on just behavior, rather than just institutions, and this can involve a huge departure from the overwhelming institutional concentration in mainstream theories of justice. And if it is the case, as seems plausible enough, that human behavior is influenced both by ethical reflections and by prudential calculations (taking note of carrots and sticks), then should the diagnosis of "just institutions" not be more linked with the variability of behavioral norms (and the deliberative basis of human conduct) than we can find in mainstream theories of justice today?[4]

Bruce Rich has given us a highly readable book on the importance and reach of some arguments in ancient India, and on their relevance for global problems today. The book fulfills some of our curiosities and whets our appetite for asking more questions, and we have reason to be very grateful to Bruce Rich for each of these achievements. I feel very privileged to have been given the role of introducing this important and enjoyable book to the general public.

AMARTYA SEN
Harvard University and
Trinity College, Cambridge
July 2007

PREFACE

This book was first published in India in early 2008, months before the recent global economic crisis. The severity and unexpectedness of the crisis have only accentuated for more and more people the realization that a global economy requires a global ethic. We live on an increasingly crowded planet, bound ever more tightly—at times uncomfortably—together in a world system turbocharged by global information networks and the Web. Yet the very forces that link for the first time in history the fate of every human on the planet to every other, have accelerated the dissolution of traditional sources of social authority and historical identity, spurring powerful countermovements to reconstitute community and form shared projects based on common values. At the same time a global order that one-sidedly prioritizes unleashed market forces over other social values has created a profoundly unstable world, a world not only of increased inequality, but one literally where the viability of whole societies, nations, and democracy itself can be put at risk.

Many of the contemporary critiques of globalization are grounded in a shared realization that a global economy calls for a global project of justice. Traditional national politics and the reorganization of all social values around markets cannot hold together the 6.5 billion inhabitants of a small planet.

How can we uphold such a world? How can we imagine alternatives?

This book is a very personal reflection on these themes, inspired by the writings and lives of too of the greatest figures of ancient India, Ashoka and Kautilya. They are unquestionably two of the most extraordinary and, at least in the West, unappreciated figures in world history. The questions first addressed by Ashoka and Kautilya have become uncannily relevant to our current situation, where the tension between economics and ethics, issues of political realism and idealism, and the role of force and violence in international relations are played out on a planetary scale. Ashoka and Kautilya provide a powerful focus and metaphor for a reflection on the overarching challenge that confronts societies in an era of economic globalization: the need to found a civil and international order on principles that transcend the goals of pure economic efficiency and amoral realpolitik.

Ashoka provides a unique example of a world ruler who tried to put into practice a state, secular ethic of nonviolence and reverence for life, which he also extended to international relations. His edicts, inscribed on rock faces and pillars all over India in the third century BC, declare even today for all to see religious tolerance and equal protection of the laws, and announce the establishment of nature reserves and protected species. His empire at the time was arguably the world's largest, richest, and most powerful multiethnic state. Its trade and diplomatic links extended over most of what was then the developed world. If we take into account the slowness of land and sea travel 2,300 years ago, administering such a vast area was the equivalent to ruling the entire globe today.

Ashoka's great ethical leap rested on the most paradoxical of foundations, a centralized government in all likelihood organized and codified by Kautilya, chief minister of Ashoka's grandfather Chandragupta Maurya. One of history's greatest political geniuses, Kautilya wrote the world's first treatise on political economy, the *Arthasastra*. The *Arthasastra* proclaims accumulation of material riches as the chief underpinning of human society, and recommends amoral realpolitik as an effective political approach.

Ashoka is a unique and revolutionary figure in history who not only renounced armed force, but also, in the words of Arnold Toynbee, made "a complete break with his dynasty's and with every dynasty's traditional policy." But Ashoka did not abolish Kautilya's administrative system; he tried to infuse it with a transcendent ethos of respect for life that encompassed every aspect of everyday activity and was strong enough to hold together one of history's first multiethnic empires. *To Uphold the World* examines the message of Ashoka for today in a dialogue with our contemporary global dilemma, a dilemma where, in the words of George Soros, "the supreme challenge . . . is to establish a set of fundamental values that applies to a largely transactional, global society."

Chapter 1 introduces Ashoka, Kautilya, and the ethical/political dilemma of globalization in the twenty-first century. It engages the reader in some of the main themes of the book and flags the lines of further inquiry and development. Chapter 2 examines the historical world of Ashoka and Kautilya: who they were, what they did, and how they responded to the challenge of their epoch, which could be viewed as the first economic globalization. Chapter 3 examines in more detail the ethical/political challenge of contemporary economic globalization through various critiques of modern political economy, many of which embody reflections on the tension between ethics and the instrumental, utilitarian logic of most economic theory and practice. Chapter 4 sets out a summary and exegesis of Kautilya's thought, the first thinker in history to place economics as the overarching organizing principle and priority of society. Kautilya was the political genius behind the creation of the empire that Ashoka inherited. Chapters 5 and 6 detail the thought and history (both in the Buddhist mythical accounts and in his edicts) of Ashoka. Chapter 7 examines Ashoka's political/historical legacy, and chapter 8, the last chapter, tries to sum up and evaluate the ultimate significance of Ashoka—the first ruler to have attempted to put into practice a global ethic, a challenge that is all the more urgent at the beginning of this century.

Distinguished historians of India have written with much more authority and knowledge than I about the period in which Ashoka and Kautilya lived. What I have hoped to do is examine them as archetypes, metaphors, and sources of inspiration for thinking about the perennial conundrums of politics, economics, and ethics in the context of a globalized world.

Ashoka called his ethic Dhamma, related to, but quite distinct from, traditional South Asian Hindu and Buddhist concepts of *dharma* and *dhamma*. (*Dharma* is the older, Sanskrit term; *dhamma* is the term used in vernacular languages derived from Sanskrit spoken in the third century BC during the time of Ashoka, such as Prakit and Pali.) For non-Indian readers, *dharma* and *dhamma* are polysemic terms with no direct translation in English: they denote a number of interrelated concepts depending on the context, including ethics, law, morality, truth, duty, and virtue. Over the years I have worked as a lawyer and international environmental advocate to promote the adoption of environmental and social standards for the lending activities of international financial institutions, both public and private. As I continued my professional work—trying to promote dhamma or dharma for financial institutions, if you will—the salience and relevance of Ashoka and Kautilya as archetypes grew in my mind.

We live in a Kautilyan world, but more than ever need an Ashokan ethic.

Washington, DC, May 2009

Transliteration of Sanskrit terms poses a challenge for any work intended for the general public. In general, Sanskrit terms and names in the text do not have diacritical marks, for example, *Ashoka* instead of *Aśoka,* except that quotations in the text maintain the transliteration of names in the original work cited. Sanskrit terms are italicized when they are first mentioned in the text, and thereafter are not italicized. In the notes, I have sought to maintain the spellings of references as they were originally published, which in some cases include diacritical marks and in other cases do not. Scholarly readers may find errors and inconsistencies in transcription, for which I am responsible and apologize.

# CHAPTER I

# Past Present

The first years of the twenty-first century dawned to uncanny and unsettling tidings.

One might begin in Kandahar, southeastern Afghanistan. It is a place that few people in the Western world had heard of before late 2001. Following September 11, 2001, Kandahar, capital of the Taliban and al Qaeda terrorist network, became synonymous with medieval obscurantism and nihilistic fundamentalism. For a few months, Kandahar symbolized the intolerance, chaos, and terrorism that threaten to erupt anywhere with repercussions everywhere in an increasingly interconnected world. As our world has become economically globalized, it is paradoxically riven more and more by disparate, sometimes violent, quests for sources of social authority and cultural identity. The invasion of Afghanistan by the United States and allied troops overthrew the Taliban, but by the summer of 2006 they were resurgent, in Kandahar and elsewhere.

For the first time in history a single state, the United States of America, achieved worldwide economic and military preeminence. In the name of democracy, pluralism, and fighting terrorism, it launched a preventative war against Iraq and declared its unilateral preemption of international law and its exclusive right to military intervention around the globe. The initial success of armed invasion soon revealed itself as illusory as the forces of the world's hegemonic military power proved impotent to control a growing, monstrous conflict of sectarian violence.

One could recall November 1999, when fifty thousand protesters stormed through the streets of Seattle, challenging the World Trade

Organization and contesting a global system in which trade and economic interests of large corporations seem to have assumed an unprecedented influence over governments and societies around the world. Their message at the most basic level was clear: social and environmental values must be pursued by governments as ends in themselves, not as adjuncts or add-ons to profits, trade, and economic growth. By the summer of 2007 the London *Financial Times* announced on its front page that opinion polls it sponsored found that large majorities of citizens of industrialized countries viewed economic globalization as "an overwhelmingly negative force." [1]

By late 2008 the growing global economic crisis unleashed the fury of the most unlikely of protesters: aging leaders of the Protestant and Catholic churches around the world. The archbishop of York, England, attacked financial traders as "bank robbers," and his colleague the archbishop of Canterbury characterized the premises of the global economic system as "fundamentalism" and "idolatry." [2] Germany's senior Protestant bishop denounced the "culture of greed," personally attacking the head of the largest bank in the country. And the pope himself also condemned the global economic system, and, talking about the collapse of banks, he quoted Jesus in Matthew 7, "Beware of false prophets, which come to you in sheep's clothing, but inwardly they are ravening wolves." [3]

This cry was echoed by sometimes unlikely spokesmen. One of the world's richest financiers, George Soros, condemns "market fundamentalism" as a greater threat to human society than any totalitarian ideology, noting that "the supreme challenge of our time is to establish a set of fundamental values that applies to a largely transactional, global society." [4] If we want to make sense of our time, Hans Küng, perhaps the leading living Catholic theologian, tells us we are faced with a simple but overwhelming proposition: "A global market economy requires a global ethic." [5]

Our path to exploring these questions returns to Kandahar. In 1957 Italian archaeologists made an extraordinary discovery there. They uncovered an ancient series of rock inscriptions in the Greek and Aramaic languages. [6] In the inscriptions, a great and ancient Indian king calls for nonviolence, including abstention from killing animals, moderation, and honoring of parents and elders. Kandahar and most of present-day Afghanistan were part of this great king's empire. It was a multiethnic, multicultural state, built on fundamental values of tolerance, nonviolence, and respect for life, as the inscriptions in

Greek and Aramaic indicate. There was more tolerance and respect for life in Afghanistan millennia ago, at least for a time, than today.

The origin of our inquiry, and the source of the inscriptions at Kandahar, is halfway around the world and very long ago. There is a hill in southeastern India called Dhauli that visitors have climbed for over two thousand years. About six miles south of the capital of Orissa state, Bhubaneswar, it overlooks a quietly beautiful expanse of bright green rice fields stretching to the horizon. It is hard to imagine a more peaceful place, but in 261 BC the green fields ran red with the blood of more than a hundred thousand slaughtered by the armies of a great king.

Today visitors climb the hill to admire the view and examine the stone edicts the great king had inscribed near the top several years after the battle. When the British deciphered the inscriptions in the nineteenth century, they were astounded to find that they commemorate not a victory but the king's conversion to a state policy of non-violence and protection of all living things. The king declares his "debt to all beings," announces a halt to almost all killing of animals on his part for rituals and food, and proclaims the establishment of hospitals for both men and animals. He declares religious tolerance for all sects and sets forth principles of good government. Over the years, he commanded similar rock and pillar inscriptions to be made from Afghanistan (including Kandahar) to the southernmost extremes of India. The king's name was Ashoka, which means "without sorrow." Dhauli was the site of Ashoka's victory over the kingdom of Kalinga, the last and bloodiest conquest he needed to unify India.

In the other rock edicts scattered over various regions of India, Ashoka declares "profound sorrow and regret" for the slaughter at Dhauli, a remorse that led directly to his conversion to a new ethic, which he calls Dhamma, "the law of piety." On several sixty-foot pillars, which can still be seen today in different parts of the subcontinent, he declares the uniform and equal application of laws and the establishment of protected natural areas. Even more remarkable from a modern perspective is a pillar edict that amounts to nothing less than a protected species act, listing all the animals the king has declared as exempt from slaughter.

My visit to Dhauli in the summer of 1991 began a quest that resulted in this book. I was touring southeastern India, particularly Orissa. Bhubaneswar, Orissa's capital, is noted for the exquisite carving of its temples. I took a day tour organized by the state government and was the only foreigner among a dozen wayfarers from all over India squeezed into a rickety, un-air-conditioned minivan. In the typical fashion of such local tours, we managed to visit every temple in Bhubaneswar and Dhauli in a single long day.

The promise of knowledge and discovery of difference are the great inspirations for travel, but tourism begins with the opposite premise, namely, eliminating the unexpected and the unknown. Economic globalization is dominated by an instrumental, utilitarian logic that seeks to reduce transaction costs and inefficiencies, and thus to compress if not abolish time, space, and difference. Travel seeks precisely what is not global, but paradoxically provides perspectives from radically different places and times that can better inform our situation. For French philosopher Alain Finkielkraut, tourism "is the worldwide victory of those who have succeeded in bringing together the same with the same over those seeking to build a common world with a shared idea of humanity."[7]

To travel in India is to encounter difference, diversity, and history as in few other places in the world. The local tours organized by Indian states and cities are a traveler's—not a tourist's—experience, and not just because of the sometimes-rickety buses. The vast majority of participants are not foreigners but Indians themselves discovering their astonishing country, a discovery where place inevitably invokes history. The guides are often quirkily well informed.

So it was that I came to visit Dhauli in the later afternoon. Our guide observed, "Well, you know, in a way you could say Ashoka was the founder of my profession," and indeed one of the pillar edicts declares Ashoka's establishment of rest houses and roads to promote travel. It was the beginning of my personal discovery of a figure who seems to have at least partly anticipated by well over two thousand years what we think of as Western concepts of nature protection, equal protection of the laws, and respect for human rights. This book is a prolonged reflection prompted by that afternoon, by Ashoka and the values he proclaimed. It is a kind of travel book, a working journey to different places in time and thought. The traveler returns understanding better the place he or she started from.

A reflection on Ashoka raises perennial issues of realism versus idealism in politics, the practical extent to which nonviolence can be practiced in governance, and the long-term influence of mythical accounts of great historical figures, as opposed to the factual, historical impact their actions had in their life span. And Ashoka poses the more disturbing—and for our self-obsessed hubristic civilization—embarrassing question of whether there has been any lasting ethical progress in the behavior of states and societies over the past millennia.

Ashoka and his edicts are the past still present, physically, but also historically. A thousand years ago Ashoka's edicts were forgotten—for centuries, the ability to read the language of the edicts was lost. Now they are timely for the beginning of a new millennium, where economic globalization, a growing global quest for identity and community, and the specter of terrorism raise the deepest questions about the guiding values of the first-ever global civilization. And in the world at the beginning of the third millennium, the end that appears to trump all others—that more and more is the global organizing principle—is the economy, or, in its extreme form, market fundamentalism. Even in a time of crisis, when economic fundamentalism appears to be failing on its own terms, there is a collective failure to imagine alternatives.

We seem to live in an epoch that in important ways gives less primacy to the respect of life than the worldview of Ashoka. Contrary to perhaps what one would expect or hope, the richer our world becomes as an economic system, the more the collective imagination of those who rule seems to atrophy so that all common goals collapse into efforts to increase production and trade. It was perhaps Aristotle who first noted this pathology, writing in his *Politics*:

> While it seems that there must be a limit to every form of wealth, in practice we find that the opposite occurs: all those engaged in acquiring goods go on increasing their coin without limit....The reason why some people get this notion into their heads may be that they are eager for life but not for the good life; so desire for life being unlimited, they desire also an unlimited amount of what [they think] enables it to go on....these people turn all skills into skills of acquiring goods, as though that were the end and everything had to serve that end.[8]

## THE FIRST ECONOMIST

It is all the more thought provoking then that Ashoka's great ethical leap rested on the most paradoxical of foundations, the work of a man who wrote that "of the ends of human life, material gain is verily, the most important."[9] The author of these words was Kautilya, the chief minister of Ashoka's grandfather Chandragupta Maurya, who founded the dynasty under which Ashoka would, after the final bloody conquest of Kalinga, unite India for the first time. Kautilya was virtually a contemporary of Aristotle, but he seems to come close to taking economic means as ultimate ends, precisely the phenomenon Aristotle witnessed personally and warned about half a world away. In Indian myth, in fact, Kautilya is represented as Chanakya, the prototype of a wily chief minister and political adviser. It is probable that Kautilya was the organizing genius behind the autocratic, centralized state that Ashoka inherited and expanded.

One of history's first and greatest political thinkers, Kautilya wrote what was arguably the first treatise on political economy, the *Arthasastra*. *Artha* means wealth or material well-being; *sastra* can be translated as "science," so the *Arthasastra* is the Science of wealth, or quite literally, Economics. Kautilya interprets *artha* as the sustenance and wealth that men produce from the earth, and, to quote him directly, "that science which treats of acquiring and maintaining the earth is the Arthasastra." Kautilya is modern in seeing economic prosperity as both the underpinning and the goal of society and the state.

To understand Kautilya's remarkable originality, it is useful to recall that in traditional Hindu culture dating back to the second millennium BC, life was seen as possessing three goals: *kama*, the pursuit of sensual pleasure, artha, the pursuit of wealth, and dharma, spiritual good through the following of the right law and duty in harmony with the order of the universe.[10] Dharma in fact is that order and harmony, so following dharma means realizing spiritual good by conforming to the universal order.[11] In ancient Hindu society (as well as modern), this in practice meant conforming with the duties appropriate to one's caste and station in life. For Buddhists, who sought to transcend the caste system, it meant (and means) realizing and practicing the truth of Buddha's teachings about the nature of human life in the world. For individuals this truth is that life is transient and characterized by suffering, and that there is a personal path of understanding and compassion for all living things that enables us to transcend this suffering and achieve enlightenment.

Both the Hindu tradition and Buddhism view dharma as superior to kama and artha, as something that overarches them and includes them in a higher spiritual order. In this context Kautilya appears as a materialist revolutionary, for he states unabashedly that "material wellbeing (*artha*) alone is supreme...for spiritual good (*dharma*) and sensual pleasures (*kama*) depend on material wellbeing."[12] (Dharma, we shall see, has many meanings; for Kautilya, a ruler has the personal ethical duty, which is also an instance of dharma, to promote the welfare of the state and people, and in practice this means making artha the priority.) He is a very modern man; his modern political avatar would probably be Henry Kissinger. Kautilya, if reborn as an economist today, would be at home with his sensibility in any high-level international meeting of finance ministers.

Kautilya also urges a ruthless realpolitik. He explicitly advocates espionage, prostitution, betrayal, and duplicity in numerous forms, burglary, political assassination, ruthless opportunism, and a long list of other tactics to advance the interests of the state. But Kautilya's realism is technocratic rather than despotic; he expounds at length on the minutiae of taxation, irrigation, foreign policy, corruption and its prevention, and sustainable management of natural resources, all as means to assure the material and political well-being of society and the state.

Shortly after Kautilya's treatise was rediscovered and translated into Western languages in the early 1900s, social thinker Max Weber marveled that "in contrast with this document, Machiavelli's *Prince* is harmless."[13] According to Indologist Heinrich Zimmer, "Kautilya brought the whole historical period into being," of which Ashoka's reign was the apogee.[14] Thus, the quandary deepens. We know that much of Ashoka's governance—in fact the organization of the society he reigned over—was based on the worldview and even the specific recommendations of the *Arthasastra*. Yet he attempted to transcend the Kautilyan view of the world through a new social ethic and politics of nonviolence and reverence for life.

Following my visit to Dhauli in 1991, my own studies of Ashoka and Kautilya convinced me that they are archetypes of political thought and action, since both were powerful historical figures whose writings reflected what they were trying to put into practice. In Western political thought these archetypes have sometimes been characterized as the utopian and the realist,[15] or in the words of theologian Hans Küng, ideal politics and real politics.[16] Ashoka and Kautilya, and the values they stood for, seem to exist together in linked contradiction, two poles in human politics.

## ETHICS AND ECONOMICS

As the international debate on economic globalization and its social and environmental consequences grew in the 1990s, the messages of Ashoka and Kautilya are growing too in contemporary relevance and meaning. The award of the Nobel Prize for Economics to Amartya

Sen in 1998 marked an official recognition of the need to restore the recognition of the framework of values and ethics within which all economic and political action takes place. Sen has been a voice for precisely this perspective, and given his South Asian origins, it is no accident that in his own writings he refers to Ashoka and Kautilya as paradigmatic figures. In a series of lectures on ethics and economics given at the University of California in 1986, Sen observed that from its origins, economic thought can be divided into two schools, one that takes the "engineering," logistical approach, and the other that takes an ethical, moral, and political stance.[17] The engineering, technocratic approach is embodied by Kautilya and is indifferent to ultimate ends, or, rather, Kautilya asserts that promoting economic gain is the primary social and ethical goal. The problem then is of means, how to promote effectively more of the same. The ethical approach can be found in Ashoka, and Aristotle. The debate between the realist and the ethical approaches to governance, economics, and politics is one that periodically recurs throughout history. The debate on economic globalization and its discontents in the first decade of the twenty-first century is its reembodiment on a planetary scale.

In fact the ethical–political approach is found especially in Adam Smith, whose writings have wrongly been distorted and misappropriated to stand for the primacy of the free market as the basis of society. Smith, in his *Theory of Moral Sentiments* (less cited than the *Wealth of Nations* but even more critical for the underpinning of his thought), goes to great lengths to emphasize the moral and collective values that are essential for social cohesion, and he attacks in some detail those who advocate the primacy of economic utility. Sen has emphasized the renewed relevance of Smith's earlier work in the debates over the future of capitalism spawned by the global economic crisis. "It would be...hard to carve out from [Smith's] works any theory of the sufficiency of the market economy, of the need to accept the dominance of capital," Sen wrote in early 2009. In *The Theory of Moral Sentiments*, Sen observes, Smith "extensively investigated the powerful role of non-profit values" and argued that "humanity, justice, generosity, and public spirit are the qualities most useful to others."[18]

MYTH AND HISTORY

Although the memory of Ashoka and Kautilya remained present and alive for over two millennia in Indian and Buddhist mythology, the historical Ashoka was reconstructed only in the mid-nineteenth century, and Kautilya even later, when long-forgotten texts of the *Arthasastra* were found in South India in the early 1900s. The historical influence of the mythical accounts of Ashoka's life is immense. Preserved in sacred Buddhist texts from Sri Lanka and India to China, Korea, and Tibet, these accounts to this day underlie the social and political expectations of government and kingship all over Buddhist-influenced Asia.[19] According to John S. Strong, the translator of one of the most important Sanskrit Buddhist religious accounts of Ashoka's life:

> Buddhists everywhere have looked back upon the Asoka-of-the-legends as an ideal king. In...Sri Lanka, Thailand, Laos and Burma, he was and still is portrayed as a paradigmatic ruler, a model to be proudly recalled and emulated. Likewise, in China, Korea, and Japan, his legend inspired and guided a number of Buddhist emperors who conspicuously patterned their rule on his.[20]

We know that Ashoka sent envoys to spread the message of his law of piety all over the subcontinent, to present-day Sri Lanka and Burma, as well as to the Middle East and eastern Mediterranean, including modern-day Egypt, Syria, and Greece. At times history and myth are tantalizingly fused, since the mythical, religious accounts have clearly had a historical and social impact as great as, and arguably longer lasting than, what we can ascertain of the real, "historical" Ashoka. The political and historical legacy of Ashoka is still a real presence in Sri Lanka and Thailand, and this legacy, like that of many great historical and religious figures, has been misused by some for sectarian, violent ends.

The mythical accounts of Ashoka and Kautilya certainly add more depth, color, and paradox to their characters: both, for example, are reported as being extremely ugly and brutally ready to act on real and imagined slights to their physical appearance. We read that when Ashoka overhears some of the mistresses in his harem mocking his rough skin and ugly appearance, he has five hundred of them burnt to death. To emphasize perhaps the total turnaround brought about by Ashoka's religious conversion, Buddhist religious treatises portray him as extraordinarily brutal and sadistic in the earlier part of his life. He establishes a special torture chamber, known as Ashoka's Hell, to slowly kill innocent people. This myth reemerges as history when we read descriptions of visits to the putative site of Ashoka's

Hell (near modern-day Patna in Bihar state) by the Chinese Buddhist monks Faxian (Fa-Hsien) and Xuanzang (Hiuan-Tsang) in the fourth and seventh centuries AD, respectively, as part of their religious pilgrimage around India. Historically, we do know from Ashoka's own statement on the rock edicts that he killed one hundred thousand people at Dhauli and deported another one hundred and fifty thousand.

According to myth recounted in Buddhist and Jain[21] chronicles, Kautilya begins his plot to put Chandragupta Maurya on the throne when the last king of the preceding Nanda dynasty dismisses Kautilya from the king's court because of his ugly physical features—a mortal slight that feeds Kautilya's hunger for revenge. On his way back from the Nanda king's court, Kautilya encounters a group of boys playing on a dusty village common a game in which one boy pretends to be a king presiding over a court where he dispenses rewards and justice and appoints others as ministers and officers. Astounded, Kautilya adopts the boy as a foster son and has him educated at the great Buddhist university of Taxila (the ruins of which are still extant in Pakistan). The boy is Chandragupta.[22]

The memory of the mythical Ashoka and Kautilya is also present in modern India, where the popularized saga of Kautilya's life was made into an immensely popular television historical soap opera series in the early 1990s, *Chanakya*. The numerous episodes portray Chanakya's shrewdness and cunning realpolitik. Archaeological symbols associated with the Ashoka of history were resurrected to serve as symbols of the new Indian state in 1947. The capital of one of the most beautiful Ashokan pillars found at Sarnath (the site where the Buddha preached his first sermon) is the Indian state seal, reproduced on official documents, stamps, coins, and banknotes.

Kautilya lives too in the names of streets and neighborhoods in Delhi: the diplomatic neighborhood is called Chanakyapuri, and one can find Kautilya Marg (Kautilya Street). Before the rediscovery of the *Arthasastra* his name continued to live in Sanskrit literature; one of the greatest of ancient Sanskrit plays that have come down to us is the *Mudraraksasa*, "The Minister's Seal," written in the sixth century AD by Visakhadeva, a high official in the Indian court. The play recounts how over eight hundred years earlier Kautilya (or, in the play, Chanakya, Kautilya's alternate, mythical name) brilliantly and ruthlessly consolidates the power of Chandragupta. A leading economic columnist in India's leading weekly news magazine writes under the pseudonym of Kautilya, and independent India's first prime minister, Nehru, thought Kautilya to be a far more penetrating political thinker than Machiavelli.[23]

PERMANENCE AND PRESENCE

Indeed, the uncanny aspect of Ashoka's edicts is their very physical presence, their permanence as cultural and human artifacts. They are written on stone at numerous sites all over India, and have survived nearly 2,300 years. They are the first written documents in Indian history, and are among the earliest archaeological monuments that one may see in the subcontinent, since most construction prior to the Mauryan dynasty was in perishable wood, mud, or brick.[24] The great irony is that 2,000 years from now they, together with the hieroglyphics on Egyptian temples that have survived and a handful of other rock and stone texts from the ancient world, probably will still be legible and read by our descendants, whereas the more data our globalized digital society produces, the more ephemeral and short-lived it becomes.

New versions of computer operating systems are only compatible with their immediate predecessor, and perhaps the one or two immediate predecessors of their predecessors. Files written fifteen or twenty years ago on superannuated computers and obsolete operating systems are for practical purposes irretrievable. Critical scientific data only twenty years old are being lost, part of a process which Stewart Brand (creator of the *Whole Earth Catalog*) calls the digital dark ages.[25] The chances that a thousand years from now there will be at least some human beings who will know how to decipher the Prakrit vernacular Sanskrit of Ashoka's edicts may be considerably greater than the existence of any knowledge of CP/M, or Microsoft Windows 2003.

The physical remnants of the world's newspapers are also in danger of obliteration. In libraries around the world the physical copies of major and minor newspapers that have been preserved for the last century and a half are being willfully destroyed and replaced with microfilm or digital records. The likelihood that a thousand years from now the text of Ashoka's edicts will be physically accessible on the great rock inscriptions he left all over India may be greater than the survival of the text in any form of today's *Washington Post* or *New York Times*.[26]

The contrast between the physical permanence of Ashoka's

edicts and the flimsy transitoriness of the growing deluge of digital data is reflected in other artifacts of our civilization. Both Ashoka's message—his Dhamma, the law of piety—and the physical rock edicts themselves seem to have inspired for the better part of a millennium physical exertions by Indian emperors to build and repair for the long term. In western India in Gujarat state there is a small mountain range, with several peaks over three thousand feet, where one of the most complete Ashokan rock inscriptions can be found. The place, called Girnar, is also a sacred site for Jains who throughout the year climb the mountain while visiting various Jain temples en route. The Ashokan rock itself is housed in a small temple-like structure, but is rarely visited. It is nonetheless one of the most extraordinary written records in India, and indeed in all of history. Centuries later, two Indian emperors wrote additional inscriptions on the Ashokan rock to describe the history of a dam and artificial lake constructed by Ashoka's grandfather, Chandragupta, and strengthened and expanded under Ashoka. The first inscription dates from AD 150, already nearly four and half centuries after the reign of Chandragupta. It describes how the emperor Rudradaman undertook major repairs to the dam and irrigation system after it was damaged by an extraordinarily violent storm and heavy rains. Rudradaman goes into some detail about the task appearing so daunting that some of his own advisers opposed it, and notes that the repairs were paid for out of existing funds "without oppressing the people of the town or the province by exacting taxes, forced labor, donations or the like."[27] Three hundred years later another emperor, Skandagupta, records further repairs to the dam, again following heavy rains and storms, undertaken in the years AD 455–58.[28]

Thus, at Girnar, we have an astounding account of the nearly continuous operation and maintenance of a dam and irrigation system for a period of over eight hundred years. It is sobering to reflect that modern-day dams, in India and elsewhere, often have an estimated useful lifetime of less than sixty years because of the siltation of the reservoirs, poor maintenance, and intended obsolescence beyond the life span of a generation or two. In India today huge amounts have been invested in large dams and irrigation systems over the past forty years with the help of loans from the World Bank and other international agencies, yet many of these systems have never been fully completed, or are already losing their usefulness because of poor upkeep and planning. Perhaps there is something to be learned from the approach of Rudradaman, who directly links his enlightened governance to dharma—as historian John Keay notes, perhaps after the example of Ashoka—and, unlike current governments, undertook his infrastructure maintenance investments without new loans or taxes burdening the body politic.[29]

IMAGINING ALTERNATIVES

To encounter the thought and historical presence of Ashoka and Kautilya is also to encounter the truly subversive role of history in liberating us from the tyranny of the present. It is natural enough to take the world as it is given or appears as the only plausible social reality. In the post–Cold War debate on economic globalization there is much talk of the End of History and the End of Utopias. The globalized economy increasingly organizes human experience in a kind of eternal, virtual present, enveloped in electronic networks. It reorders the physical world and everyday life for growing numbers of individuals in networks of homogenized consumption, communication, and travel, in which one moment is not qualitatively different from another, nor one place different from another. Much has been written on its implications, for example by the Catalan social philosopher Manuel Castells in his three-volume opus, *The Information Age: Economy, Society and Culture*. Huge populations are increasingly excluded from this world, only appearing as irrational, inefficient, and above all unprofitable intrusions from another dimension. But these intrusions increasingly take the form of protest or, for the most excluded and violent, terrorism.

Imagining concrete social alternatives means positing an elsewhere. It is always difficult to imagine alternative societies or worlds that do not yet exist, but the past provides us with a store of human experience that can be truly subversive of the present. The social ruins of post-Taliban Kandahar appear not so bleak if we recall the Kandahar of Ashoka's time, for if values of nonviolence and ecumenism reigned there in the distant past, it is not unimaginable that they could also triumph in the future.

A leading American popularizer of Tibetan Buddhism, Robert Thurman, wrote in 1998 that the principles to be found in Ashoka's edicts could serve as the basis for a modern progressive "politics of enlightenment."[30] In fact, Ashoka himself came to power in a period that has certain analogies with our own, for the India of his time was one of the first examples of a large region undergoing large-scale and, for the times, rapid technological, social, and political change. It was a period marked by important advances in metallurgy; irrigated agriculture replaced less intensive cultivation. Urban populations were growing, and international trade routes proliferated. The increasing spread of markets and trade weakened smaller political units and states. India at the time of Kautilya still consisted of many smaller petty kingdoms and republics (historians have pointed out some parallels with Greek and Italian city states at the time of Pericles and Machiavelli) known as *ganas*, and Kautilya has specific recommendations on how to manipulate and subdue these political units.

Economic expansion and integration were accompanied by greater specialization in occupations, the rise of the precursors of merchant banking, and new forms of financial management, again analyzed by Kautilya. The originality of Kautilya in this regard continues to be discovered. Kautilya's *Arthasastra* describes the world's first customs tariff, one that a contemporary Indian analyst argues was, 2,300 years in advance, fully in conformity with the customs valuation principles of current international trade law as codified in the General Agreement on Trade and Tariffs (GATT)![31]

The Mauryan Empire was the political embodiment of internationalizing currents, a multicultural mix with important Persian and Greek influences. The Persian Empire occupied part of northwest India for over two centuries, from the mid-sixth century BC to the invasion of Alexander the Great in 326 BC. Mauryan architecture reflected Persian design, and Ashoka's penchant for inscribing rock and pillar edicts, though new for India, was a standard practice of Persian emperors. The Greek influence was the afterglow of the conquests of Alexander the Great and his successors, who set up Greek dynasties following Alexander's death, stretching from present-day Pakistan to the eastern Mediterranean. We know from several Greek and Roman historians that Ashoka's grandfather Chandragupta Maurya waged a war of liberation against Alexander's successors to rid India of foreign domination on its western front, and, according to Plutarch, Chandragupta as a youth even met Alexander personally. Ashoka himself may very well have been one-quarter Greek (the wife of Chandragupta was the daughter of the Greek king Seleucus Nikator, a general of Alexander the Great who reigned over a kingdom that included parts of present-day Pakistan).[32] There was clearly an unprecedented mixing of populations and cultures. In fact, the *Mudraraksasa* describes

Kautilya as helping to mobilize for Chandragupta's cause not only straggling Greeks and Persians, but also Scythians, Gurkhas, Cambodians, and Bactrians.[33]

Between 800 and 200 BC there was a unique period of worldwide psychological and spiritual transformation, a transformation that German philosopher Karl Jaspers called the Axial Age.[34] It was literally the axis or hinge of history, marking the psychological and spiritual coming of age of much of humankind. In the world's major civilizations—China, India, Greece, and the Near East—a simultaneous coming to self-consciousness and ethical spiritualization occurs: it is the time of Confucius and Lao-Tsu, the Upanishads and the Buddha, Zarathustra, the Hebrew Old Testament prophets, and the beginnings of Western philosophy from the pre-Socratics through Plato and Aristotle.[35] On one level Jaspers notes, "Rationality and rationally clarified experience launch a struggle against...myth....religion was rendered ethical."[36] Philosophers appeared and the emergence of speculative thought meant that "man becomes conscious of Being as a whole, of himself and his limitations."[37] On the political level, Jaspers points out, this uniquely creative ferment in its earlier and middle stages was associated with the existence of many competing small independent states and the expansion of trade in Greece, India, and China. History, governance, and politics for the first time become the subject of independent analysis—as we see in the case of Kautilya and his contemporary, Aristotle. Near the end of the period, in the fourth and third centuries before the Common Era, these small contending states and cities were consolidated into large centralized empires in China, Greece (under Alexander and his successors), and India, through the subcontinent's unification under Chandragupta Maurya and Ashoka.

The essence of the Axial transformation lay in the opposition of increasingly independent rational thought with existing myth and tradition. A new relation between society and religion evolved, one based, according to Karen Armstrong, on "the idea of a single universal transcendence...internalized spirituality...and practical compassion."[38] Although many peoples and cultures lay initially outside the Axial cultures—the relatively uncivilized peoples of northern Europe and the Amerindian societies of the New World, for example—Axial religions and ethics over the next millennia came to be the core values of nearly all peoples on the planet. The Axial period, Jaspers asserts, was the ethical coming of age of humanity, and Ashoka is one of its last great manifestations.

To a large extent, we are still attempting to live on the spiritual capital of the Axial period, a capital that is increasingly exhausted. The Axial world ethical systems were anchored in the belief in a universal transcendent reality and authority. They have lost over the past hundred years most of their following in the secular West, a loss of belief that with the spread of Western secular values, has extended over most of the globe. The rise of religious fundamentalism is a late twentieth-century phenomenon, a reaction against an increasingly pervasive global market secular culture. Fundamentalism, while claiming to revive religion, constitutes a defensive identity against global secular market values, while rejecting much of the universality and compassion of the great Axial ethical systems.[39]

Jaspers intimated, and many contemporary religious thinkers such as Hans Küng argue, that the social and cultural transformations associated with economic globalization have pushed us to the edge of a second Axial Age, which will and must lead to new values, ethics, and politics based on a new vision of universal transcendence. There is a tension between a world dominated by a market-based instrumental, transactional framework of social relations, and the need for a social ethic rooted in the transcendent, in a greater reality beyond immediate knowledge, control, and use.

Perhaps nothing embodies the international, value-grounding spirit of the Axial period better than the capital of the Ashokan pillar at Sarnath, which was almost miraculously resurrected in 1947 as the symbol and seal of the newly independent Indian nation. Sarnath, literally, the Deer Park, is a few miles outside the Hindu holy city of Varanasi. Here, Buddha gave his first sermon, setting into motion the sacred wheel of Dharma, the law and order of the world, and the doctrine that achieves knowledge of that order. We can still see this resplendent pillar capital in the museum at Sarnath, and the original column itself—inscribed with Ashoka's edicts—was over seventy feet high, and was still standing nearly a thousand years later in the seventh century AD when the Chinese Buddhist pilgrim Xuanzang described it in the account of his travels to Buddhist sites and monasteries in India. The Ashokan pillar capital at Sarnath is the symbolic embodiment of the spreading of Ashoka's secular law of piety beyond the farthest reaches of ancient India. The capital is crowned by four majestic lions on a disclike plinth, symbols of imperial authority; on the side of the plinth four wheels separate a lion, a bull, an elephant, and a horse, each symbolizing in India since the second millennium BC the four corners of the known earth. The lion is the north, the bull is the west, the elephant is the east, and the horse is the south. The wheel motifs separating each animal are a prehistoric sun symbol, a Mesopotamian symbol for God and knowledge, as well as for Buddhists symbolizing the wheel of Dharma. The same motif, the Ashokan wheel of the Sarnath capital, stands today in the middle of the Indian flag, evoking four millennia of history.

The recurrent emphasis on authority and law facing in the four directions also embodies the ancient Indian ideal, refined by Buddhism, of the *chakravartin*, the universal king who pacifies and reigns over the four corners of the world. *Chakravartin* literally means "setting the sacred wheel in motion," from the Sanskrit roots for wheel, *chakra*, and *vrt*, to turn or revolve. In Buddhist tradition the universal emperor is a worldly homologue to the Buddha, and just as there can be different reincarnations of the Buddha, there appear chakravartins at different times in history.[40] It is the mythical image of Ashoka as the world-liberating chakravartin in Buddhist religious texts that has had the profound historical impact on ideas of governance and kingship all over Asia mentioned above. Yet the pillar capital at Sarnath shows that the myth was partly based in fact, or at least in the image that Ashoka wished to present of himself. Ashoka, after the slaughter at Dhauli, became fully convinced of the truth of Buddha's teachings[41] and promoted a secular Dhamma or law of piety as a new ethic to guide his kingdom. But most authorities agree that Ashoka's law of piety, while inspired by Buddhism, is a practical, secular social ethic quite distinct from Buddhist doctrine.

The plinth in turn stands on a bell-shaped lotus flower. Art historians have noted that that motif of heraldic animals on a lotiform bell is similar to the capitals of columns found at Persepolis, the great palace of the Persian emperor Darius the Great, with resonances dating back to more ancient Mesopotamian civilizations. The rather formal and imperial sculptural depiction of the lions is also similar to Persian sculpture of the same epoch. The animals on the side of the plinth are depicted in a much more lively and realistic style, typical of Hellenistic sculpture.[42]

The archetypal symbolic power of the Sarnath pillar capital, and the chakravartin ideal it embodies, can be seen in the fact that as late as the nineteenth century, the king of Siam was invested with a magic ceremony involving his perambulation of an artificial hill with fountains on each side embodying the same animals on the Sarnath plinth: a lion, a bull, an elephant, and a horse. According to art historian Benjamin Rowland, "The artificial hill in Bangkok was the world mountain Meru [a mythical mountain in Tibet], according to ancient cosmology towering like a pillar between earth and heaven; the four beasts stood for the four quarters and four rivers of the world, so that the whole structure was a kind of replica of the world system." [43] It is thought that both Persian and Greek artisans worked on and influenced the design of the capital, a design which embodied a new cultural synthesis that was uniquely Indian, one rooted in Ashoka's conversion to Buddhism and his attempt to create a common ethos for a multicultural empire. Societies, if they are to survive, need to recognize as an organizing principle and transcendent goal, something that goes beyond the short-term calculations of realpolitik and economic advantage. For Ashoka, this "something" was Dhamma.

A detailed analysis of the texts of the Ashokan rock edicts and columns reveals a remarkable system of governance and social organization. Paradoxically, most scholars agree that to understand Ashoka's reforms, the best complement to the rock and pillar edicts are the more detailed prescriptions of Kautilya's *Arthasastra*. Ashoka's reforms are not contradictory to Kautilya's system but build upon it and attempt to transcend it. Nevertheless, a certain tension always remains between the Ashokan ideal and Kautilyan realpolitik.

Both Ashoka and Kautilya assert that they are promoting dharma, which besides meaning law, virtue, duty, ethics, and truth, is based on the Indo-European root *dhr*, meaning "to hold, to bear, to carry." Dharma is an underpinning concept of South Asian civilization over the millennia, whose specific interpretation in specific contexts evolved over the centuries. There is a Hindu, pre-Buddhist conception of dharma, and a post-Ashokan, post-Buddhist Hindu reinterpretation. It is nothing less than an integrated conception of the structure of society and the world, and the duty of each human being in that structure in specific situations and roles. Much of this book is also an exploration of the inflections of dharma, and its contradictions. It is a dialogue with the past to better understand the questions we face concerning the relation of politics, ethics, and economics at the beginning of a new millennium.

Dharma, literally, upholds the world.

CHAPTER 2

# The Age of Transcendence

Our age, ever more obsessed with the present and the immediate, seems to have little time or use for ancient history. In the West, the history of the Indian subcontinent and its neighbors still seems to be a quaintly esoteric topic, despite the newly found infatuation for India's future as an economic superpower in the twenty-first century. Yet the cultural and social crisis of the epoch of Ashoka and Kautilya has important parallels for the dilemmas of today.

Ashoka and Kautilya can be seen as a culmination of the whole historical period of major economic, technological, and cultural change, not just in India, but in what was effectively the known world, stretching from the Mediterranean to China. India in Kautilya's and Ashoka's time—the fourth and third centuries BC—lay at the center of this world. Traditional accounts of Western history in this period tend to focus on Greece, which, through the short-lived, meteoric conquests of Alexander the Great in the 320s of the fourth century BC, extended its cultural influence all the way to India. But India throughout most of this time was arguably the richest and most powerful economy on Earth, rivaled earlier only by ancient Persia, whose imperial preeminence lasted less than a hundred years, dominating the late sixth and early fifth centuries BC.

By the middle of the first millennium BC the Brahmin (referring to the priestly caste) social and religious order had pervaded most of the subcontinent for the better part of a thousand years. This order is also often called Vedic, referring to the ancient ritual and mythic literature—*Vedas*, meaning "knowledge"—of the Indo-European pastoral peoples who migrated to the subcontinent around 1500 BC.[1] It emphasized the strict respect of caste and the critical role of priests in performing rituals and animal sacrifices to uphold the social and religious order, based on what were by then already age-old customs and mores of agricultural and pastoral life in village India. It was a society already guided by the grand concepts and religious–philosophical ideas that characterize South and Southeast Asian civilization—of which the two most important were perhaps dharma (law, ethics, order, what upholds the world) and karma (causality in the broadest sense). An interpretation of karma as the influence of actions in past lives on the present justified the Brahmin social system, particularly caste. But new political and economic forces were brewing, which set the stage for a period of intense religious and philosophical questioning, culminating religiously in the Buddha and later, politically, in Ashoka.

In the first millennium BC much of the subcontinent was organized in numerous clan affiliations and networks that formed oligarchic tribal republics governed by assemblies; membership in the governing assembly was restricted to members of the same clan or confederacy of clans. By the sixth century BC these clan-republics had coalesced, according to tradition, into sixteen larger states.[2] By the early decades of the fifth century BC, one state would emerge preeminent: Magadha. Magadha's rise was favored both by aggressive and ambitious monarchs and clear natural advantages, such as its critical control of the central-eastern Ganges valley and access to territory (through marriage and conquest) that was rich in forest resources, ivory, and iron and copper ore deposits.[3] By the late fourth century BC Magadha was an imperial force to be reckoned with.

Meanwhile, in the west a new imperial state also flourished, the Achaemenid (Persian) Empire, founded by Cyrus the Great in 559 BC. Cyrus, and his successor Darius (reigning from 521 to 486 BC), built the largest empire the world had seen until then, extending from Egypt and conquered Greek cities in Asia Minor to the Indus River, with tributary states extending farther east to the Jhelum River. Trade flourished between the two imperial states.[4] Only a single pillar still stands from Chandragupta and Ashoka's palace, but it is a pillar in the style of Persepolis, the great palace of Darius built around 500 BC whose ruins still stand in southern Iran.[5] The pillar can be seen at the archaeological site of Kumrahar outside of Patna, the capital of today's Indian state of Bihar. Around 330–326 BC, following Alexander the Great's conquest of Persia and its northwest Indian territories, many Persian aristocrats and artisans fled to Magadha and played in subsequent years an important role in the increasingly cosmopolitan Mauryan state. Tushaspa, Ashoka's governor of what corresponds to today's Gujarat state, was "undoubtedly a Persian."[6]

The most important influence of the Persians on Ashoka may have been their extraordinary policy of religious and ethnic tolerance.[7] In 539 BC Cyrus conquered Babylon, at the time the richest, most populous city in the Near East. Cyrus issued a victory proclamation that has come down to us recorded on an inscribed clay barrel, the famous Cyrus Cylinder, excavated in the ruins of Babylon in 1879 and brought to the British Museum, where it remains today. It is a proclamation of justice, tolerance, reconciliation, and religious freedom. Cyrus announces that he frees the people of Babylon from the "shameful yoke" of slavery imposed upon them; he orders the return of the images of various gods of different peoples and sects to their rightful places and proclaims his support for the restoration of their temples. The proclamation of the Cyrus Cylinder is viewed by many as the first charter of religious freedom and human rights, and in 1971 the United Nations had it translated into all its official languages. A replica of the cylinder is on display in one of the corridors leading to the meeting room of the Security Council.[8] One cannot help but think of another leader of a dominant global empire (George W. Bush) who, like Cyrus and Alexander the Great, also invaded Babylon, putatively under divine guidance, in the name of freedom and tolerance. In terms of post-conquest planning and management, Cyrus comes off as much more successful. In the Cyrus Cylinder (lines 24–26) he declares, "My numerous troops walked around in Babylon in peace, I did not allow anybody to terrorize the country of Sumer and Akkad...I brought relief to their dilapidated housing, putting thus an end to their main complaints."[9]

Around the same time—mid-first millennium BC—a technological revolution centered in Magadha was transforming economic life: the transition from the Bronze to the Iron Age. The invention and use of iron ploughshares, hoes, and axes contributed to agricultural production. Iron technology also improved the quality and efficiency of the manufacture of everything from—in the words of a leading historian of ancient India—"the making of beams for ceilings to improving the structure of the chariot, cart and possibly even river craft. Interdependent technologies, such as the firing of superior pottery and the making of glass, were probably also tied into experiments to improve iron artifacts."[10]

These technological and economic changes fostered urbanization, greatly expanded trade, and led to the rise of new social classes—merchants, traders, a proliferation of artisans—that challenged the Brahmin orthodoxy, which was rooted in a simpler agricultural and pastoral life. Artisan and merchant guilds emerged as a new and powerful force in urban life.[11] Concentration of wealth in the new towns and cities also increased, weakening tribal clan relations and traditions of equality within the oligarchic ruling castes.[12] Rulers, who traditionally came from the Kshatriya (warrior) caste, were usurped by new dynasties of lower birth. Most notably, this occurred in Magadha, where at the beginning of the fourth century the Nanda dynasty, Sudras, of the lowest caste origin, seized control of the most powerful state on the subcontinent.

In China and Greece there were similar economic and political trends. The sixth and fifth centuries BC in China saw the rise of expansionist, rival states—Chu, Song, Jin, Qi, and Lu. Agricultural and administrative reforms in some states fostered greater prosperity, but civil wars raged, and, in the words of historian Karen Armstrong, "old political and social structures were disintegrating."[13] In Greece, the late sixth and early fifth centuries BC saw the displacement of "the descendants of Bronze Age aristocrats...by populist movements amalgamating clannish movements into democratic polities."[14] Subsequently, the expanding economic and trading power of various Greek city-states in Asia Minor, Greece itself, and Sicily spurred armed rivalries and wars.

New thinkers arose in China with new solutions to ethical and religious uncertainty, of which the most renowned was Confucius (551–479 BC), virtually contemporaneous with the birth of Western philosophy with the pre-Socratic philosophers in Greece (e.g., Heraclitus, 540–480 BC, and Parmenides, born circa 515 BC). And it was precisely in the latter half of the sixth century BC, during the years of their captivity in Babylon and subsequent liberation by Cyrus, that the ancient Hebrews experienced their most intense and revolutionary period of religious thought and ethical debate.[15]

In this same period in India, Magadha became a cynosure of cultural ferment. A new sense of individual consciousness emerged, and the old sacrifices and rituals lost their ability to convince a growing part of the population.

In Magadha, the Brahmin ideological center could not hold.

CULTURAL CRISIS AND CREATIVITY

The economic, social, and political changes in the Ganges Valley in the mid-first millennium BC led to nothing less than a counterculture, dropout movement of ascetics, wanderers, and thinkers who posed radical alternatives to the dominant Brahmin orthodoxy.[16] Some wandered alone, others congregated in loose associations following a teacher or guru. It was a time of extraordinary intellectual ferment; the tame media-ritualized discourses of what passes for public debate in industrially developed societies today might not favorably compare. According to historian Romila Thapar,[17] the main function of these wanderers and sects, "apart from acquiring knowledge, was to participate in discussion and debate. They were such an established institution that some of the towns and larger villages associated them with *kutuhala-salas*, literally places for exciting curiosity or interest," that is, public debating halls that were in parks or groves at the edge of towns. Some sects also tried to reassert, or reinvigorate Vedic orthodoxy. The culture of vigorous public philosophical debate became an important part of everyday life, with local rulers holding regular contests. These were not sedate affairs, but, in the words of one historian, "virulent, gladiatorial contests."[18] Women were active participants too: we hear of the account of four Jain sisters versed in one thousand different philosophical theses, wandering around India challenging anyone to win a debate with them.[19]

These sects included not only what we would think of as followers of differing religious beliefs but also different schools of philosophy. They came to be characterized as *astika* ("yes") sects that accepted or reaffirmed Vedic traditions, and the *nastika* ("no") sects that denied the authority of the *Vedas* and in some cases questioned the existence of any deities. *Brahmanas* and *Sramanas* are two other terms that later became current to characterize these contending currents of thought, corresponding roughly to those following and not following Brahmin traditions. From the sixth to the fourth centuries BC the differences and tensions between these groups, and the social classes that supported them, became more intense. From today's standpoint, the most important of the Sramana, nastika sects, were the Buddhists and the Jains. Respecting, reconciling with, and giving equal support to both Brahmanas and Sramanas are major aspects of Ashoka's promulgation of religious tolerance in his edicts.

Among the numerous materialist, atheistic sects, one of the most important, with many followers for nearly two thousand years until the fourteenth century AD, was that of the Ajivikas ("way of life"). The most famous Ajivika teacher, Maskarin Gosala, was a contemporary of the Buddha. Gosala taught that natural events and human actions were all bound in a chain of total predetermination, so that in effect there is no such thing as independent human agency, free will, or choice. Every sentient being achieves eventual liberation from the cycle of births through the same number of myriad reincarnations taking place during 8.4 million aeons (*mahakalpas*). Gosala is reputed to have said that "just as a ball of string will, when thrown, unwind to its full length, so fool and wise alike will take their course, and make an end of sorrow." [20]

One of the most intriguing questions posed by the proliferation of contending philosophical sects in sixth-century India is the question of cultural cross-fertilization with pre-Socratic Greek philosophy. French historian Alain Danielou observes that the Greek Christian Gnostic philosopher Clement of Alexandria (AD 150–215) "does not hesitate to say that 'the Greeks had stolen their philosophy from the Barbarians,'" and observes that already in the nineteenth century the German scholar Schroeder "noted that almost all the philosophical or mathematical doctrines attributed to Pythagoras [sixth century BC] were current in India at the time, in a much more developed form." [21]

These traditions are at odds with the one-sided, at times caricatural Western stereotype of ancient Indian thought as predominantly mystical and religious. Amartya Sen notes that Sanskrit "has a larger volume of agnostic or atheistic writings than in any other classical language." [22]

RISE OF THE PEACOCK DYNASTY

The cultural, social, and political turmoil of the age was compounded in the fourth century BC when a historical supernova bathed much of the ancient world in its intense but short-lived brilliance: Alexander the Great. Alexander conquered an area corresponding to the entire Persian Empire at its apogee in Cyrus's time, from Egypt to the Indus Valley, sounding its death knell, as well as sealing the long-drawn-out demise of the tribal republics in northwest India. After Alexander's death in 323 BC his surviving generals divided up his conquests, one of whom, Seleucus Nikator, asserted sovereignty from what is modern-day Syria to northwest India. The political upheaval caused by

Alexander's invasion and the subsequent fragmentation of his empire facilitated the rise of Ashoka's grandfather Chandragupta Maurya.

Starting from the northwest provinces and Punjab, Chandragupta launched a military campaign that succeeded in overthrowing the ruling Nanda dynasty in Magadha in 321 BC. He was able to recruit tribesmen whose livelihoods had been disrupted by the Greek-Macedonian invasion.[23] What is striking is how the ancient descriptions of these mountain tribal peoples parallel what we hear of the unruly tribal areas on the Pakistan–Afghanistan border that even today are not completely under the control of any state. The fourth-century-BC Sanskrit grammarian Panini characterized them as kingless gangs that live by arms, and the Roman historian Justin describes Chandragupta's recruiting efforts in the region as "collect[ing] a band of robbers."[24] Osama bin Laden is only the latest in a long series of rebels who have used these tribal areas in the northwest of the Indian subcontinent as a base.

Chandragupta was the first Indian king to enter the stage of world history, and it appears that he is mentioned in the firsthand accounts of the companions of Alexander—but these direct sources are lost. The most important ancient Greek account of India and its history, the *Indika*, was written by Megasthenes, the ambassador of Seleucus to Chandragupta's capital, Pataliputra, on the outskirts of modern-day Patna. The *Indika* is also lost to history but large portions of it are either quoted verbatim or paraphrased by many subsequent Greek and Roman historians. The classical accounts that have survived are mainly concerned with the life of Alexander or the geography of India, but we do learn that Chandragupta mustered a huge army to reclaim the territories in the Indus Valley that Alexander occupied and Seleucus sought to reclaim, and that the Nandas were of lowly birth and highly unpopular with their subjects. The Roman historian Curtis (first century AD) recounts a tale worthy of Shakespeare's *Richard the Third*: the first Nanda king was a barber in the court of his predecessor, became the lover of the queen (who is alleged to have been a former courtesan), conspired with her to assassinate the king, and then as guardian of the surviving child princes murdered them, too, paving his way to the throne and the founding of a new dynasty.[25]

Buddhist texts have Chandragupta descended from a Kshatriya clan called Moriya, meaning those from the place of the peacocks. In Jain accounts, Chandragupta was the grandson of the chief of a village of peacock breeders. In any case, peacocks have been found both at the base of at least one Ashokan Pillar, and sculpted in several places in railings at the great ancient stupa at Sanchi in central India, in carvings associated with the story of Ashoka's life. It would appear likely that the peacock was indeed the emblem of the Mauryan dynasty.[26] Chandragupta's rise, told in Buddhist and Jain chronicles, is very much linked to the ambition and skills of Kautilya. According to these sources, and the text of the *Arthasastra* itself, Kautilya appears to have been the political and administrative genius behind the rise of the Mauryan Empire, the creator of the system that Ashoka inherited and built upon.

In all of the Greek and Roman accounts where Chandragupta is mentioned, there is no reference to Kautilya. Our only properly historical text is the *Arthasastra* itself, which ends with Kautilya's personal claim that "This science [i.e., the science of wealth, *Arthasastra*] has been composed by him, who in resentment quickly regenerated the science and the weapon [military power] and the earth that was under the control of the Nanda kings."[27] So it is from the *Arthasastra* that we know Kautilya's thoughts and opinions. What we know of Kautilya's life and biography—apart from his claim to be the real force that overthrew the Nandas—is semimythical but could very well correspond to a number of actual events and encounters.

The first mention of Kautilya is in later Brahmin, Sanskrit texts of the fifth century AD, the *Puranas*, which are miscellaneous collections of mythical-historical and religious writings.[28] The *Mahavamsa-Tika*, a Buddhist Pali (Sri Lankan) text of the tenth century AD, places Kautilya as growing up in what was probably the ancient world's greatest university town—Taxila (located in the Punjab in today's Pakistan). The young Kautilya is described as displaying a precocious talent in reciting the *Vedas* and other sacred Brahmin texts but is also characterized as a physically hideous and disgusting person, with an ugly complexion and twisted, crooked limbs. Even the name Kautilya means "crooked" in Sanskrit.[29]

The turning point in Kautilya's life—and one might say in South Asian ancient history—occurs when, according to the *Mahavamsa-Tika*, he ended up in the Pataliputra court of the last Nanda king, Dhana Nanda. Dhana Nanda, whose rule was characterized as unpopular and stingy,[30] was paradoxically extremely generous as a patron of learning, setting up a foundation called the Danasala, which awarded grants to scholars—a kind of U.S. National Science Foundation or National Endowment of the Arts in the fourth century BC. The awards were administered by a council, and Kautilya became its president. According to one account, the president of the Danasala was entitled to occupy the traditional honorary seat reserved for the leading Brahmin in the king's court, but when Kautilya tried to take his seat in royal ceremonies, Dhana Nanda found him so uncouth and repulsive that he threw him out. Kautilya cursed the king, and escaped his imminent arrest by fleeing Pataliputra that night disguised as a naked Ajivika ascetic.[31]

Historian Abraham Eraly suggests that it would not have been out of character for Kautilya to have embezzled funds from Dhana Nanda's scholarly foundation and that that was the real reason for his rude ejection from the royal court.[32] This conjecture at least gives an explanation for the next episode in the *Mahavamsa-Tika*: Kautilya's revenge. Fleeing into the wilderness, Kautilya uses his knowledge of metallurgy and recasts a treasure of coins he had somehow amassed into denominations worth eightfold their original worth. We hear thus that (1) Kautilya is a counterfeiter, and (2) he escaped Pataliputra with an already substantial horde of coins.[33]

Kautilya, having amassed a war chest through these extraordinary means, looked for a champion who could overthrow the Nandas. Kautilya knew he had found the person he needed when he came upon Chandragupta as a young boy in a dusty village organizing his playmates into a royal court with himself playing king. He adopted the boy and financed his education at the great Buddhist university at Taxila. The Jain account of Kautilya's first encounter with Chandragupta adds a revealing detail: Kautilya decided to test the boy playing king by asking him for a gift. Chandragupta points to a herd of cattle—obviously belonging to an adult proprietor—and tells Kautilya to take them, proclaiming "the earth is for the enjoyment of heroes."[34]

Two other legendary incidents give further insight into the wily nature of Kautilya's intelligence. According to the *Mahavamsa-Tika*, Chandragupta's early military campaigns were not successful: he would attempt to attack and seize cities and towns head-on, spurring counterattacks that left his forces in disarray. Kautilya and Chandragupta retreated into the wilderness, resolving to "acquire a knowledge of the sentiments of the people."[35] They encountered a mother scolding her son for trying to eat a cake by nibbling at the center and discarding the edges; in effect, the boy, according to the Jain account of the same story, burns himself by grabbing at the hottest part of the dish rather than starting with the cooler edges. The mother chides the boy for being as foolish as Chandragupta, who, rather than conquering the countryside first, tried to take the center of towns, leaving himself open to destructive counterattacks launched on the frontiers. Kautilya and Chandragupta changed their strategy.[36]

Jain sources recount an even more revealing anecdote. Despite Chandragupta's repeated attacks, a town stubbornly holds out. Kautilya disguises himself as a wandering monk, enters the town, and is questioned by the beleaguered citizens about how long he thinks the siege will continue. Kautilya, having spotted the main temple as he walks into the city, tells the people that victory will be assured when they remove the idols from the temple. The townspeople rush to move the idols outside, while Kautilya manages to send a message to Chandragupta to withdraw his forces from the siege. The gullible inhabitants are soon reveling in a victory celebration, at which moment Chandragupta's army storms and takes the town.[37]

Both the historical and mythical accounts of Chandragupta's ascension to power and the mythical accounts of Kautilya's biography reinforce and confirm the politically, culturally, and morally unsettled nature of the fourth century in northern India, a situation that had been brewing for two centuries and that reached a kind of apogee in the chaos following Alexander's invasion and Chandragupta's revolutionary overthrow of the Nandas.

Kautilya found a number of novel solutions to the issues of his day, issues that Ashoka would also face. First and foremost, there was the question of how to deal with the shifting social order and the cultural uncertainties and politically destabilizing forces it fostered. Kautilya's approach in the *Arthasastra* is to reaffirm the old Brahmin order through radical, revolutionary means.[38] Although the *Arthasastra* is a description of an ideal state, it is clear, for example from the accounts of Megasthenes that have come down to us, that the Mauryan Empire under Chandragupta and later under Ashoka reflected many of Kautilya's prescriptions.

Kautilya seeks to uphold and restore a framework of dharma, which reaffirms the primacy of Brahmins and Kshatriyas. The ruthless, unsettled nature of the age allowed Kautilya to observe human behavior in all its extremes more clearly than in peaceful, culturally stable times. He formulated and systematized a radical notion of the state, whose goal is to reinvigorate the conservative dharmic order through the systematic pursuit and management of artha, material wealth, coupled with the adoption of realpolitik in diplomatic relations and extensive internal espionage to guarantee security.

The goal of all these machinations is the welfare of the people. Kautilya states that "in the happiness of the subjects lies the happiness of the king and in what is beneficial to the subjects his own benefit. What is dear to himself is not beneficial to the king, but what is dear to the subjects is beneficial (to him)."[39] But everything depends on how this welfare is defined and on what specific measures are advocated to achieve it. For Kautilya the king has a preeminent duty to ensure that the special duties of each individual in each caste are adhered to and not transgressed. Kautilya himself appears to have been of Brahmin origin, and he concluded the *Arthasastra* with a couplet proclaiming that it was he who liberated India from the grip of the Nandas. The Nandas were Sudras, the lowest caste, a living affront to the tradition that a king should be a Kshatriya, a warrior.

In keeping with this reaffirmation of Vedic values, Kautilya prescribes the harshest discrimination against outcastes ("Chandalas") and "heretics," which included the major Sramana sects—Buddhists, Jains, and Ajivikas. There is a heavy fine for feeding Jains, Ajivikas, and other heretic monks (i.e., Buddhists) at religious festivals or ceremonies honoring ancestors. Heretics and Chandalas are banished to live on the outskirts of cremation grounds, considered to be the most impure, unclean area by the higher castes.[40] In keeping with this conservative social outlook, Kautilya expresses in numerous passages his low regard for merchants and artisans, who, he assumes, have a propensity to cheat and illicitly pocket excessive profits. His disdain mirrors traditional Brahmin disdain for the Vaisya (merchant) caste, trade, and usury. He mistrusts the power of the tradesmen and artisan guilds; they are to be strictly regulated, and no guild can change its location without state permission.[41]

There is a certain unintended irony and paradox in these attitudes, however, since it was precisely the rise of the mercantile and artisan class that reflected much of the economic and consequent political might of Magadha. Kautilya in fact recognized the primacy of this new social-political force and hence put forth the proposition that artha, not dharma, is the real underpinning of the state and society. But the control of artha is to be taken out of the hands of its creators and administered by the state to restore and uphold the old Brahmin, Vedic order.

Kautilya's reading of human nature is also rather cynical, or some would say, pessimist or realist.[42] In a chapter on criminal law and procedure in the *Arthasastra*, Kautilya states that if a woman shows conspicuous grief after the sudden death of her husband, she should be investigated as a suspect in his possible murder.[43] No one is to be trusted. We shall see that a significant part of the *Arthasastra* is an encyclopedia of different kinds of cheating, betrayal, and treason that every economically and politically active person in Kautilya's state may be tempted to commit. Given this view of human behavior, the state's rational response is to set up an enormous Stasi-like apparatus of internal espionage.

But Kautilya's prescriptions are also for his times enlightened and in many instances relatively humane. He itemizes numerous measures for the protection of weak members of society (widows, the old, children, the sick, and the handicapped). Women enjoy more rights than they would for most of the next 2,300 years (under certain conditions they could divorce and own property). There are measures for protection of animals and nature, consumer protection regulations, labor laws, housing standards, and financial incentives to foster international trade. Compared with previous customs and the recommendations of earlier thinkers—which he often reiterates before stating his view—Kautilya frequently chooses the more moderate, less harsh option.[44]

Thus, by singling out the amorality or morality of Kautilya's specific recommendations, it is easy to misunderstand him, since, in Amartya Sen's words, he is "the ultimate consequentialist" where "it is hard to disentangle Kautilya's ultimate values from the practical reason he presents, especially in governance and politics, where the instrumental and strategic connections are played out much more prominently than valuational priorities."[45] Although Kautilya states his ultimate values quite clearly in the *Arthasastra*, he does not repeat himself on these issues, so it is easy to get lost in the enormous detail with which Kautilya describes his ideal state.

*Consequentialism* is a specialized philosophical term for one of the two mainstreams in the philosophy of ethics: in broad terms it connotes pragmatism or realism; that is, actions are right or wrong judged exclusively or primarily on the basis of their consequences. The utilitarian calculus of Jeremy Bentham and his followers is a simple form of consequentialism.[46] Most forms of modern economic thought are also, in theory, consequentialist. Much of the so-called market fundamentalism condemned by critics of one-sided economic globalization is utilitarian and consequentialist in its assumptions. The other great current of ethical thought is deontology (from the Greek root *deon-*, meaning "obligation," "necessity"), whose variants hold that actions must be judged according to certain normative values and universal ethical rules or obligations. Kautilya is probably the ancient world's greatest consequentialist, while Ashoka provides one of history's greatest examples of a deontological approach in statecraft—he tries to put into practice a universal, normative ethic. One of the best examples of this difference is the differing approach of Kautilya and Ashoka to protecting species: Kautilya prescribes certain protective regulations because of their ultimate economic utility, while Ashoka does so on the grounds of a normative, universal ethic of care for the welfare of all living, sentient beings. But a caveat here is also in order: as with any great historical figures, an attempt to categorize Ashoka and Kautilya too facilely—as acting exclusively from deontological or consequentialist assumptions—misrepresents the complexity of their thought. Ashoka's Dhamma, while apparently grounded in a universal, normative ethic, is also inspired by practical, "consequentialist" considerations of governance, and Kautilya's prescriptions do not in all cases reflect only a calculating, instrumentalist approach.

Kautilya was not only the world's first economist, but also, as proclaimed in the title of a book by Robert Boesche, "the first great political realist." [47] In the ancient world, perhaps only Thucydides and Sun Tzu are his rivals. But Thucydides wrote a history, not a systematic work on politics and economics. Sun Tzu was an astute theorist of war and politics, but his work does not have the comprehensive economic and social breath of the *Arthasastra*. Kautilya has been compared to Machiavelli and Bismarck, certainly great realists, and to modern political theorists and practitioners of realism, such as Hans Morgenthau and Henry Kissinger.

Did Kautilya succeed in the effort to restore and uphold Brahmin values? It is hard to say. The appeal of the nastika sects, favored by the rising merchant classes, appears to have continued unabated. According to Jain tradition, Chandragupta became a Jain monk near the end of his life and starved himself to death—the traditional form of Jain suicide—around 297 BC. Today one can still visit the hill, Chandragiri, in Karnataka state, where Chandragupta died. Near the top is a twelfth-century temple with carved panels that narrate the story of the Mauryan king and his Jain teacher. His son, Bindusara (Ashoka's father), extended the conquests of his father, and according to some accounts continued to employ Kautilya as an adviser. Given the discrimination that Kautilya urges against heretical sects, it is perhaps ironic that not only did Chandragupta probably die a Jain, but Bindusara was reputedly a patron of the Ajivikas.

Bindusara is most remembered in history for the request he sent to Antiochus I, the Greek Seleucid (one of several Greek successor dynasties that administered the fragments of Alexander's empire after he died),[48] king of Syria and the Near East. Bindusara asked Antiochus if he could send a supply of figs, wine, and a philosopher. Antiochus replied that he would gladly send the figs and wine but Greek philosophers were not for export. Even then, intellectual property was a contentious trade issue.

## A ONCE FORGOTTEN EMPEROR

As with Kautilya, we know little of Ashoka's life except from Buddhist and Jain semimythical accounts. What we know directly of the historical Ashoka comes from his various inscribed edicts inscribed on rocks and pillars.[49]

The Buddhist texts were written and compiled centuries after Ashoka's death. The most important are the Pali-language[50] chronicles of the history of Sri Lanka and Buddhism; and a saintly history of the life of Ashoka, the *Ashokavadana*, written in Sanskrit in northern India in the second century AD. Later historical accounts—for example in the travel writings of the Chinese Buddhist monks Faxian (Fa-Hsien, fifth century AD) and Xuanzang (Hiuan-Tsang, seventh century AD), and the history of Buddhism written by the Tibetan Lama Taranatha in the sixteenth century AD—draw on these and other earlier Buddhist religious texts, and recount a number of the mythical events that are found in these earlier chronicles.[51] These texts often differ in both the events and chronology of Ashoka's life, but where they concur we can conjecture that they recount an occurrence or date that may have some basis in fact.

Bindusara died in 272 BC, and afterward, all the Buddhist chronicles agree that there was a bitter struggle for power that lasted three or four years. The chronicles also agree that Ashoka was not the heir to the throne and had to eliminate his brothers as rivals. Accounts differ as to how many brothers were in his way—one source says he killed six brothers, another ninety-nine. What appears to be historically likely is that there was a succession struggle in which Ashoka triumphed in 269 BC, perhaps by murder, certainly using the Kautilya-esque intrigue that was the mark of the Mauryan court.[52]

Ashoka's life prior to his father's death is shrouded in myth. The northern Buddhist sources recount a revolt during Bindusara's reign in the great Buddhist university city of Taxila. Ashoka was sent to quell the rebellion and demonstrates superior diplomatic skills. The Sri Lankan Pali chronicles have Ashoka as his father's envoy to the commercial city of Ujjain, where he falls in love with Devi, the beautiful daughter of a merchant. They have two children, Mahinda and Samghamitta. The same religious-mythical accounts describe Devi as helping to win Ashoka over to Buddhism. How much of this actually happened is hard to say, but we can quote the opinion of the most authoritative historian of ancient India, Romila Thapar: "The tradition of Devi could well be true, since it does not interfere with the flow of events concerning the life of Aśoka." [53]

But the Buddhist chronicles also describe Ashoka a few years later, in the early part of his reign, as an extraordinarily cruel, sadistic man, whose conversion to Buddhism produces a complete transformation of character. We also have no way of knowing to what extent this was true or not; we do know that the putative ruins of what was allegedly a special torture center built by Ashoka, "Ashoka's Hell," was a well-known tourist site for Buddhist pilgrims in the early centuries of the first millennium AD, with recorded visits by both Faxian and Xuanzang in the fifth and seventh centuries, respectively.

The seminal event of Ashoka's reign was the great Kalinga war in 260 BC. Several years later, Ashoka declared on rock edicts all over India his remorse for the death and suffering caused by the Kalinga war and proclaimed his new policy of nonviolence and tolerance, Dhamma. Vincent Smith, author of the original *Oxford History of India* in the 1920s, characterized Ashoka's bloody conquest, his remorse and conversion to a new ethos, as "one of the decisive events in the history of the world." [54] We do not know the motive for this war, apart from simple expansion of imperial rule over a weaker state. One leading historian, Stanley Wolpert, speculates that he was simply following the ruthless prescriptions of the *Arthasastra*. [55] The major rock edicts (which number fourteen, plus two separate, alternative versions found in some sites of two of the edicts), as they are called, were inscribed at sites all over the Indian subcontinent in 256–255 BC, the fourteenth year of Ashoka's reign. In the thirteenth rock edict, where Ashoka expresses his regret for Kalinga, he also lists the regions outside and inside his empire where he has sent envoys to spread the word of his new policy: these include the lands of all of the Hellenistic states

established by Alexander's generals and their descendents—the Seleucids in the Mid-East and Syria, the Ptolemies in Egypt, and three
other Greek monarchies controlling areas corresponding to Libya and
Western Egypt (Cyrene), Macedonia, and Western Greece and Alba-
nia (Epirius). He also mentions sending a mission to what is today Sri
Lanka. Pali Sri Lankan Buddhist chronicles describe at length Ashoka's
friendly contacts with the Sri Lankan king Devampiya Tissa. Ashoka
helps to convert Devampiya Tissa to Buddhism, culminating in his
sending his son (conceived with Devi), Mahinda, as a special envoy to
the island. Mahinda is thought to have made this voyage around 249
BC.[56] Another semimythical account in the Pali chronicles recounts
how the daughter of Ashoku and Devi, Sanghamitta, became a Buddhist nun and brought a sprig of the Bodhi tree—under which the
Buddha experienced his enlightenment—to Sri Lanka.[57]

Ashoka's personal conversion to Buddhism was no doubt given a
great impetus by his remorse after the Kalinga war, but it is thought to
have been gradual, his interest and involvement having preceded the
war, growing more intense over several years following it.[58] His conversion and subsequent patronage of Buddhism was a turning point
in its becoming a world religion. Later in his reign, Ashoka regularly
undertook pilgrimages to the sacred sites of the Buddha's life and
generously endowed the construction of thousands of stupas, not only
in India but in Southeast Asia and China. Material evidence of this
activity remains to this day, not only in the form of ruined stupas,
but also, for example, a memorial column Ashoka had erected around
250 BC in Lumbini, the birthplace of the Buddha in northern India
near the current Nepalese border, commemorating his pilgrimage
there the year before.[59]

In the twenty-seventh and twenty-eighth years of his reign,
around 242 and 241 BC, Ashoka had erected in different sites of the
subcontinent a number of sixty-feet-high polished stone pillars, inscribed with seven new edicts. They restate and add more detail to his
policy of Dhamma, and seem infused with a greater sense of urgency
in wishing to see his policies carried out. After the pillar edicts, we
again have no real historical record of the remaining years of Ashoka's
reign except Buddhist religious chronicles. They recount that Ashoka's main queen, Asanhimitta, died and was replaced by a younger,
attractive wife named Tissarakha around 237 BC, five years before his
death. Both the Pali chronicles and the *Asokavadana* give engrossingly
horrifying accounts of the wickedness of the new queen, who plots to

destroy the Bodhi tree because she is jealous of Ashoka's regard for it, and who, after failing to seduce Ashoka's son Kunala, tricks Ashoka into having him blinded.

There is considerable evidence that Kautilya's prescriptions helped build an unprecedentedly prosperous, well-managed empire. Megasthenes describes the Maurya capital, Pataliputra, as the richest and best-run city in the world. But there are also signs of underlying social and political discontent. Chandragupta, according to the Roman historian Justin, began his reign as a liberator of northwest India from Greek rule, but in his later years was a tyrant and oppressor. The realism of Kautilya may have degenerated into despotism, one of the dangers of a purely realist approach untrammeled by ethical limits. The revolt at Taxila, which Bindusara sent Ashoka to put down, shows that these tensions persisted.

The accounts of Megasthenes reveal that the Mauryan Empire, while not a copy of the ideal state described in the *Arthasastra*, did reflect in surprising detail a good number of Kautilya's prescriptions. We can speculate that Kautilya's emphasis on *"artha* above all" may have accentuated the amorality of the new mercantile economy in Magadha, which, in the words of Armstrong, "was fueled by greed, and bankers and merchants, locked in ceaseless competition, preyed on one another." [60] The fatalistic, deterministic Ajivikas prosper and are clearly one of the leading, most influential Sramana sects under the Mauryas. The Ajivikas are said to have practiced both extreme forms of asceticism as well as indulging in what their critics claimed were unseemly indulgence of food, drink, singing, dancing, and sex. Their popularity and some of their practices may be explained by roots in earlier Dravidian, Bronze Age culture; indeed, they may have preserved even more ancient remnants of Shamanism. [61]

Thus, the Sramana–Brahmana tension persisted. The second-century Sanskrit grammarian Patanjali—also the author of a seminal text on yoga—refers to the Sramana–Brahmana enmity as one of several examples of irreconcilable natural enemies, along with the cat and the mouse and the snake and the mongoose. [62]

The bloody massacre at Kalinga perhaps was only the last and most severe in a series of incidents that convinced Ashoka that the Kautilyan approach could not work to hold together a multiethnic empire riven by new philosophical and religious ideologies. The proliferation of these movements, Thapar notes, "has been explained as due to the breakup of tribal society and its consequences." [63] The new sects sought to reconstitute community and identity for more and more people, mainly in towns, whose lives no longer could be situated, or made sense of, in the traditional Vedic framework.

In retrospect, the rise of Buddhism in the Mauryan Empire seems if not inevitable, likely; a society grounded in Kautilyanism alone would appear to provide bitter spiritual sustenance. We have seen that the continued political and social turmoil associated with the economic and political transformation of the sixth to third centuries BC in the Ganges plain created the need for a new social ethic. A number of the Sramana sects, but particularly Buddhism, through its relative egalitarianism and emphasis on individual ethical responsibility and effort, responded to this need. It provided the antidote to untrammeled amoral individualism, expressed either in the ruthless pursuit of power or wealth, or the hedonism that was a logical consequence for some of the followers of the materialist sects.

Several contemporary historians describe Buddhism's role in Magadha in terms that appear almost analogous to that of Protestantism in the growth of a mercantile, less hierarchical, more open society in the West. Gail Omvedt refers to Buddhism's appeal in reinforcing the "moral sentiments" of Justice, Prudence, and Beneficence that Adam Smith, in *The Theory of Moral Sentiments*, maintained were essential for the survival of society—and for the ultimate survival too of economic activity and the market, which, after all, are embedded in society.[64] "Buddhism," Omvedt concludes, "acted not so much to promote [economic] growth as to give it an ethical foundation while endorsing it; in contrast Brahamanic Hinduism pushed the society back into stagnation. Buddhism, in discouraging ritualism, in countering birth-based ascription, in setting its face against all notions of purity-pollution, gave positive encouragement to the developing society of openness, equality and mobility."[65] We almost hear an echo of Karl Popper and his followers (like George Soros) in this characterization. Ashoka's propagation of these broader Buddhist values—witness his emphasis on tolerance and open debate—may make him indeed one of the first defenders of the ideal of the Open Society against its enemies.

Finally, Ashoka's reign continued and expanded the growth of international trade that had also played a major role in the profound cultural upheaval of the mid- to later first millennium BC. The Mauryan Empire reached its peak under Ashoka, and India can be seen at that time as one of the economic centers of the world, linking Egypt,

Ethiopia, Rome, Greece, and the Selucid Empire with the Silk Road, central Asia, and China. One could say that he presided over the high point of the first economic globalization.[66]

An excursion into the historical context of the times of Kautilya and Ashoka leads us back to the major themes of the present: we too live in an age where a newer, more encompassing phase of economic globalization fueled by new technologies poses new challenges of identity and community, ethics and economics, for large portions of the earth's population. A global economy now more than ever requires a global ethic. In their ethical approaches we can view Kautilya as an archetypal "consequentialist" and Ashoka as an equally archetypal "deontologist," and they were practitioners, not just theorists. They both wielded extraordinary political power, and thus what we know of their lives and writings may have much to tell us even today.

After so many centuries we still live in a Kautilyan world and we often appear to be further away than ever from reconciling it with a higher ethic. The challenge Ashoka faced when he inherited an empire built on Kautilyan principles is a metaphor for the one a globalized planet faces today. The planetization of market-based economies and social values has also created a crisis of meaning, authenticity, and authority, spawning countermovements seeking to establish individual and group identities and new sources of political authority from the fragments of ground-up traditions and histories.

This tension grows as every event in our world seems to become connected with and bound to an interdependent network of other occurrences. The compression of time and space that accompanies economic and technological globalization has, as it were, karmic effects. More and more we live with, encounter, pay for, or benefit from the individual and collective impacts of our actions and of the actions of others in this life, rather than, as classic Hindu or Buddhist doctrine maintains, in past or future lives. But the awareness of this condition and the ability to act on it often seem paradoxically weakened by the very economic and communications processes producing it. Everyday experience and life in Web- and image-linked societies are dominated by an expansion of the immediate self and its imagined possibilities, accompanied by a reduction of the world.

For the world's richer populations, the shrinking of the lived world into an everyday experience increasingly dominated by mediated images poses social and psychological dilemmas as the historical and cultural sources of individual and community identity dry up. For billions of poor and the socially disenfranchised, access to a globalized world of images portraying limitless virtual possibility collides with a shrinking horizon of real social and economic opportunity. This is planetary nitroglycerin.

More self for less world is a fool's bargain.

# CHAPTER 3

# The Great Dilemma

There have been signs for years. Originating in different perspectives, they seem to point toward the same deepening dilemma, the overarching quandary of the present moment in history. In the spring of 2000, Bill Joy, one of the entrepreneurial leaders of the entire Internet economic revolution, the cofounder and chief scientist of Sun Microsystems, published an article in *Wired* titled "Why the Future Doesn't Need Us." He warned that the lead twenty-first-century technologies that may spur still greater global economic growth—nanotech, robotics, and genetic engineering—also threaten the survival of the human species. Quoting Thoreau and Aristotle, he called for alternative social goals "beyond the culture of perpetual economic growth" before it is too late, and citing the Dalai Lama he implored that "our societies need to develop a stronger notion of universal responsibility and of our interdependency." [1] The recent global economic crisis has only brought home the huge risks of global economic interdependency in its current form, driven by the profound lack of responsibility for societies and the earth that has characterized the past decades of market fundamentalism.

After September 11, 2001, more thoughtful observers began to link the violent eruption of fundamentalist terror with growing disjunctures in the global system. George Soros, the billionaire hedge fund investor and currency speculator who now is better known as a philanthropist and globalization critic, writes that there is an overarching message from 9/11 that world politicians and international organizations still are mostly ignoring. The asymmetric threat of fundamentalist terrorism arises out of a fundamental asymmetry in globalization: "We have global markets but we do not have a global society. And we cannot build a global society without taking into account moral considerations."[2] Soros had also warned for years about the purely economic dangers of the naïve belief in the benign self-regulating nature of markets, and was one of the few who lambasted, before the economic crisis, luminaries such as U.S. Federal Reserve chairman Allan Greenspan as free market fundamentalists. A shamefaced Greenspan confessed before the U.S. Congress on October 23, 2008, that he and others who believed that markets would not spiral into self-destructive behavior were "in a shocked state of disbelief." Belatedly, he discovered the importance of history: "The whole intellectual edifice, however, collapsed. . . . because the data inputted into the risk management models generally covered only the past two decades."[3]

But the greater risk in the model is not economic; it is the threat to the viability of societies everywhere. For foreign affairs commentator Robert Kaplan, Islamic fundamentalism is an increasingly important source of "moral and psychological support" to hundreds of millions of formerly rural people congregated in poor urban slums uprooted from their old values and exposed to a global secular consumerism that is basically valueless. "While our elites babble about globalism," he concludes, "new class struggles arise, tied to religion and the tensions of Third World urban life."[4] The market-led growth of the past decades has led just as often to greater inequality and poverty as to the realization of the utopian promises of economic progress espoused by its proponents. As German economics commentator Gabor Steingart notes, "economic imbalances—both within and between nations— have incredibly explosive potential." In fact, in the one region of the world where wealth has indisputably increased most rapidly, Asia, there has been "a rebirth of nationalism . . . never before has so much money been spent on new weapons systems, including nuclear warheads."[5] *New York Times* Africa bureau chief Alex Perry (and former South Asia bureau chief in the early 2000s) concluded in 2008 that "the shared truth that links conflict zones as distant as the Himalayas and the Sahara is that globalization starts wars. . . . Globalization is not about integrating the world. So far, it is about integrating the rich."[6]

Is globalization then an enemy of social justice, equity, and environmental conservation, a threat to community, society, and cultural identity, or an ally, or both, or neither? Is globalization about unleashing free trade and markets around the world, as the United States and other Western elites preached for the past three decades? Or will it be in the future about building a global system of governance, as some European leaders are now espousing? Is it inevitable and uncontrollable, or is the issue what kind of globalization, and for whom?

FALSE DAWN

Nearly two decades ago, the end of the Cold War marked the triumphalist promotion of a global market system led by the United States and international financial institutions like the International Monetary Fund, World Bank, and World Trade Organization. Key players and commentators like Larry Summers and Francis Fukuyama heralded the dawn of a new era, where the entire world was converging on a consensus of the same market-based economic system and of Western values of democracy that putatively were somehow bound to markets. But in the words of John Gray, professor at the London School of Economics, it was a false dawn.

Gray was a prominent conservative political thinker and former adviser to Margaret Thatcher, but did an about-face in 1998 in his impassioned denunciation of free market globalization, *False Dawn*. "Democracy and the free market are rivals," he warns, "not allies." [7] He concluded that the global triumph of markets trumpeted by former U.S. treasury secretary Lawrence Summers is leading us to a nightmarish dystopia.

And of all people billionaire George Soros emerged in the late 1990s as one of the most eloquent oracles of global dystopia. In a February 1997 article in the *Atlantic Monthly*, and then a full-length book in 1998, *The Crisis of Global Capitalism*, Soros attacked the dominant ideology of "market fundamentalism" as the greatest threat to social and political stability worldwide. Soros castigated the increasing extension of market and economic reasoning to all areas of social activity, including professions like medicine and law, which formerly were guided by historically rooted, semiautonomous ethical codes. Indeed, the penetration of market, transactional relationships has become so pervasive in Western society, and particularly in the Anglo-American world, that family and personal relations are increasingly atomized and replaced by market-derived transactional interactions. If these trends are not countered, the "destructive and demoralizing social effects" of market fundamentalism will undermine the social cohesion on which civilized existence depends; in fact, this process is already well underway. Presciently, he warned that "market forces, if they are given complete authority even in the purely economic and financial arenas, produce chaos and could ultimately lead to the downfall of the global capitalist system."[8]

In a world menaced by this increasingly transactional corrosion of human relations, the urgent challenge is to reassert politically and culturally the primacy of social, ethical and political values, to rein in the market and the primacy of the economic that has mesmerized politicians and governments. In fact, Soros, putting his money where his values are, notes that the large foundation he supports, the Open Society Institute, is committed in its work in the United States to "challenging the intrusion of marketplace values into inappropriate areas" and "dealing with the inequities in the distribution of wealth and social benefits that arise from market fundamentalism."[9]

## MARKET MONOTHEISM

Up to a point, the reasoning of market fundamentalists that the market is the primary social value is remarkably similar to Kautilya's: wealth or artha (or economic growth) is what society needs first in order to address other worthy goals: social order and welfare (which it is the king's, duty or dharma, to assure in Kautilya's world) and leisure time resources for individual pleasure and enjoyment (kama in ancient India). Kautilya himself would be amazed at the extent to which his basic thesis has triumphed in our world. But even more than in Kautilya's vision, means have become ends.

Theologian Harvey Cox has pointed out that in mainstream social discourse the market has assumed many of the attributes that used to be attributed to a transcendent God: omnipotence, omniscience, and omnipresence.[10] The market is omnipotent as First Cause, more and more the prime force in all areas of human activity. Its underlying principle and force is to convert everything into an exchangeable commodity. In a reversal of the Christian sacrament, which converts ordinary wine and bread into pathways to union with God, the Mass of the market takes the most sacred areas of life and transforms them into marketable goods and services.

The market is omniscient because it mysteriously and ceaselessly computes the wishes and desires of billions of human beings in an incalculable series of interactions into perfectly balanced prices reflecting aggregate demand and supply for every human good and activity. The most decadent Roman emperor never put so much faith in the readings of chicken entrails as the leaders of the Western world in ambiguous economic indicators. If there is a crash in the stock market, we read in the newspaper that "the market" is speaking as an oracle; it is telling us something, predicting the next recession, or higher inflation six months ahead. If stock prices in a particular investment sector fall or rise, the market is announcing a future change in demographic trends, or signaling otherwise unfathomable currents in long-term collective social choices. And the market is omnipresent, extending its reach into hitherto untouched areas, such as childbearing and now, through biotechnology, the modification of existing life and even the creation of new life.

The triumph of market monotheism is not without irony. As in Hinduism, for the enlightened (professional economists, perhaps) there is one ultimate cause and reality, but this doctrine is too austere and abstract for the uninitiated to fully appreciate. For the majority, the meaning of the new religion is revealed and made tangible through the colorful and ever proliferating polytheism of commodities.

In one sense this ideology, which even in the present crisis is now global, is the logical extreme of a current at work in Western history since the seventeenth century: the rationalization of all spheres of social life, and the accompanying disenchantment of the world associated with the withering of traditional religious beliefs and community custom. A qualitative leap occurs in the nineteenth century with the first attempt in history in Britain to erect market principles as an autonomous sphere, disconnected to almost all social, ethical, and political constraints. The economic view of society, to become economics, had to emancipate itself from subservience to any other principles of politics and morality.[11]

The triumph of the market has been the triumph of the economic, and of the instrumental, utilitarian social rationality that permeates it. The notion of utility dates back to the late eighteenth century and the dawn of modern economic thought in Great Britain through such figures as Jeremy Bentham and John Stuart Mill. For Bentham and Mill, utility was simply the principle of rationally pursuing the greatest happiness or good for the greatest number. More modern versions of the theory take an operational approach—utility is whatever makes an individual choose one thing or option over another, which must be what in that instance makes him or her happy. The key question, of course, remains how one defines at the individual level this happiness or good, and then what social mechanism allows the most effective realization of this good for the greatest number.

Market monotheism, at least in times of economic stability, is immensely attractive—it appears to make the world fully intelligible, and to offer a hardheaded, practical way of enhancing human welfare. There is no better description of the psychology of the attractiveness of the economistic, utilitarian approach than the account John Stuart Mill gives of it in his *Autobiography*. The young Mill developed an intellectual friendship with Jeremy Bentham, the founder of utilitarian philosophy. Mill slowly comes to an epiphany whereby Bentham's principle of utility, of a rigorous rational analysis and reduction of all social institutions according to the "greatest happiness for the greatest number, fell into place like a keystone which held together the detached and fragmentary component parts of my knowledge and beliefs. It gave unity to my conception of things." [12] More specifically, Bentham defines utility, and happiness, as the principle that derives all individual and social behavior from "the governance of two sovereign masters, pain and pleasure. It is for them alone to point out what we ought to do, as well as to determine what we shall do." [13] Bentham's relentless analysis applies not only to political economy, but to justice, legislation, and the entire organization of society. Values like natural law, or "the moral sense," are shown to be irrational and founded in sentimentality rather than reason; only a consistent, rational analysis along the lines of social utility can found a social science worthy of the name. Worldview is too weak a term to describe Mill's epiphany:

> I now had...a creed, a doctrine, a philosophy; in one among the best senses of the word, a religion....and I had a grand conception laid before me of changes to be effected in the condition of mankind through that doctrine...there seemed to be added to this intellectual clearness, the most inspiring prospects of practical improvement in human affairs. [14]

One could venture that Mill's intellectual infatuation with utility presaged the seduction of our entire civilization by the same principle. However, in early adulthood, Mill underwent a tremendous personal, psychological, and intellectual crisis, which led him to totally reconsider and reevaluate everything he thought and wrote before. It began with a sense of emptiness or lassitude: he realized that if all his Benthamite goals were achieved for the reform of society, he personally would not be happy. He even considered suicide. (We would call his crisis today a severe depression—a mental affliction that has become endemic in the Western world over the past three decades.) He discovers that, paradoxically, directly seeking one's personal happiness—the ground assumption of Benthamite utility—is futile, since it can be achieved only by having another, transcendent goal.

Mill reorders his priorities, embracing the moral goals that as a good Benthamite he previously denounced as "sentimentality" and "vague generalities." The problem with the Benthamite view is that it is based on an extremely narrow, crippled view of human motivation and potentiality, both individual and social.[15] Bentham's "knowledge of human nature," Mills wrote, "is bounded. It is wholly empirical; and the empiricism of one who has little experience." Bentham suffered from a huge "deficiency of imagination" in his understanding of the lives and feelings of humans different from himself. The lack of comparative historical perspective is equally fatal: "Other ages and other nations were a blank to him from purposes of instruction." There was something almost autistic in his attempt to create a philosophy "wholly out of the materials furnished by his own mind, and minds like his own."[16]

Mill's description of Bentham's intellectual and cultural deficiencies eerily evokes the well-intentioned but one-sided, one-dimensional thinking of many of our leading policymakers and technocrats, whose intellectual and career experiences often resemble one another much more than those of the rest of the inhabitants of the earth whose lives their decisions affect. The Benthamite view of utility as the basis of individual and collective happiness remains alive today in the crude assumptions made about economic man and rational choice in much contemporary economic theory. The fact that most economists view history as irrelevant is particularly disastrous, literally a form of idiocy, of self-referential ignorance.

In the current economic crisis, these assumptions are being challenged. Thus, Mill's personal transformation has newfound timeliness. He realizes that human motivation is more complex, and less rationally focused on self-interest, than the Benthamite model assumes. For Mill, the challenge of the future becomes "how to unite the greatest individual liberty of action, with a common ownership in the raw material of the globe, and an equal participation of all in the benefits of combined labor."[17] We could say that Bentham was Mill's Kautilya, and that like Ashoka he experienced a deeply personal conversion, resulting in transformative change in political perspective.

THE GREAT DECEPTION

Consider the following tale, which recalls a common version of the American dream. The son of a poor man is wracked by dissatisfaction with his miserable circumstances. He admires the condition of the rich, and "heaven in its anger" instills him with burning ambition. He resolves to "devote himself to the pursuit of wealth and greatness." Years follow of disciplined study, constant work and self-sacrifice: "With the most unrelenting industry he labors day and night to acquire talents superior to all his competitors." But to rise he must also "serve those whom he hates, and is obsequious to those whom he despises." He looks forward to the day when his success will be consummated, when the wealth and prestige of his station will finally quell the gnawing anxiety and drive to achieve that consumes him day and night. After many years, "in the extremity of old age," he achieves his dream.

But the teller of this tale appears to be moralistic, pessimistic, and skeptical, certainly not the sort of person you would want to have as a speaker at the chamber of commerce, or for that matter appear before the management or directors of any mainstream institution in America in the age of hedge funds and dot.com entrepreneurialism. For the life of this Horatio Alger–style hero ends thus:

> It is then in the last dregs of life, his body wasted with toil and diseases, his mind galled and ruffled by the memory of a thousand injuries and disappointments which he imagines he has met with from the injustice of his enemies, or from the perfidy and ingratitude of his friends, that he begins at last to find, that wealth and greatness are mere trinkets of frivolous utility, nor more adapted for procuring ease of body or tranquillity of mind, than the tweezer-cases of the lover of toys.[18]

Is this from Balzac or Stendahl? Or is it an unpublished short story of Leo Tolstoy, perhaps an earlier version of *The Death of Ivan Ilych*, the account of a prosperous lawyer who on his deathbed recognizes the vanity of the wealth and prestige he devoted his life to? No: it is from Adam Smith's *The Theory of Moral Sentiments*. In *The Theory of Moral Sentiments*, which preceded the publication of *The Wealth of Nations* in 1776 by seventeen years, Smith makes clear his personal view that the real satisfaction of most things that money can buy is "in the highest degree contemptible and trifling."[19] For beyond basic physical needs, money and material wealth can do little to fend off personal anxiety, sorrow, disease, and death. For the rich man, whose dismal fate Smith so vividly portrays, peace of mind and happiness were at all times within his reach, a matter of attitude, not wealth and possessions. This is a view much influenced by Stoic philosophy, Epictetus, Seneca, and Marcus Aurelius.[20]

What is even more remarkable about this passage is that it introduces Smith's first mention of the workings of the invisible hand. It is for the imagined—and false—pleasure of riches, and the misplaced social esteem of wealth, frivolous and spiritually empty as it may be, that a great "deception . . . rouses and keeps in continual motion the industry of mankind." It is this delusion that has transformed the world, "turned the rude forests of nature into agreeable and fertile plains, and made the trackless and barren ocean a new fund of subsistence."[21] He describes the "natural selfishness and rapacity" of the rich, their "vain and insatiable desires" as the motor behind the economy that, "led by an invisible hand," nevertheless advances the interests of society and affords "means to the multiplication of the species."[22]

There is much to reflect on here. First, unlike the paeans to free market entrepreneurialism, Smith clearly has a low opinion of the rich as human beings, characterized as they are by "natural selfishness and rapacity." Rather than a moral hero, the entrepreneur appears as a tragically deluded character who realizes too late that he has sought happiness and peace of mind in the wrong objects. Most importantly, the ultimate good that Smith saw resulting—the "multiplication of the species" through the razing of forests and the exploitation of oceans, and other resources—are now trends that will lead us to planetary disaster if not abetted. Clearly we have come to the point where the fueling of infinite desires for consumption and material wealth is producing more and more socially and ecologically dysfunctional effects that in many cases already outweigh the benefits of increased economic growth. If the objects of what Smith[23] calls "the economy of greatness" are in reality "trinkets and baubles," then it is all the more insane to continue undermining the biological support systems of the planet for such ends.

"WHAT IS THE END OF AVARICE AND AMBITION?"
The Adam Smith of this earlier work is an untimely thinker who in the late 1990s and 2000s has been rediscovered. It is no understatement that the Smith of *The Theory of Moral Sentiments* has become more relevant for understanding the challenges of the current global

economic crisis than the technical works of numerous contemporary economists. In early 2009 Chinese premier Wen Jiabao told the *Financial Times* that he always carries a copy of *The Theory of Moral Sentiments* with him when he travels. Among the lessons of the book, Wen Jiabao observed, is that "Adam Smith wrote that in a society if all the wealth is concentrated and owned by only a small number of people, it will not be stable."[24]

The Smith of *The Theory of Moral Sentiments* is very different from the caricatural prophet of the unleashed market that was trumpeted by the supporters of Ronald Reagan and Margaret Thatcher in the 1980s. In fact, the critics of market fundamentalism have pointed out that Adam Smith can more appropriately be viewed as an opponent of untrammeled free markets rather than a proponent. Both Amartya Sen and theologian Hans Küng emphasize that Smith was a professor of moral philosophy at the University of Glasgow, and that economics in the eighteenth century—and for Smith—was viewed as a branch of philosophy and ethics. Sen puts Smith strictly on the side of an ethical, political approach to economics, as opposed to the Kautilyan "engineering," instrumental approach.[25] Smith grounds much economic activity in a profound insight of social psychology:

> What is the end of avarice and ambition, of the pursuit of wealth, of power, and pre-eminence? Is it to supply the necessities of nature? The wages of the meanest laborer can supply them....It is the vanity, not the ease or the pleasure, which interests us. But the vanity is always founded on the belief of our being the object of attention and approbation. The rich man glories in his riches, because he feels that they naturally draw upon him the attention of the world.[26]

These insights are if anything even more pertinent today than in the eighteenth century. The enormous competition for salaries by corporate heads, professional athletes, entertainers, and entrepreneurs is driven not by material necessity but by a socially generated need for comparative ranking and approval

Smith emphasizes the key roles of the three values of Justice, Prudence, and Beneficence in underpinning the social order. Justice is by far the most important; a society can exist without Beneficence (magnanimity, compassion, public spiritedness), though it will be "less happy and agreeable," based on short-term mercenary concerns where no man feels he owes society any obligation. But a society where people are not restrained from hurting one another soon disintegrates. "Justice," he emphasizes, "is the main pillar that upholds the whole edifice....[I]f it is removed, the great, immense fabrick of human society...must in a moment crumble to atoms."[27]

One could say that Smith would reorient the Kautilyan trilogy of artha, kama and dharma, to put the priority on dharma as the absolute underpinning of all social and political activity. Justice secures wealth, not the other way around. And indeed, a primary meaning of dharma is law, a kind of natural law. The Indo-European root *dhr*, we recall, means "to hold, to bear, to carry," and Smith reiterates that it is Justice that upholds society, not the pursuit of economic gain.

Smith's analysis gives an insight into the dilemma that Ashoka faced. Ashoka inherited and expanded a multinational, multiethnic empire, characterized by historian Gail Omvedt as a "new mobile society with no established moral-philosophical code."[28] We shall see that Ashoka's Dhamma can be viewed as an attempt to develop a shared social ethic grounded in commonly accepted "moral sentiments," a secular code to put into practice Justice, Prudence, and Beneficence.

Of all qualities, Prudence is the most useful for the individual, Smith writes. Prudence in turn is based on the union of understanding, of being able to foresee the consequences of our actions, and of self-command, the ability to undergo present pain or forgo present pleasure in order to obtain greater pleasure or avoid greater pain in the future.[29] In effect, Prudence restrains the individual from actions that may bring him short-term advantage but longer-term harm. Smith points out that Prudence is not the same as mere self-interested pursuit of utility; he maintains that the understanding and self-command of which it consists are motivated by approbation as much as self-interest. Thus:

> The pleasure we are to enjoy ten years hence interests us so little in comparison with that which we may enjoy day to day...that the one could never be any balance to the other, unless it was supported by the sense of propriety, by the consciousness that we merited the esteem and approbation of every body, by acting in the one way, and that we became the proper objects of their contempt and derision by behaving in the other.[30]

Smith develops the notion of approbation to include a kind of socialized superego that does not need actual reinforcement from society.

Beneficence and Justice are reinforced by our perception of the sentiments of other people, but also by

> the sentiments of the supposed impartial spectator, of the great inmate of
> the breast, the great judge and arbiter of conduct....it is this inmate who,
> in the evening, calls us to an account for all those omissions and viola-
> tions...both for our folly and inattention to our own happiness, and for our
> still greater indifference and inattention, perhaps, to that of other people.[31]

All in all Smith portrays the combination of the desire for approbation and self-interest that drives economic behavior as embedded in
a framework of more complicated motivations and values: sympathy
and benevolence are as ingrained in human nature as selfishness and
self-interest, and Justice must be the underpinning of any society;
he expounds at some length on the role of conscience and duty. He
goes to considerable lengths to denounce the view of society as being
based purely on self-interest and utility, though in a limited context
these motivations work for the general good through the workings of
the invisible hand. Paradoxically, he denounces the views of Bernard
de Mandeville, to whom he owed the most for his conception of the
"invisible hand," or the harmony of private and public interest.

Bernard de Mandeville was born in the Netherlands but lived in
London in the early 1700s; by profession he was a physician. In 1723
he published a tract in verse which soon became infamous all over
Europe, *The Fable of the Bees: Or Private Vices, Publick Benefits*. His
satirical poem describes a beehive (a metaphor for human society)
where each bee, pursuing its corrupt and private interests, contributes
to a social organization that thereby thrives and prospers. A great
curse falls upon the hive, whereby its members desire to become virtuous, honest, and altruistic; their prayers are granted, and calamity
ensues. The disappearance of individual vice undermines individual
industry and activity; the life of the hive implodes in sloth, poverty,
and finally a demographic collapse. Thus the moral: "Fraud, Luxury
and Pride must live, While We the Benefits receive." [32]

Smith's objection is that Mandeville goes too far, by denying the
validity of benevolence, duty, and any kind of non–self-interested social motivation, "all publick spirit, therefore, all preference of publick
to private interest, is, according to him, a mere cheat and imposition
on mankind." [33] Margaret Thatcher would state two and a half centuries later that "there is no such thing as society. There are individual

men and women and families," pursuing their interests.[34] "It is thus that he [Mandeville] treats every thing as vanity which has any reference, either to what are, or what ought to be, the sentiments of others," Smith continues. "It is by means of this sophistry, that he establishes his favourite conclusion, that private vices are public virtues." [35]

These distinctions seem to have often been lost in the ideological debate over the role of markets over the past two decades, though thinkers like Sen and Hans Küng have recalled them. Nonetheless, more and more the rationalizations put forth to enshrine the dominion of an unregulated global market economy (or rather, a global economy regulated to prohibit socially based limits on markets), are in spirit closer to Mandeville's beehive than to Adam Smith. For the proponents of unlimited trade and the unleashing of markets in every area of human activity, social and environmental standards, protection of cultural values, and historic community are among the kinds of well-intentioned but disastrous "virtues" that Mandeville portrayed as bringing about the downfall of the hive.

## THE DOUBLE MOVEMENT

Many of the critical commentators on the distortions wrought by economic globalism have invoked the Adam Smith of *The Theory of Moral Sentiments* as an ally. For Soros, Gray, Küng, and other like-minded thinkers, transcending what we might call the Kautilyaism of the present age is the "supreme challenge" and "great dilemma" of our time. These critiques also owe much explicitly and implicitly to the seminal work of Karl Polanyi, *The Great Transformation*. Polanyi's classic account of the government-organized triumph of free market economics in nineteenth-century Britain was first published in 1944, and in recent years has been rediscovered with fresh urgency.

There are three fundamental points in *The Great Transformation* that today are more relevant than ever. First, the triumph of national market capitalism in Britain in the early 1800s was not a natural, social evolution involving the enlightened recognition of the state to finally allow socially deep-rooted and natural market behavior to flourish and benefit all. On the contrary, it was the result of a historically unprecedented, brutally engineered, top-down, systematic set of political and legislative interventions. It involved the completion of the enclosure movement, "a revolution of the rich against the poor," [36] whereby the lords and nobles further consolidated large landholdings, ejecting rural populations from the countryside; the abolition of existing poor laws and social protections to create a more fluid and amenable labor market; and the repeal of the Corn Law, which opened agriculture to free trade, abolishing protectionist measures that had existed for hundreds of years. The social upheaval and misery these measures caused were immense, equaled only by the growth in profits and economic power of the industrial owners.

Over the past three decades, the same process has been occurring on a global scale. The agencies that furthered the unleashing of markets from all controls are the Bretton Woods Institutions—the World Trade Organization, International Monetary Fund, and the World Bank—and the finance ministries of the leading industrialized countries, led by the United States. Already by the summer of 2000 the United Nations Economic and Social Council released a report, *Globalization and Its Impact on the Full Enjoyment of Human Rights*, which was remarkably critical of this multilateral system and its reinforcement of profoundly unequal positions of bargaining power for poor countries vis-à-vis the rich. The WTO is described as an entity that has ensconced the values of free trade and commerce to overrule considerations of human rights, even though its decisions have "serious human rights implications." "For certain sectors of humanity," the UN report concludes, "the WTO is a veritable nightmare." [37]

Polanyi's second point is that in all human societies from the most primitive to advanced civilizations, economic relations, and transactions had hitherto been *embedded* in an overarching cultural and social framework, which set limits to market activities. Anthropological and historical research showed that "man's economy, as a rule, is submerged in his social relationships. He does not act so as to safeguard his individual interest in the possession of material goods; he acts so as to safeguard his social standing, his social claims, his social assets. He values material goods only in so far as they serve this end." [38] This view is actually quite close to Adam Smith's in *The Theory of Moral Sentiments*. Its corollary is that disembedding the economy from society as an autonomous, and then totally dominant sphere undermines the society on which it is based. [39]

His third major point is that very quickly, within two decades in the case of nineteenth-century Britain, the untrammeled domination of market values produced a countermovement of social activism and legislation to rein in the depredations of the market based on "the principle of social protection aiming at the conservation of man and nature." [40] The whole process of government promotion of unencumbered freeing of markets from all social constraints and the social reaction against it Polanyi called the "double movement."

Polanyi viewed this double movement as inherent in the evolution of market capitalist societies. But the reaction of society to protect itself against the socially corrosive and disruptive effects of the market does not always end benignly, as it did in the case of nineteenth-century reform legislation in Britain, the New Deal, or the creation of social market economies in much of Europe in the last fifty years. Polanyi wrote his masterwork as a central European refugee living in Canada during World War II. His painstaking reexamination of economic history was motivated by a desire to understand the forces behind the apocalyptic self-immolation of European civilization in the 1930s leading to the most devastating war in history.

His thesis—of striking importance again today—was "that the origins of the cataclysm lay in the utopian endeavor of economic liberalism to set up a self-regulating market system."[41] For a century—the nineteenth century lasting until the First World War—the world economy expanded, supported by an uneasy, and in Polanyi's view, fundamentally unstable tension between the push toward a utopian self-regulating world market and the domestic social measures undertaken progressively with the spread of democratization, by major industrialized countries. The measures that countries took to defend social cohesion (protectionist tariffs, for example) undermined the stability and functioning of the international market economy, and exacerbated the social crisis rather than alleviating it. The ultimate consequence was the downward spiral that led to fascism and the Second World War. The fundamental quandary is that a society based on the preeminence of the market over the social undermines the social cohesion necessary not only for the functioning of the market but for the survival of society itself. The fatal dilemma is that early twentieth-century attempts to mitigate the disruptive impacts of the market undermined the functioning of the world economy and created even more social disruption. The key to understanding this quandary is that the utopia of the free market was itself a governmental, social project, created and maintained through "an enormous increase in continuous, centrally organized and controlled interventionism."[42] It is through the rediscovery of society, the abandonment of the vision of an autonomous market utopia, that some hope for a more stable order can be found.

We are now faced with a crisis of similar dimensions, with similar opportunities and dangers. We should not forget that the need to reassert social values of identity, community, and equity in response to the social failure of the market in the 1920s and 1930s became a worldwide phenomenon in industrialized and in many developing nations. We have forgotten too soon that not only communism, but especially fascism was a response to this challenge. Indeed, Polanyi reminds us that "if ever there was a political movement that responded to the needs of an objective situation and was not a result of fortuitous cause it was fascism."[43] Many parts of the developing world, particularly the Arab world and Latin America, have flirted for the past sixty years with elements of a governmental and social approach more akin to national socialism than market liberalism, from Peronism in Argentina, to the Båth parties in Syria and Iraq. National Bolshevism is a not-so-latent threat that can thrive in the ongoing social disruption and cultural anomie unleashed by the economy of Mafia capitalism in much of the former Soviet Bloc.

The recent economic crisis tested governance and an already weakened social contract in many nations. Without major reforms in national and global economic governance, even more severe crises await us. The challenge of the coming years may well be a race between a reactionary and nationalistic populism—and worse—and an instauration in and among nations of a new order based on principles that must be the underpinnings of any sustainable global society: Justice, Beneficence, and Prudence.

THE WEB AND THE SELF

*Global networks of instrumental exchanges selectively switch on and off individuals, groups, regions and even countries, in a relentless flow of strategic decisions. It follows a fundamental split between abstract, universal instrumentalism, and historically rooted, particularistic identities. Our societies are increasingly structured around a bipolar opposition between the Net and the Self.*
—Manuel Castells[44]

Thus, the tension between the economy as an increasingly dominant domain and other social values is a constant theme, from Kautilya and Ashoka, to Adam Smith and John Stuart Mill, through Karl Polanyi and contemporary critiques of globalization. The first decade of the twenty-first century has not transcended this tension, but accentuated it in a total, globalizing process.

New information technologies in particular have played a central role in this evolution. There is no more comprehensive attempt to understand this process than the work of Manuel Castells, a Catalan sociologist-philosopher at the University of California, Berkeley. The perspective of Castells is hardly a matter of theoretical interest; already in 1998 one could read in the *Wall Street Journal* that he was widely read by Silicon Valley scientists and executives, viewed as the Adam Smith and Karl Marx of the information age.[45]

The underlying elements of Castells's thesis are relatively few and all-embracing. New information technologies have extended the reign of economistic, instrumental reason to envelop and unify the entire planet. The logic of these technologies is functional and transactional; it is the Net and Web itself that counts, not the particular meaning or content of what it carries or transmits. Again, it is the Kautilyan, "engineering" or logistical approach to economics and society that is ascendant here, in unprecedented scope and scale. Above all, as never before in history, the new information technologies reduce transaction costs, the friction and inefficiencies of communication and economic exchange. The two greatest obstacles to such efficiencies are the constraints of space and time; the workings of the Net and the Web tend toward an idealized eternal simultaneity of "Timeless Time" in an electronically mediated "Space of [informational] Flows."[46] The world of electronic financial flows, for example, appears to virtually abolish the constraints and differences of time and space that until recently always characterized social and economic life on the planet.

The End of History is more than the post–Cold War hypothesis —that is ageing rather poorly—that democratic capitalism is the triumphant world system with no serious ideological competitors. Rather, what has come to pass is the reality of working and living in a world more and more shaped by the Net and the Web, in which history and the past are absent or irrelevant or at best live on in an Internet collage of fragmented virtual artifacts available for recreational consumption.

Timeless Time involves the elimination of sequentiality; in the global electronic network economy, past and future tend to disappear and events appear to happen almost simultaneously, rather than in slower chains of cause and effect. It is paradoxically a culture of the eternal ephemeral.[47] It involves the denial of death and mortality, which would otherwise rudely erupt to break the flow of the eternal consumption of images and commodities as if there were no tomorrow, or rather as if today is tomorrow is forever. Although most of humanity continues to live everyday life under the "clock time" of industrialized modernity and according to the natural rhythms of biological time, the emerging, dominant processes in the global network society operate in Timeless Time. Castells's observation is by now hardly original. For example, Klaus Schwab, the Swiss business professor who founded in 1970 the World Economic Forum that meets annually in Davos, Switzerland, talks of "ever increasing time-compression and complexity . . . the death of sequentiality. . . . this leads to an increased collective vulnerability, especially in that zone where governments and business interface."[48] He suggests the international system must deal with this challenge if future global economic meltdowns are to be avoided. Displaying a lack of imagination all too typical of our globalized elites, he suggests the solution is to amplify still further the current order of things: to deal with the effects that the expansion of electronic communications has created we must further intensify electronic communications.

The Space of Flows, in turn, involves the delocalization of traditional places, disembedding local places from their connections to history and culture. It is the material, spatial organization of the privileged places in the globalized network economy. For Castells the Space of Flows consists of the telecommunications, computer, broadcasting and high-speed transportation networks, as well as the privileged space of hubs and nodes in these networks (suburban edge cities, global financial capitals, research centers, airport hubs, etc.). The Space of Flows finds its aesthetic expression in the monotonous, globally interchangeable architecture of the privileged places of consumption and exchange for delocalized global elites: airport terminals, shopping malls from Singapore to San Francisco to Sao Paulo, the growing global networks of fast-food chain outlets, designer boutiques, shopping malls and five-star luxury hotel chains.[49] We also encounter it directly in the disembedding and delocalization of electronic commerce: for the consumer at least the shop is no longer a physical, local place, nor is his or her purchase embedded in any locality where state and municipal taxes would be charged. The transaction takes place, and exists, in the Space of Flows.

As everyday life becomes more and more characterized by interactions with the Net and Web in work or leisure time, our shared culture becomes one of "Real Virtuality." "It is so," Castells observes, "and not virtual reality, because when our symbolic environment is, by and large structured in this inclusive, flexible, diversified hyper-text, in which we navigate every day, *the virtuality of this text is in fact our reality*, the symbols from which we live and communicate."[50] The reality of our daily experience is more and more that of images and appearances mediated by global networks of communication. Political power in turn increasingly becomes concentrated in those who control the creation, distribution, and transmission of these images, be it through the Web, telecommunications companies, Hollywood, and the media.

The other side of this all-embracing process is starkly dystopian: those places, groups, even whole countries left outside the dizzying global integration of the Network Society are increasing marginal-ized and impoverished, sociocultural black holes in the new world economy. Inequality increases both within and among nations. The weakening of the nation state and the failure of any transnational regulation and control leads to a nightmarish proliferation of social pathologies and environmental destruction. In particular, the pau-perization of the most vulnerable, the less fit to compete in a global market, has led to the unprecedented destitution and exploitation of hundreds of millions of women and children, and a worldwide explo-sion in prostitution. The brave new global information economy is accompanied by the increasing marginalization of whole continents such as Africa, large swathes of the former Soviet Union, as well as the collapsing Detroits and other old industrial areas of some industrial-ized nations. Among the most skillful and successful groups in adapt-ing to and profiting from the rise of the global network economy are ruthless new international mafias trafficking in drugs, prostitution, smuggling, terrorism, and the appropriation of entire national econo-mies and nation states; Colombia, Mexico, and Russia are just three of a growing number of examples.[51]

For Castells the social reaction to this globalizing process of "ab-stract, universal instrumentalism,"[52] is increasingly based on the de-fense of identity, as defined by history and locality, or by a search for new—or renewed—collective identities of spirituality and meaning. Thus on the one hand we see the revival of tribal conflicts and af-firmations of regional autonomy, as well as religious fundamentalism, Islamic and Christian—for short, the "Jihad versus McWorld" dichot-omy.[53] Concurrently, the so-called new social movements such as en-vironmentalism and feminism seek to defend the integrity of natural places (including the entire atmosphere and oceans) or gender.[54] One could characterize all these movements as being based on either—in Castells's words—resistance identities or project identities.

These social movements are all attempts to reappropriate space and time on different terms than the dominant forms of the omnipresent space of electronic flows or the eternal present of Timeless Time. They involve the defense of specific localities and places, and the reclaiming of time as tradition, or (in the case of environmentalism) as a longer-term future horizon for decision making. Local movements to assert cultural and political autonomy, fights to save historic places from dam reservoirs or shopping malls, and movements to save national and regional cuisines from McDonaldization are all identity-based movements to preserve the heterogeneity of place against the dominant organization of the Space of Flows.

The world of the Network Society appears to exist in the realm of an electronic ether rather than rooted in a world of stuff and matter. There is an associated tendency to represent society itself as somehow finally liberated from historical material and natural constraints. Castells himself claims that we are on the edge of a "qualitative change in human experience" that amounts to the final autonomy of culture and social organization vis-à-vis the material bases of existence.[55] History, he says, has been characterized first by societies where Nature dominated Culture (or Society); then, beginning with the modern age and the Industrial Revolution, the domination of Culture over Nature. Now the claim is made that in effect Culture has so domesticated Nature that Nature itself is only another cultural category, that we are entering a new age where Culture only refers to Culture.[56]

This, of course, is preposterous; we have become so inured and ensconced in our own images and messages that there is a tendency to take the images for reality, in fact to lose the ability to discern between images and reality. For most civilizations Nature has always been a cultural category in one form or another, but we are at the point where the physical collapse of whole ecosystems and unprecedented changes in climate could threaten the material underpinnings of global society. At the moment of our putative declaration of independence from matter and nature, the entire natural underpinnings of our social existence are deteriorating, changing and destabilizing the material foundations on which we have so precariously constructed a gigantic planetary social and economic edifice. It is as if a man inside a house were to spend so much time watching television and surfing the Web that he would declare that from his daily experience he felt secure and independent, all the while not taking measures to protect his house against an oncoming torrential storm and flood. And the storm and flood may be social as well as natural.

## THE SOCIETY OF THE SPECTACLE

*In societies where modern conditions of production prevail, all of life presents itself as an immense accumulation of spectacles. Everything that was directly lived has moved away into a representation. . . . The spectacle is not a collection of images, but a social relation among people, mediated by images. . . . It is no more than the economy developing for itself.*
—Guy Debord[57]

Much of the reality of the Network Society was uncannily foreseen by a small group of French avant-garde thinkers in the early and mid-1960s, known as the Situationists. It was an artistic and political movement with roots in surrealism and anarchism. The analysis of the Situationists seemed to anticipate the totally unexpected general strike and mass student movement that nearly brought down the government of Charles de Gaulle and the Fifth French Republic in May 1968. In the aftermath of the events of May 1968, the works of the leading Situationist thinkers, particularly Guy Debord, became better known in France, and in certain left-wing circles in Britain and the United States for some time, but by the 1980s faded into the obscurity from which they had briefly emerged.

Debord's chief work, *The Society of the Spectacle*, sets forth the organizing theme and critique of Situationist thought, the notion of the Spectacle. Economic and political relations, Debord maintained, were in a period of historical transition whereby power and the experience of everyday life in postindustrial societies were being transposed from the possession of things and the ownership of the means of industrial production to the control of a proliferating network and exchange of images through which all social and economic life would increasingly be mediated—the Spectacle.[58] The Spectacle generates an "eternal present" of "frozen time"; authentic history is its enemy. Socially, it produces the isolation of individuals, the delocalization of space, and the destruction of identities not mediated through itself. More and more "images chosen and constructed by *someone else* have everywhere become the individual's principal connection to the world he formerly observed for himself." [59]

The Spectacle is the culmination of a society based on the production of commodities: it is the point at which "the commodity has attained the *total occupation* of social life. Not only is the relation to the commodity visible, but it is all one sees: the world one sees is its world."[60] It creates a world characterized by "generalized autism."[61] The media of course reinforce the Spectacle particularly through their emphasis on the immediate and through the denial of history.

Part of Debord's inspiration for *The Society of the Spectacle* came from a 1961 work of the American historian Daniel Boorstin called *The Image: A Guide to Pseudo-Events in America.*[62] Boorstin described the increasing unreality in American society and politics associated with the proliferation and increasing dominance of media-generated images. He coined a new word, *pseudo-event*, which increasingly characterized even in the early 1960s individual and collective experience in America. Pseudo-events are synthetic happenings arranged or instigated to advertise something, to sell something, to influence public opinion—public opinion itself being a kind of a pseudo-event built up from numerous other pseudo-events. In this culture, experience takes place as pseudo-events mediated and manufactured through images, and these images become our reality. In fact, pseudo-events, because they are media and image generated, tend to be simpler, more believable, more dramatic, and more intelligible than other forms of experience. Images become more important than ideals, "personality" more valued than character, the hero is replaced by the celebrity (a person who is well known because he or she is well known), travel by tourism, and the authentic by the inauthentic. Decades later, in the United States, the generation and manipulation of pseudo-events has become the dominant mode of political discourse.

Debord built on Boorstin's observations to elaborate a more radical, even more prescient critique. The most thought-provoking comment of Debord goes to the heart of the entire enterprise: the society of the Spectacle values the immediate, the demonstrable, the quantifiable; yet in reality it masks enormous and dangerous ignorance: "In this world which is officially so respectful of economic necessities, no one ever knows the real cost of anything which is produced. In fact the major part of the real cost *is never calculated*."[63] As we now witness the growing and ultimately unpredictable consequences of global warming, tropical deforestation, and the emergence of new infectious diseases associated with patterns of economic misdevelopment, not to speak of the incalculable human suffering unleashed in the marginal-ized "black holes" of economic globalization, the full weight of this observation becomes apparent.

In an epoch that more and more is imprisoned by immediacy, Debord saw history as the most subversive discipline, as the knowledge that genuinely aids in understanding what is and what is to come. In this he echoes (and cites) Thucydides,[64] who declared in the first pages of *The Peloponnesian War*: "I have written my work, not as an essay which is to win the applause of the moment, but as a possession for all time." [65]

### THE RECOVERY OF BEING

Whether in the criticisms of market fundamentalism gone awry, the reflections of Adam Smith on Justice, or Polanyi's call to rediscover society, we rediscover underlying archetypes of the tension between artha and dharma, between the Kautilyan approach and a higher Ashokan ethos. The search for this ethos begins not just in the unease we experience in witnessing the growing instability and inequity of a world dominated by an instrumental, transactional market-based logic. The quest for a framework of social meaning beyond the market begins with a personal questioning that prompts us to search for a solid ground to found our identities in such a world. In this respect we can understand better the crisis of John Stuart Mill, which was a very modern personal identity crisis that led him to reconsider what he viewed as important for human beings, individually and collectively.

If social countermovements begin in a quest to recover or redefine individual identity, this quest inexorably extends beyond the self and the present to an identity to be defined in terms of others and in an expanded notion of time, either in recovering history or seeking a social project that is to be realized in the future. But history itself, through its very concreteness, has a more powerful subversive value: it shows unequivocally that the ruling assumptions of the world in given societies in given times were different, and thus our lives are not imprisoned by the present, that the future is not merely an extrapolation of the same. The recollection of the past to inform our perception of the present opens up horizons of possibilities that otherwise are not visible. We see the present with new eyes. To understand the recent economic crisis we find little useful guidance in many of the assumptions that reigned over the past two or three decades; instead policymakers, journalists, and thinkers have turned to the almost forgotten events and lessons of the Great Depression, and even of depressions past such as that of 1873, to be reexamined and reinterpreted with fresh immediacy.

If we believe that the creation of national markets was the gradual, inexorable evolution of a natural process or social propensity, breaking down the barriers erected by parochial local interests, the current evolution and crisis of economic globalization appears inexorable, a virtual force of nature that cannot be stopped or modified. But if we accept Polanyi's thesis that the nineteenth-century creation of national markets was the top-down creation of the state, an unprecedented series of continual interventions serving the ascendant interests of a subset of society, a horizon of new and different possibilities is disclosed. The expansion of the current global market, the move toward global deregulation in the international system over the past three decades, has been a conscious project orchestrated through specific national and international institutions. The multiple crises engendered by this project will require even more concerted and coordinated national and international efforts to restore a balance between society, nature, and human livelihood.

Castells suggests that the environmental movements offer hope to transcend the opposition between the global market network economy and fundamentalist movements rooted in religious or cultural identity. Many environmental movements are simultaneously localist and globalist in the protection of specific places and of the global commons such as the atmosphere and the oceans. Similarly these movements assert a longer-term, intergenerational perspective in decision making that challenges the eternal present of the culture of real virtuality. Environmental movements propose a project of global human identity as a biological species, one that includes all humans regardless of cultural, historical, or gender identity. But the global environmental project at the same time subsumes, includes, and indeed reaffirms individual identity-based cultures rather than obliterating them. In short, Castells maintains, we see the beginnings of a global "green culture" that has the potential at least "to weave threads of singular currents into a human hypertext, made out of historical diversity and biological commonality." [66]

The theme of the reappropriation of space and place is a critical one. The logic of the global network economy is one of delocalization, of the disembedding of the cultural, historical, and biological specificity of places. The architecture of new towns and buildings around the world looks increasingly similar. The destruction of the biological diversity of ecosystems produces wastelands that resemble each other more than what existed before in each particular locality. Thus, environmental and cultural heritage movements focus on defending the nonnegotiable, nonexchangeable integrity and specificity of local places.

The most potent global counter and double-movements in the age of the net have their source in and derive their force from a profoundly felt need to encounter community rootedness and authenticity of experience. These movements seek overarching ethical norms in a global transactional culture that uproots and disembeds community, place, history, and identity. In fact, the Greek word *ethos* originally refers to place, to the customs and mores associated with a particular locality; the notion of an abstract ethos that does not reflect the adaptation of a particular community to a particular place was originally foreign to Greek culture. A placeless world of real virtuality is one cut off from the foundation of ethics. At the same time, an ethic must be founded in something outside the self and mere relativism, in a reality that encompasses the local but that transcends it.

Although there is much talk of "community" on the net, cyber-"communities" by their nature do not satisfy the human need for groundedness in place and time, and for physical face-to-face interaction with a small group of cohorts. These are needs that almost seem to be biologically hard-wired, perhaps from many millennia of human evolution in small hunter-gathering groups.[67] The Net can facilitate the coming together of communities, but their way of being, origins and goals lie outside, or beyond the world of Real Virtuality. Community is not a collection of e-mail addresses.

Finally, it is poets who tell us that the loss of reality and a hunger for being grows with our collective, global distancing from lived, particular experience. Czeslaw Milosz observes that we live in a world where increasingly we talk about and swim in a world of images and texts, of cultural references referring to cultural references, rather than lived experience or the encounter with things themselves.[68] This enormous cloud of cultural references, encountered through the media, television, movies, and the Web, is continually expanding, becoming more and more the staple of everyday experience for people in the postindustrialized and industrializing countries of the world. In other words, our world more resembles Debord's vision of the Spectacle. Such a world, Milosz notes, is gray; in fact, "grayness covers not only things of this Earth and space, but also the very flow of time, the minutes, days and years." [69]

The hunger for being grows, and poetry becomes critical "in the face of this deprivation because it looks at the singular, not the general." It encounters what is particular, unique, irreducible, variegated, "it cannot reduce life with all its pain and ecstasy into a unified tonality. By necessity it is on the side of being." [70] Poetry is the opposite of the transactional, instrumental logic and language that dominates our world. The poet's attitude constitutes a kind of reverence for life, a mindfulness of being. For Milosz, this mindfulness and reverence is found in the original spirit of Buddhism; we also find this mindfulness in the pietistic traditions of Christianity, in the thought and practice of Saint Francis of Assisi, for example. In 1999 an interviewer asked Milosz what prospects there were for reverence for life or mindfulness, given that the globalizing world embodies the opposite: speed, acceleration, noise. Milosz replied: "This is true. Yet at the same time, one cannot deny one very great and hopeful tendency—the ecological consciousness. Ecology is basically a call for mindfulness." [71]

So, we have called upon a number of thinkers, contemporary, as well as two of the founders of political economy, to help us reflect on the dilemma of the present moment. Economic forces, and the force of economic logic, have created ever-growing tensions between the ways of wealth and the values the pursuit of wealth originally was supposed to serve: We call them society, community, and as individuals, identity and connectedness to being. It is not a new dilemma, only one that has taken new and unprecedented forms. Let us examine then the thought of Ashoka and Kautilya in more detail. As remote and different as their world was, perhaps from long ago they have more to say to us then we suspect.

CHAPTER 4

# The *Arthasastra*
## *Wealth above All*

In the summer of 2000 the two newest, most popular television shows in America were *Who Wants to Be a Millionaire* and *Survivor*. *Who Wants to Be a Millionaire* was dropped from U.S. prime time two years later, but became the most popular new television program on the planet, with national versions in thirty-one countries, including Japan, Israel, Finland, and India. The Indian version became the most popular show in the history of the country's television, with a regular audience of over 100 million people.[1] The program inspired both a popular novel, *Questions and Answers*, and the 2009 international film of the year, *Slumdog Millionaire*. *Survivor*, based on a Dutch television program, also spawned clones around the globe.

The continued popularity of such reality TV programs provides an interesting insight into the collective psyche of our world, and of America, in the first years of the millennium. *Millionaire* was a classic quiz show, but its immense popularity seemed to confirm that money indeed is the first or at least most desired goal in contemporary life.

In *Survivor*, the prize was also a million dollars but the struggle to win it is more complicated. In the last episode (in 2000), a real-life corporate consultant triumphed to emerge as the lone survivor in an artificial, made-for-television "tribal" society of fifteen people on an island off the coast of Malaysian Borneo. The victor won through a strategy of calculated plotting and deception over fourteen fellow contestants who put a higher value on personal relationships, honesty, or honor, or who were not as skilled in scheming. Each week, after a series of tests and competitions, the participants would have to vote to eject one person. Richard Hatch, the winner, succeeded in outlasting all the others and claiming the prize money through a series of manipulative alliances and betrayals that his coplayers and the media characterized as Machiavellian. As the core group of survivors grew smaller, it was not lost on the 51 million television viewers that Hatch's alliances, betrayals, and manipulative instrumentalizing tactics resembled nothing so much as office politics in the corporations and bureaucracies where most Americans work. That the winner should be of all people a corporate consultant was seen by many commentators as a confirmation that the television show was a mirror of dominant American values in the age of the global market. Nor was it entirely surprising that six years later Richard Hatch would be indicted and convicted of tax evasion on his winnings and sentenced to over four years incarceration in a federal prison.

A prominent cultural anthropologist lamented that the game mirrored the approach of economic analysts whose theories become more elegant if grossly simplistic assumptions are made about human nature, for example, that people always seek profit maximization. Indeed, "if the outcome of 'Survivor' convinces people that there is something fundamentally, primarily human about competition that legitimizes betrayal, it moves us one step further into being a society whose values are defined by the economists." [2]

From the vantage point of 2009, we can view Hatch as a media harbinger of much more grandiose confidence schemes to come, an emanation of the same culture that produced Bernie Madoff and Allen Stanford. And in the romanticized Indian quiz show saga of *Slumdog Millionaire*, we realize that the contestant hero's triumph is all the more improbable as we learn, from the mouth of the quiz show host himself, that the game is rigged—a realization that is also beginning to dawn on much of the American public concerning the market excesses of the past decade.

If we could somehow acculturate Kautilya in a visit to the twenty-first century, he might in some ways feel very much at home in the tactics of such games, or as a real-life corporate consultant or confidence man. For Richard Hatch was as much an unknowing disciple of the *Arthasastra* as of Machiavelli's *Prince*. Kautilya radically reordered the three traditional Hindu life goals to value wealth and material well-being above righteousness and pleasure, at least in the conduct of the game of politics and in the management of society. Kautilya advocates too the opportunistic use of alliances to advance one's cause—and the intentional making and breaking of treaties and agreements under certain circumstances with the goal of increasing the vulnerability of opponents for future betrayal: "Wishing to over-reach an enemy...he should create confidence with a treaty, saying 'we are in alliance,' without the fixing of place, time or object, and after finding the enemy's weak point, strike at him."[3]

But corporate consulting and rigged reality shows would have been child's play for Kautilya; departing from certain assumptions—basically the need to preserve the state internally and to ensure its security and aggrandizement externally—he goes much further. He warns that the ruler must protect himself from the machinations of his own wife and family, particularly his sons, for "princes devour their begetters, being of the same nature as crabs."[4] His prescriptions for tactics to maintain internal order and acquire new territory are perversely ingenious and cold blooded even by the standards of the former KGB or Gestapo: he advocates the creation of an enormous internal espionage establishment, the use of prostitutes, fake holy men and ascetics, murder, burglary, bribery, and deceptions of all kinds to ensure state security. Spies posing as holy men or ascetics[5] should ascertain who among the ruler's subjects are content and malcontent; the most recalcitrant should be put to work in mines, their fami-lies hostage to the state.[6] The best spies and security agents, Kautilya recommends, are orphans who are raised by the state.[7] More than two millennia later, the KGB and Ceaucescu's Securitate in Romania would follow this principle; particularly in Cold War–era Roma-nia the most feared agents were those taken out of Romanian orphan-ages as children by the regime and raised in special hostels, ensuring their single-minded loyalty and implacable ruthlessness.

Even a millennium and half ago, Kautilya was a highly controver-sial character. In the seventh century AD, Bana, one of the greatest of ancient Indian prose writers and adviser to one of the greatest of Indian kings, Harsha, expresses his contempt: "Is there anything that is righteous for those for whom the science of Kautilya, merciless in its precepts, rich in cruelty, is an authority...?"[8]

ORIGINS

Kautilya's *Arthasastra* had been lost to history until 1904 when a na-tive Indian official discovered an ancient Sanskrit manuscript writ-ten on palm leaves in a monastery in southern India. The curator of the government library in Mysore, Dr. R. Shamasastry, translated the manuscript, and it caused a sensation among scholars around the world, including Max Weber, one of the founding fathers of modern sociology. It revolutionized the perceptions of Western Orientalists, who had before them a detailed, highly sophisticated manual for statecraft that evoked an Asian civilization that in the fourth century BC, in Weber's words, "went far beyond what was familiar and average practice for the *signore* of the early Italian Renaissance."[9] An Italian scholar commented at the time that the discovery of the *Arthasastra* marked the end of "the prejudice against the Hindu character as being devoid of force and vitality."[10]

The manuscript that has come down to us is in one sense the product of many authors; it is thought to reflect writings and an evolution of political thought that preceded Kautilya's time by perhaps two or three centuries. In fact on a number of issues Kautilya cites other sources and opinions and then gives his view. Some scholars assert that it is a composite manuscript, reflecting revisions and additions through the third and fourth centuries AD.[11] Nevertheless, Kautilya states throughout the text that he is the author and several subsequent commentators in Indian literature and philosophy claim the same. So we can accept as more probable than not that this is the work of a single historical person, one of the most important and unjustly neglected figures in world history. Kautilya was the political genius behind the creation of one of the world's first and greatest empires.[12]

The *Arthasastra* is divided into fourteen books; the first five books comprise about two-thirds of the text and deal with domestic economic, social, and legal policy; the latter part of the work is concerned with foreign policy. At the outset Kautilya states that the *Arthasastra* is the science of politics, which deals with the "acquisition and protection of the earth."[13] He reformulates this at the very end of the treatise, stating: "The source of the livelihood of men is wealth, in other words, the earth inhabited by men. The science which is the means of the attainment and protection of the earth is the Science of Politics."[14] So artha is wealth, but wealth is based on the earth as it is inhabited and worked upon by humans. The goal of politics is to acquire and maintain the earth inhabited and developed by humans. Kautilya's conception of wealth and politics includes sustainable management of natural resources, the protection of other species of life, plant and animals, and social welfare measures.

A good part of the rest of the first book, after passages describing the duty of the king to uphold the traditional social order of castes and their duties, deals with the daily routine of the king and the establishment of an elaborate system of internal espionage for state security. The daily routine Kautilya prescribes is one that would have exhausted even Bill Clinton when he was president. After only three- to four-and-a-half hours of sleep, the day begins at 1:30 a.m. with religious reflection and review of the day's agenda. At 3:00 a.m. our ideal ruler starts conferring with his secret agents, and by 6:00 a.m. he has his first meeting with military and financial advisers. Between 7:30 and 9:00 a.m. he should have an open audience with any subject of the kingdom who has a matter to discuss, and breakfast is at 9:00 a.m., after he already has been working for over seven hours. So the day goes on in an endless round of activity; from 6:00 to 7.30 p.m. he is to have a second meeting with his secret agents, followed by a sec- ond bath of the day, dinner, religious meditation, and repose at 9:00 p.m., accompanied by music, and falling asleep by 10:30.[15] Amazingly, there is some historical evidence (for example, in the *Indika* of Meg- asthenes) that the actual schedule of Chandragupta—and Ashoka— may have had some resemblance to the ideal described by Kautilya. But we do not know whether other colorful details recounted by Kautilya also matched reality. For example, the king's inner circle of personal security is to consist of armed Amazons, reinforced by a second circle of "eunuch servants wearing robes and turbans, in the third [circle] humpbacks, dwarfs...in the fourth, ministers, kinsmen and door-keepers, lances in hand."[16]

For Kautilya the king's duty and happiness lies exclusively with the happiness of his subjects, "what is beneficial to the subjects [is] his own benefit." The king's duty is ceaseless exertion and attention to "the management of material well-being"; inactivity brings material disaster.[17] Ashoka utters similar sentiments in his edicts. Yet for Kauti- lya the duty of the ruler to uphold the welfare of the state and its sub- jects relies heavily on a monstrous apparatus of secret agents and spies. He recommends the establishment of two major espionage corps, with nine categories between them of secret agents. The first corps con- sists of a fixed, centralized group, which includes bogus monks and ascetics, and networks of students, farmers, and merchants reporting continually to the government. The second corps, described as "Rov- ing Spies," handles assassinations and dirty tricks of all kinds; it cor- responds to the special actions agents of the CIA or KGB. The main function of these agents is to constantly ferret out—and act on—any signs of disloyalty to the king. The list of possible suspects starts with the crown prince, the commander in chief, the chief of the palace guards, and extends to the entire government administration as well as the population at large. Agents are to be planted among the king's foreign enemies *and* allies; to guarantee the foreign agents' loyalty, their families should be kept hostage.[18]

This atmosphere of generalized paranoia and the details of organization and tactics bear in many regards a startling resemblance to what we have learned of the organization of the security apparatus in modern totalitarian states. The extensive networks of student, farmer, and merchant informants, for example, recalls the networks of the Stasi in East Germany, so extensive that according to some estimates 20 percent of the population served as informants in one way or another. Holding families hostage at home was another standard operating technique for foreign agents of former East Bloc countries posted abroad.

Thus, we see that although the ultimate goal of Kautilya's system is the welfare of the people, both the assumption of what that welfare consists of and the means that are necessary to realize it bear troubling resemblances to the worst excesses of modern regimes. Indeed, Kautilya also sets forth a rough notion of the origins of the social contract, and of the role of force and violence—*danda*, literally, the "rod" or the "stick"—in protecting the state born of this contract.

A not uncommon sight in India today are members of an order of yellow-ochre robed mendicants known as *dandins*; they carry a staff or rod, also wrapped in yellow cloth, that must never touch the ground.[19] The now archaic meanings in English of *wand* are similar; we can find in the *Oxford English Dictionary* old uses of *wand* to denote the scepter of the king; a symbol of the authority of high legal office, as in a sheriff's wand; a rod or switch for punishment; and, as in *wand of peace*, an ancient term of Scots law: "a silver tipped baton delivered to an outlaw in token of his restoration to the king's peace; also carried by the king's messenger as the symbol of his office, and broken by him (by way of protest) if was resisted in the execution of his duty." One scholar has noted that the restraint of the dandins in never allowing their emblematic wand to touch the ground is a metaphor for the moral restraint that should be exercised in the use of all force and authority, particularly that of the state.[20]

Kautilya devotes a whole chapter to danda, for "on it is dependent the orderly maintenance of worldly life."[21] The social order, the four castes, and their respective duties—all depend on the skillful use of the rod, the coercive force of the state. Use of force in the right amounts in the right circumstances is not easy; clearly the king who is "severe with the Rod, becomes a source of terror to beings," but the king who is "mild with the Rod, is despised."[22] Well-being and spiritual good for the kingdom ensue with the judicious use of force, but use "in passion, or anger, or contempt" enrages even otherwise mild forest anchorites and wandering ascetics.[23] But worst of all, Kautilya says, is the total lack of coercive force, and of kingly authority to use it, because this entails a state of Hobbesian anarchy, which in ancient India was called the "law of the fishes," where "the stronger swallows the weak in the absence of the wielder of the Rod."[24]

Although Kautilya's notion of the use of force in practice appears at times extraordinarily repressive, he reaffirms a truism of political thought through the ages, that Justice, the protection of the weak from the arbitrary depredations of the strong—based ultimately on the wealth and coercive power delegated to the state—is the underpinning of all social and economic order. We are reminded of Adam Smith's observation in the *Theory of Moral Sentiments* that "justice is the main pillar that upholds the whole edifice . . . if it is removed, the great, immense fabrick of human society . . . must crumble to atoms."[25]

No Justice, no peace.

GROWING THE ECONOMY

The longest and in many ways most fascinating section of the *Arthasastra* is the second book, which deals with the duties and activities of various government department heads; it is nothing less than a comprehensive description of the ideal administration and economy of Mauryan India. A surprising number of measures appear not only to have been actual features of the empire of Chandragupta and Ashoka, but persisted for many centuries if we believe the Chinese pilgrims who visited India hundreds of years later.

One of the most important functions of the state is to promote the expansion of agriculture and rural development in general. Kautilya advocates an active policy of new land settlement; the new settlers should be mainly low-caste Sudras—the caste of peasants and land cultivators—and they should be resettled in villages ranging in size from one hundred to five hundred families. He recommends a series of land development incentives such as tax exemptions, state-backed loans of grain, cattle, and money, and land reform, i.e., confiscation of land "from those who do not till them and give them to others." Irrigation is a major part of the rural development strategy: "He should cause irrigation works to be built with natural water sources or with water built from elsewhere." [26]

The trade director "should encourage the import of goods produced in foreign lands by (allowing) concessions." Goods arriving via ship or caravan are to be granted tax exemptions to enable a profit to be made by their owners. And foreign traders are to enjoy immunity from lawsuits regarding money matters. [27]

The king is to develop "mines, factories, produce-forests, elephant-forests, cattle-herds and trade-routes and (establish) water-routes, land-routes and ports." [28] The government director of metals is to establish "factories for copper, lead, tin…brass, steel, bell-metal and iron, also (establish) trade in metal ware." [29] Mining is a particularly key sector, because it is the most important source of revenue for the treasury. The treasury in turn is the underpinning of the army, which is one of the manifestations of danda, the Rod, state coercion. Once again Kautlilya articulates how artha is realized: "With the treasury and the army, the earth is obtained." [30]

In fact, Kautilya's development agenda more than two millennia later has an eerie resemblance to the policies of the World Bank over many years. For decades, particularly the 1970s and 1980s, rural development, agriculture, and land settlement were the number one lending priorities for the bank in developing countries. Irrigation was also a major sector, as well as infrastructure such as roads and ports. Mining has also been a favorite investment for the bank's rapidly increasing subsidization of private-sector investment in developing countries. Kautilya's aggressive policy of new land settlement was a major feature of the Mauryan Empire, and the economic decline of the empire following Ashoka's death has been linked in part to the growing economic burden placed on the state treasury by these schemes. [31] Like modern land settlement projects promoted by international development agencies, Kautilya's new settlements seemed to have required subsidies, loans, and tax holidays for an indefinite period. Just as in modern times, many of these new settlements may have proved to be environmentally and economically unsustainable.

Kautilya's pursuit of artha is by no means one of unprincipled greed or exploitation; on the contrary, in a number of areas he advocates rational, long-term sustainable use of resources, including conservation of forests and protection of various species of animals and plants. Kautilya recommends, for example, the imposition of user fees for irrigation waters, above the normal one-sixth tax imposed on all agricultural produce. These water use fees apparently applied to all irrigation works, whether built by the state or by the individual farmer. It is interesting to note that in modern times water shortages have been caused by the practice of providing free water or water at extremely inexpensive rates; a major economic and environmental reform has been the attempt of development agencies and governments to encourage less waste and more sustainable use by charging water use fees. In fact, the U.S. federal government could learn something from Kautilya, since profligate water use by farmers in the American West has been encouraged by the supply of irrigated water at the cost of the government to farmers in highly arid regions where conservation should be encouraged.[32]

Kautilya advocates the establishment of various kinds of protected forests, "one for each kind of forest produce."[33] The kinds of forest produce include, besides hardwoods: reeds and bamboo; creepers and cane; fibers, such as hemp; materials for ropes; leaves for writing, such as palm leaves; flowers used in dyes; medicinal plants and herbs; and plants used for poisons.[34] Again, there are interesting modern correlations here, since in the whole area of international forest conservation the issue of sustainable use of nontimber resources has become increasingly important since the early 1990s. The setting aside of "extractive reserves" for nontimber resources such as natural rubber in the Amazon, chicle in the Guatemalan Peten rainforest, and ratan in Borneo, has become an important alternative in the struggle to promote conservation of forests that will allow economic benefits for local populations from the sustainable harvesting of nontimber products.

Kautilya also advocates the creation of protected reserves "where all animals are welcomed as guests and given full protection."[35] There is to be imposed "the highest fine...for binding, killing or injuring deer, beasts, birds or fish for whom safety has been proclaimed and who are kept in reserved parks, the middle fine on householders (for these offences) in reserved park enclosures."[36] Apparently the fine for householders for poaching was less because it was assumed the motive would be personal use rather than sale.[37] Of great importance too is the setting aside of special reserve forests for elephants, well guarded, with the death penalty for poaching. Having a sustained supply of elephants was a matter of state security, for military victory "depends principally on elephants."[38]

Kautilya has a whole list of species "which should be protected from all dangers of injury." These include, besides cattle, various kinds of birds and deer.[39] Beyond the protection of specific species, Kautilya also sets forth general rules against cruelty to animals. Causing hurt to small animals is punished by a fine of one *pana*, two panas if blood is drawn; hurting animals entails fines of two and four panas (for drawing blood), and the offender has to pay for the treatment and recovery of the injured beast.[40] (The pana was a coin of silver that was the standard unit of currency in the *Arthasastra*.) Even individual plants and trees enjoy protection, and if the scale of fines is indicative, they rank higher than animals, at least in urban areas. Cutting the shoots of shade, fruit or flowering trees in city parks is punishable by a fine of six panas, small branches twelve panas, and big branches twenty-four panas. All of this is to be overseen by several special departments of government, including a chief superintendent of forest produce, a chief elephant forester, and a chief protector of animals and controller of animal slaughter.[41]

We have here a whole program of resource management and conservation that is more sophisticated and farsighted than anything found in the United States until the late nineteenth century. Kautilya's approach might be compared to that of the utilitarian conservationists of the Gifford Pinchot school. Pinchot (1865–1946), the founder of the U.S. Forest Service and of America's first graduate school of forest management at Yale, was a close friend of Theodore Roosevelt. He is widely viewed as the founder and most eloquent spokesperson of his time for multiple-use management of natural resources in the United States. Pinchot literally coined the term *conservation*, defining it as "the use of the earth for the good of man,"[42] a definition that almost paraphrases Kautilya's description of artha. In fact, the story of how Pinchot chose this word to describe the then new approach to sustainable land and resource management a century ago relates to Indian history. Apparently Pinchot and a forester named Overton Price were discussing the need for a new term to describe their philosophy of resource use, and they remembered that in India the government forests were called *conservancies*.[43]

The essence of Pinchot's approach was rational, multiple use of resources for economic and other ends, with careful attention to their stewardship. His former friend, John Muir, later became his greatest opponent, for Muir was one of the first of whom we would call today deep ecologists, advocating the protection of nature and species as a value in itself, not as something that should be justified on any economic or utilitarian grounds. We will return to this theme later, since Ashoka's approach to conservation builds on that of Kautilya, but also transcends it in a higher ethos of respect and care for all life with which John Muir would have agreed.

REGULATION: ALE HOUSES AND PROSTITUTION, CONSUMER PROTECTION, LABOR LAW, AND ACCOUNTING

The economy of Kautilya's ideal state is a highly regulated one, with government ministers and administrators overseeing and collecting revenue from every conceivable activity. The second book of the *Arthasastra* describes some thirty odd administrative departments that besides traditional areas such as agriculture, forests, and mines, also include prostitution, liquor and alehouses, and gambling. For every activity where money or goods can be collected, the state is present. Gambling, the sale of liquor, and prostitution are such lucrative activities that in modern times they have traditionally attracted organized crime; Kautilya, with his typically cynical view of human nature, establishes them as state monopolies. The detail he lavishes on their management is fascinating reading, giving a unique insight into the details of daily life on the subcontinent nearly two and a half millennia ago. The controller of spirituous liquors, for example, "should cause ale-houses to be built with many rooms, (and) provided with separate beds and seats, (and) drinking bars provided with perfumes, flower and water, (and) pleasant in all seasons."[44] This is certainly a step up from your average cocktail lounge, and so are the refreshments. Kautilya lists the ingredients and instructions for an impressive variety of mixed drinks, including ones made with mango juice and essence of mango liquor, jaggery ("a coarse dark brown sugar made in India by evaporation from the sap of various kinds of palm," according to the *Oxford English Dictionary*), honey, rice, various kinds of peppers and spices, betel nuts, grapes, and turmeric (the chief ingredient in curry powder), to name a few.[45] The consumption and manufacture of alcoholic drinks is strictly regulated, but manufacture is not a state monopoly. The state alehouses, however, have other goals besides concentrating public drinking; they are prime sites for state espionage. Secret agents are to be posted to follow the conversations and the expenditures of customers, merchants are to find out "through their own female slaves of beautiful appearance, the intentions of strangers and natives...when they are intoxicated or asleep in secluded parts of the [alehouse] rooms."[46]

Prostitution offers too many opportunities for both taxation and espionage not to be closely regulated by the state. Prostitutes are classified, according to their beauty and jewelry, in the highest, middle, or lowest rank, and paid accordingly. The superintendent of courtesans is to keep track of all payments, gifts, and income for prostitutes, and each prostitute, if working independently and not for the state, should pay a monthly tax equal to double the standard fee they charge for a single visit. Courtesans and prostitutes proficient in languages are to be used for spying, and murder of enemies of the state.[47]

The lot of a prostitute in Kautilya's society, however, was more desirable and less risky than that of the vast majority of prostitutes in the world today, because the state guaranteed her economic security and that of her children in her old age, and applied strict penalties for any violence and abuse on the part of clients. When a prostitute loses her beauty, she is to secure the job of "mother" or "nurse" in brothels. There are fines for statutory rape, and "if a (man) robs a courtesan of her ornaments, her goods or the payment due to her, he shall be fined eight times (the amount)."[48]

Traders and merchants are also strictly regulated. Conspiracies to fix prices, to lessen the quality of goods sold for the same price, and to create artificial scarcities in goods to raise prices, are all punished by very high fines.[49] Goods that are highly beneficial to the country—for example, seeds and medicinal plants—should be duty free; the import of harmful or worthless goods, such as poison or alcohol, should be banned.[50] Thus, trade is encouraged, but notions of the public good set limits to free trade.

Physicians are also regulated, and there are penalties for malpractice: there is a middle-level fine for death caused by a mistaken treatment, and "in case of injury to a vital part or causing a deformity [on the part of a physician], the (magistrate) shall treat it as (a case of) physical injury."[51]

We also find what may be the first written description of export-import insurance. Customs officers at the frontiers are to charge, after obtaining statements of the quantity and quality of goods from merchants, a road toll, the amount of which corresponds to the quantity and nature of the goods. The customs officers then have the obligation to make good what may be lost or stolen on the way within the area of their jurisdiction.[52] Similarly, "what is stolen or killed between villages, the Superintendent of Pastures (shall make good)."[53]

Interest rates too are strictly regulated, the standard rate for personal debt being 1 and 1.25 percent per month, or 15 per-cent a year— a rate that does not compare unfavorably with modern credit card rates. Loans for riskier activities are entitled to higher rates: 5 percent a month for trade, 10 percent for transport through forests, and 20 percent for transport over the sea. There are separate rules for rate of return on capital that is lent: half of one year's profit. Kautilya's treatment of economic issues is in some respects much more modern than that of Aristotle, and of the classical and medieval Western world in general: the medieval church condemned the charging of interest as a source of income, and Aristotle expressed a disdain for commerce as an end in itself, an attitude that pervaded Western culture for many centuries.

Kautilya also sets out a whole code of labor relations. Certain fines are stipulated for noncompletion of work, but agreements and contracts for jobs can be annulled by the laborer in case of illness or calamity, or if the work is "vile," which presumably refers to unconscionable conditions not anticipated in the agreement. Or, alternatively, the laborer who is incapacitated has the right to get someone else to do the work in his stead.[54] Labor disputes "shall be settled only on the testimony of witnesses. In the absence of witnesses, the (judge) should inquire at the place where the work (was carried out)."[55] Kautilya also refers to the existence of labor guilds or unions, which negotiate work agreements on behalf of laborers.[56] Although the India of Kautilya was a society markedly differentiated by caste hierarchies, one can only marvel at the degree to which labor rights and a certain freedom to contract on the part of laborers, both individually and collectively, are respected.

On the other hand, besides caste differences, there is also considerable material inequality built into Kautilya's vision of the Maurya state. Kautilya enumerates the grades of pay for the entire civil service, ranging from forty-eight thousand panas for the prime minister, commander in chief of the army, and crown prince, to sixty panas for laborers and cowherds.[57] The highest-paid officials of the Maurya state were thus to be paid 800 times more than the lowest, a ratio not quite as extreme as the much-criticized growing gap between CEOs of American corporations and their workers. In 2006 the average American CEO was paid 821 times the salary of minimum wage workers, up from seventy-eight-fold in 1978.[58] But these ratios still understate the pay disparities in the global economy since rich country multinationals increasingly move their labor-intensive operations to developing nations. For example, the average American CEO is paid over two thousand times the average salary of an industrial worker in Mexico, a country with middle-income wages in global terms.[59] Once again a comparison with Kautilya's world reveals that the twenty-first century does not seem to have advanced as much as we like to think; indeed, as the globalization critics maintain, we seem in some respects to be heading in the wrong direction.

Even more disturbing are certain estimates that laborers in fourth-century-BC India had a higher standard of living than they do today in the heartland of Chandragupta and Ashoka's empire, which corresponds to the modern state of Bihar. According to one Indian researcher, the minimum wage of sixty panas was almost exactly the equivalent minimum wage paid to laborers by the British East India Company in the eighteenth century.[60] In the 1990s, public works laborers in Bihar were "paid almost the same amount in money as their forefathers were paid in silver two-and-a-half millennia ago!"[61] In fact, they are worse off, since in ancient times much food was gathered from the land, whereas the destruction of forests and common lands has made modern laborers much more dependent on their wages and the market for survival than their ancestors.[62]

There is a class of indentured servants or serfs in Kautilya's world, who could even be characterized as slaves; their working conditions and rights are also regulated. What is remarkable is that even for these individuals at the bottom of Maurya society, there is more freedom than existed in contemporaneous Greek society, not to speak of American society up to the Civil War.

Visitors to Washington sometimes make a day excursion to an eighteenth-century manor house that can rightfully be considered in some ways the birthplace of the Declaration of Independence and the Bill of Rights. The elegant country house was the home of the man who wrote these words in May 1776: "that all men are by nature created free and independent and have certain inalienable rights ... the enjoyment of life and liberty ... and pursuing and obtaining happiness." The country estate is not Monticello or Mount Vernon, but Gunston Hall, and the author of these words, who inspired his younger friend Thomas Jefferson two months later in drafting the preamble to the Declaration of Independence, was the Virginia planter George Mason. The document Mason drafted is the Virginia Declaration of Rights. Mason refused to ratify the U.S. Constitution in 1789 because it lacked an explicit bill of rights that he incorporated in the Virginia declaration. The adoption of the first ten amendments to the Constitution ten years later, guaranteeing freedom of speech, worship, assembly, and so forth, was in no small part due to the principled stand and advocacy of Mason. A dynamic, rapidly growing public university in northern Virginia—home to two Nobel laureates in economics—bears Mason's name.

Genteel female volunteers in colonial garb escort tourists on tours of the interior of the house, explaining that Mason's Virginia Declaration of Rights is the predecessor of not just the Declaration of Independence but of the French Declaration of Human Rights in 1791 and of the Universal Declaration of Human Rights of the United Nations in 1946. In contrast, one of the exhibits outside displays more words penned by George Mason: an advertisement on behalf of him and his son in the *Virginia Courier* of September 14, 1778, offering a reward for the capture of two escaped Negro slaves, complaining that they had left with items of clothing belonging to Mason and warning ship owners and captains on Chesapeake Bay not to embark them.

In this regard Mason was no different from Washington, Jefferson, or James Madison, who also owned slaves. In the 1850s, American proslavery apologists such as George Fitzhugh argued that slavery was preferable to the degraded conditions of "free" workers in the new global market of industrial capitalism and on humane grounds should be extended to the working men of the northern states and Europe.[63] Such views had an echo a century earlier among some of the English and Scottish political economists who were contemporaries of Adam Smith. The Anglo-Irish philosopher Bishop Berkeley advocated that beggars should be enslaved for at least a period of several years, and Francis Hutcheson, the Scottish moral philosopher, advocated perpetual slavery for the vagrant class.

Perhaps we should not judge the contradictions of Kautilya too harshly. The contrast between his proclaimed goals of social good and the unsavory methods he sometimes advocated is hardly as glaring as the spectacle of a new country 2,200 years later that claimed to be the cradle of human liberty, but that tolerated a system of slavery harsher and more absolute than anything that existed in Kautilya's India.

While most commentators agree that a kind of indentured servitude did exist in Mauryan India, it was indeed qualitatively different from the slavery that existed in much of the ancient world, particularly Greece, not to speak of the southern United States millennia later. The Mauryan economy did not depend on a system of slave labor, as did Greece and the antebellum South. Kautilya speaks of *dasas*, who are unfree laborers who toil together with free laborers in agriculture and in state enterprises, and who are entitled to the same pay. Normally Aryas—who comprised most of the population belonging to the four main castes, including Sudras, or peasants—could not be subject to permanent servitude, but they could be pledged to labor for a certain time period to pay back a debt or pledge themselves in the case of economic destitution.[64]

The indentured servants of colonial times might be an analogy. Permanently unfree labor seems to have been the fate of some unassimilated tribal and foreign laborers, *mlecchas*. But even they had many rights not associated with slaves: they could own, inherit, and pass on property, and their children were free, unless, in the case of mlecchas, they were sold as pledges. They were paid the same wages as free laborers. If an indentured woman had children with her master, both she and her children were to be set free. Those who were pledged as servants should not be forced to do certain kinds of unclean labor (picking up a corpse, dung, urine, or leavings of food), and they are to be liberated if subjected to any corporal punishment or sexual abuse.[65] The dasas of Kautilya's India enjoyed significantly more freedom and human dignity than the slaves of Thomas Jefferson and George Washington.

The dasas, however, were not at the very bottom of society; those outcastes who did unclean jobs—disposal of human wastes and corpses, leather workers, and so forth—were excluded from day-to-day contact (which the dasas necessarily had) with most of society, and were forced to live outside the city limits.[66] Nevertheless, even the outcastes did not belong to a master and also had a degree of autonomy and independence not granted to slaves in the classical or antebellum worlds.

As appropriate to a state and society based on the acquisition and management of material wealth, financial management and accounting are highly developed in Kautilya's ideal government. In Kautilya's administrative hierarchy, two finance officials, the collector-general and the treasurer-general rank right beneath the prime minister, chief priest, and commander in chief of the army. The collector in particular oversees the gathering and increase of revenue from various sources, while the treasurer manages funds once they have been received.[67] There are definitions of accrued revenue, outstanding revenue, expenditure, and balance received and carried forward that remind one of the U.S. Internal Revenue Code.[68]

The standard tax, we noted earlier, was one-sixth of agricultural produce, with additional fees for use of irrigation waters and tax holidays for investments in irrigation infrastructure or land improvement. In the early eleventh century AD, the Arab traveler and scholar Alberuni wrote an account of India that confirmed that 1,400 years after Kautilya, Indians still typically paid a sixth of their income to the king.[69] If the king is short for cash, Kautilya recommends hitting up the rich in proportion to their wealth and flattering them in return with awards of high positions, "umbrella, turban or decorations in consideration of money."[70] Bill Clinton's inviting rich Hollywood moguls to sleep in the White House's Lincoln Bedroom for a night in exchange for financial contributions to the Democratic Party was only a new variant on a very old theme.

The government administration also includes an accountant-general who is to build a records office where detailed financial records of all government departments are to be kept, as well as up-to-date information on the prices of all commodities in the kingdom and rates for different types of labor and legal records of all kinds. He is to oversee the finances of all works, appointing superintendents as well as monitoring the management and honesty of government departments through a network of spies.[71]

At the end of the fiscal year, the chief accountants of different departments are to meet in the records office with the accountant-general and present their accounts in sealed boxes. They are not to talk with one another and each is to give an oral recital of the written financial statements they have submitted. The accountant-general then checks the financial statements, auditing every work and undertaking.[72] He levies fines on the department accountants for discrepancies and for late submission of records.

Although Kautilya's description may be an idealized model, one can only admire the almost fanatical financial scrutiny and accountability that he prescribes. Kautilya would be appalled at the spectacle of a state treasury (such as our own) knowingly handing out hundreds of billions dollars to bail out entities such as banks with no rules for providing an exact accounting of how the money is used.

Even with such rigorous accounting procedures, Kautilya singles out corruption as a major threat to the state. He enumerates forty varieties of embezzlement and recommends again an elaborate system of espionage, paid informants, and incentives, both negative and positive, to check corruption. Penalties range from death for theft of objects of high value in state mines and factories to a varying scale of fines. Other penalties include publicly smearing the corrupt official with cow dung and ashes and "proclaiming his guilt," shaving his head, and exiling him.[73] While a system of informers and publicly smearing corrupt officials with dung may not be politically correct in today's mores, these approaches would certainly be more effective than the halfhearted measures we see today in the international system. Over the past forty years there has been very little accountability for many of the corrupt officials and rulers of the world, both in developing and industrialized countries, and international financial institutions until recently virtually ignored the issue. The question of controls and incentives is critical. Kautilya realized that corruption was a deadly threat to the state and that it is extremely hard to detect and requires rigorous controls, penalties, and incentives to keep it in check.

LAW AND ORDER

Books three and four of the *Arthasastra* set out what is in some respects a remarkably evolved legal code, dealing with areas that today we characterize as rules of pleading, civil procedure, rules of evidence, law of contracts, law of defamation and slander, law of nuisance, law of assault and battery, inheritance and family law, and the analysis of conflicts of laws, among others. A tribunal of three judges, to be appointed in major towns, oversees most kinds of civil and criminal actions and litigation.[74] There are rules stipulating when and how legal agreements and contracts are valid, including the invalidation of agreements made with parties of diminished mental capacity.

Kautilya's views on punishment combine aspects that we would view as barbaric and others as enlightened. He endorses torture and a caste-based discriminatory scale of punishment for the same crime. But there are other aspects that are remarkably progressive, even by contemporary American standards. For example, there is a whole code of prison administration, from which some American states and municipalities could learn: "For the hindrance of sleep, sitting down, meals, answering calls of nature or movement and for binding, in a judge's lock-up or in a prison-house, the fine shall be three panas increased successively by three panas for him that does it and for him who causes it to be done." [75] There are explicit penalties for violating women prisoners, although the higher the caste of the prisoner, the more stringent the penalty.[76] Prisons are to be constructed with separate facilities for men and women, and the inmates are to be provided with adequate latrines, bathing rooms, and arrangements for religious worship.[77]

Even more important is the conclusion of some commentators that imprisonment was a relatively infrequent form of punishment, the standard punishment for most criminal offences being a fine, or capital punishment for the most serious such as murder and arson. Prisons appear to be reserved for pretrial detention, and for those who, unable to pay a fine, work off what they owe in state agricultural enterprises (men) and textile concerns (women).[78] Here, contemporary America does not compare well, with more than 2.3 million people incarcerated, over 1 percent of the adult population. Kautilya also would have disapproved of the easy availability of guns in America society: "(People) shall move about unarmed, except those permitted with a sealed license." [79]

The *Arthasastra* sets out a law of defamation and libel, but again the degree of punishment is related to caste, the libel of a lower-caste person by a higher-caste individual subject to a lesser fine than the converse. We also find what may be the first statute in recorded history against what we would today call hate speech, namely politically incorrect discriminatory language against the disabled, or derogatory remarks based on ethnic or national identity:

> Among abusive expressions relating to the body, habits, learning, occupation, or nationalities, that of calling a deformed man by his right name, such as the blind, "the lame" etc, shall be punished with a fine of 3 panas; and by false name, 6 panas. If the blind, lame etc. are insulted with ironical expressions such as "a man of beautiful eyes"...the fine shall be 12 panas. Likewise when a person is taunted for leprosy, lunacy, impotency and the like....If abuse is due to carelessness, intoxication, or loss of sense etc., the fines shall be halved.[80]

Thus all abuse is punished, though the fine is doubled if the epithet is not true (i.e., the insulted party is not blind, lame, etc.), and mitigating circumstances such as drunkenness reduce the penalty.

But Kautilya has little tolerance for different religious sects, particularly Buddhists, and severely limits freedom of political speech: those who insult the king either directly or behind his back are to have their tongues cut out. There is the same penalty for "licking anything in a Brahmin's kitchen"![81]

The heavy hand of danda, coercive force, in Kautilya's state becomes apparent again when we read that for serious offences torture is a standard method of interrogation:

> The ordinary fourfold torture is: six strokes with a stick, seven lashes with a whip, two suspensions from above and the water tube [pour salt water through the nose]. In the case of very grave offenders (there may be): nine strokes with a cane, twelve whip-lashes, two thigh-encirclings, and two hangings up, needle in the hand, burning one joint of a finger of one who has drunk gruel, heating in the sun for one day for one who has drunk fat, and a bed of blabaja [coarse green grass] on a winter-night....He should cause torture to be given on alternate days and one only on one day.[82]

The reference to pouring saltwater through the nose must be one of the earliest-recorded mentions of waterboarding, a torture that has received much notoriety through its use by American forces in Iraq and in the prison camp at Guantánamo Bay. Minors, the aged, the sick, the intoxicated, the insane and pregnant women are not to be tortured, and women in general receive only half the standard prescribed torture. Brahmins are exempt from torture.[83]

Not surprisingly, Kautilya advocates capital punishment. For killing someone in a fight, the penalty is death with torture. Arsonists are to be burnt alive, saboteurs of dams, drowned.[84] Sex is regulated too. Abortion,[85] as well as homosexuality and sodomy, is punished by fines: "For one approaching a woman elsewhere than in the female organ, the lowest fine for violence shall be imposed, also for misbehaving with a man. A fine of twelve panas for the senseless wretch who carnally approaches lower animals, and double (that) for misbehaving with images of gods."[86] And woe to him who has relations with the king's wife: "The (punishment) in all cases (shall be) cooking in a big jar."[87]

## FOREIGN AFFAIRS AND WARFARE

*I am conscious of the fact that even 300 years before Christ, India had a diplomat who wrote . . . that a ruler should do nothing to displease the people. . . . The government of India has done a great service to mankind by bringing all diplomatic missions together in an integrated colony for the purpose of improving relations among representatives of various nations . . . India has paid a fitting tribute to . . . the celebrated sage diplomat who was the minister of Emperor Candragupta Maurya and author of the* Arthasastra.
—Earl Warren, former U.S. Supreme Court chief justice[88]

So spoke Earl Warren in 1956 when he laid the corner stone for the new U.S. Embassy building in the diplomatic quarter of New Delhi—known as Chanakyapuri, Chanakya being the popular, mythical name for Kautilya. One would hardly surmise from his words that Kautilya's diplomacy was notorious for ruthless realpolitik, intrigue, and deception, but then again Warren was also being diplomatic. Yet even with respect to diplomacy and warfare, Kautilya combined cold-blooded realism and treachery with some remarkably enlightened policies.

There are seven constituent elements of the state for Kautilya: the king, the ministries, the territory, the fortified city, the treasury, the army, and the ally (interstate relations).[89]

Kautilya gives a detailed description of the Mauryan army—including kinds of weapons and administration, details that Megasthenes in part confirms. Kautilya recommends training the army every day, except holidays, with frequent inspections by the king.[90] What is most astounding about the Mauryan army was its size; Chandragupta may have mustered as many as seven hundred thousand men, including nine thousand elephant cavalry, and according to Megasthenes they were all regularly paid, an enormous testament to Kautilya's financial management.[91] By contrast, the standing army of the Roman Empire at its apogee is estimated to have been three hundred thousand, which is also the approximate size of the current American armed forces.[92] Kautilya's admonitions about sound management of the treasury underpinning the army, and daily training for recruits, are as relevant as ever. One may contrast the sorry decline of the Russian army today, poorly paid and ill trained.

Kautilya also gives elaborate descriptions of the kinds of construction and fortifications appropriate for a fortified city, and again Megasthenes corroborates a number of details, as do modern archaeological excavations at Chandragupta's (and Ashoka's) capital, Pataliputra.

The heart of Kautilya's diplomacy lies in what he called the circle or mandala of kings (*rajamandala*), and the six different policies of foreign affairs in dealing with these kings. He formulates a theory of geopolitics that in some ways has never been surpassed—or in practice and in history, proved wrong. At the center of the circle or mandala of states is the king who is the "would-be conqueror." His immediate neighbor is a natural enemy, and the neighbor of his immediate neighbor is in turn a natural ally; the third outlying state is the natural enemy in turn of his ally, and thus also an ally of his immediate neighbor and enemy—and so on. In total, Kautilya describes twelve states (including the state at the center that is trying to acquire, consolidate, or defend its power), allied or opposed along the old principle that the enemy of one's enemy is an ally, and that neighbors are natural competitors.[93] Certainly the history of much geopolitics confirms this basic insight; one need only look at much of the history of competing alliances in Europe—France and Poland, for example, having been natural allies against Germany for hundreds of years.

Every state is in a given moment in a condition of decline, stability, or advancement, and the policy of the would-be conqueror at the center of the mandala is contingent on these circumstances.[94] Peace through treaties, hostility short of war, neutrality, armed attack, defensive alliance with another power, and simultaneous pursuit of peace with one state and hostility with another—these are the six policies of geopolitics. Which policy a state pursues is a function of its relative strength or weakness vis-à-vis the other states in the mandala, particularly its natural enemies, its neighbors. Thus, peace is for a weaker state, biding its time until it grows stronger; everything else being equal, a strong state should seize the moment and wage war. As noted earlier in this chapter, Kautilya advocates making peace treaties with the goal of buying time to build up one's forces to wage war, or even in the spirit of immediate deception to lull the enemy into a state of unpreparedness to increase the chances of success for a planned attack. He anticipated many infamous and cynical betrayals in history, the Molotov–Ribbentrop pact between Stalin's Soviet Union and Nazi Germany in 1939 being only the most notorious.

Although the goal of foreign policy is the expansion of the wealth and territory of the center state, peaceful means are preferable to war when they can work. (Kautilya certainly would have advised against the U.S. invasion of Iraq, both because other means were available and because of the excessive costliness, weakening the treasury, the underpinning of the state.) Kautilya identifies four strategic means to bend the will of another state, each more costly than the preceding: conciliation, gifts (*dana*), sowing dissension, and force (danda). He implies that conciliation should be tried first, resorting to force only when the first three have been tried and failed—a principle that seems to be rediscovered in the diplomatic overtures of President Barack Obama.[95] But in many cases, one of these measures is usually the most appropriate: for example, sowing dissension is the best approach for breaking up alliances, and gifts can be used to create traitors in the enemy camp. In general, conciliation and gifts work with weaker states, but sowing dissension and armed force are the appropriate ways to deal with stronger states.[96]

Kautilya's approach to foreign relations, then, is eminently rational, instrumental, and realistic: he believes that wealth and might triumph over courage and the energy of those who believe they have a just cause. He states that previous sages were wrong to think that valor triumphs over brute force, since the king who has might—which he sees as rooted in economic power—can hire heroic men, pay for a well-equipped army, and more easily make alliances with other powerful states. Thus, "winning over and purchasing men of energy, those possessed of might, even women, children, lame and blind persons, have conquered the world."[97]

History has proven him right time and time again: the Union forces in the American Civil War initially fought on most occasions with less audacity than the Confederate army under the leadership of brilliant and inspired generals like Stonewall Jackson and Robert E. Lee; but eventually the economic juggernaut of the ascendant North and the war of attrition led by Grant defeated superior valor. In World War II the allied victory over Germany and Japan was not due to superior bravery or spirit on a man-to-man basis; most accounts testify to the fanatical, in some case literally suicidal, fighting valor and initially high morale of the Axis troops, which was more than a match against allied armies. But final victory was assured by the enormous economic and manpower superiority of the allies.

While brute force defeats courage, cunning and knowledge can triumph over both: "The king, with the eyes of intelligence and science, is able to take counsel even with a small effort and to over-reach enemies possessed of energy and might, by conciliation [with allies] and other means and by secret and occult practices."[98] Thus, Kautilya, while taking a totally unsentimental view of the material basis of power, is quite modern in seeing technology and intelligence (in both the national security and more generic sense) as ultimately determining factors.

In fact, in an amazing admonition for his time, he warns against the uselessness of astrology, stating it is a foolish person who consults the stars to seek an auspicious time to undertake an action. Kautilya reminds us this is a material world: the only auspicious "constellation" for "achieving an object" is another object, i.e., material means.[99] And to drive the point home, he emphasizes: "Men, without wealth, do not attain their objects even with hundreds of efforts; objects are secured through objects, as elephants are through elephants set to catch them."[100]

Kautilya is really almost a contemporary of ours in his view of the world as material, as dominated by might, wealth, and the cool, rational application of technical, instrumental reason. His analysis of power politics and the circle or mandala of states appears as relevant as ever, speculation on the postmodern decline of the nation-state notwithstanding. A number of treatises on post–Cold War geopolitics published in the 1990s and early 2000s unconsciously evoke Kautilya's analysis, except that the entire planet is now the area of play for the mandala of states, rather than, as in Kautilya's time, the Indian subcontinent. Samuel Huntington, for example, in *The Clash of Civilizations and the Remaking of World Order*, describes a planet divided among nine geopolitical, civilization-based groupings, each maneuvering in a complex web of alliance, competition, neutrality, and hostility toward one another. The civilizations in his schema embody the resurgence of identity-based politics on an international level.

On a global level, Huntington's groupings and alliances tend to follow Kautilyan principles; for example, the Orthodox world led by Russia seeks alliances with India and China as counterweights to its neighbors Japan and the West (non-Orthodox Europe and North America). He sees each civilization as consisting of core states surrounded by a concentric circle of sympathetic states meeting up against the "fault line" where different civilizations border on one another, frequently with hostility or conflict—Bosnia being one such example. Each of Huntington's civilizations is in a state of decline, dominance (the West is in a transition from dominance to decline), or ascendancy and resurgence (Islam, and the Sinic cultural area, for example), corresponding to Kautilya's categories of decline, stability, or advancement.[101] But Huntington's "civilizations" are crude, clumsy constructs, not really corresponding to the much more heterogeneous cultural and historical reality of the regions he describes;[102] Kautilya's approach is much more situational and pragmatic.

Zbigniew Brzezinski has written of the need for a new U.S. geo-politics, focusing on "the grand chessboard" of the Eurasian land mass as mandala of states that the United States cannot allow to come under the domination of any hegemon—the failed project of both Hitler and Stalin. Thus the primary task of U.S. foreign policy and diplomacy should be to first "identify the geostrategically dynamic Eurasian states that have the power to cause a potentially important shift in the international distribution of power.... and to pinpoint the geopolitically critical Eurasian states whose location...[has] catalytic effects on the more active geostrategic partners," and second, "to formulate specific U.S. policies to offset, co-opt, and/or control the above [states]."[103] This is a modern reformulation of the overall ap-proach behind Kautilya's six policies and four strategic means to deal with other states.

Just when we are ready to conclude that Kautilya is the advocate of the cold-blooded, amoral imposition of force and instrumental use of reason to gain wealth and advantage without regard for humanitarian ideals, he surprises us—characteristically, one might add. His rec-ommendations for warfare, for example, show a remarkable sense of restraint and even compassion for the injured, fallen, and conquered. The attacking army should be accompanied by a kind of Red Cross, with physicians with surgical instruments and medicines, as well as women in charge of food and drink, stationed in the rear.[104] The at-tacking army is to grant safety to the enemy injured, and to those who have lost their weapons, who retreat or surrender, or who have ceased fighting.[105]

Kautilya calls for the protection of the countryside of the enemy territory, particularly of farmers. The attacker should not use fire in-discriminately, for fire destroys "innumerable creatures, grains, ani-mals, money, forest produce, and goods. And a kingdom, with stores exhausted, even if obtained, leads only to loss."[106] We are reminded that artha for Kautilya is above all the land inhabited and used by people. "There is no country without people, and no kingdom with-out a country," he observes.[107] He would not have approved of the massively destructive tactics of modern war.

Kautilya's insight that wealth is the underlying basis and goal of politics, and that the material and social well-being of the defeated state is in the interest of the victor is one that would have to be learned anew through tremendous suffering in the twentieth century. We only need to recall the Treaty of Versailles, with its economically ruinous consequences for defeated Germany after the First World War, and the totally different—and successful—approach of the Marshall Plan after the Second World War.

All in all, as we wade through the *Arthasastra* we are overwhelmed by an almost obsessive attention to detail and regulation; Kautilya leaves little to the imagination, or to discretion. His is a command and control world, and the economy he describes is heavily regulated, with a large state sector. Yet, despite the huge distance of more than two millennia, his age was, alas, no more barbaric or brutal than ours; when compared with the most ruthless statesmen of the past hundred years, Kautilya is a paragon of moderation and balance.

POLITICS AND ETHICS

Kautilya advocates rather enlightened provisions for the physical and economic protection of the weak, some of the elements of what we would view as a welfare state. The king, for example, "should maintain children, aged persons and persons in distress when these are helpless, as also the woman who has borne no child and the sons of one who has (when these are helpless)." [108] Moreover, the state is to ensure child and wife support, and support of aged parents on the part of those who have the means to do so. [109] Children, the old, the sick, wandering monks, pregnant women, and Brahmins are to be granted free passage on river ferries by the controller of shipping. [110]

Kautilya's recommendations for preventing famines "remain relevant even today," according to Nobel economics laureate Amartya Sen. [111] Sen in particular admires Kautilya's colorful injunction to "thin the rich by exacting excessive revenue or causing them to vomit their accumulated wealth." [112] The king should also provide the population with seeds and provisions, help them through the distribution of his own wealth and together with his subjects resettle on the banks of rivers and lakes where available water will help grow crops. He can also launch large-scale hunting and fishing expeditions. [113]

How are we to understand Kautilya, then? In reading him we are constantly torn between unease, at times bordering on repulsion, for his apparently ruthless and cynical approach to power; and admiration, for eminently rational, indeed enlightened and practical policies. In reality, there is no contradiction, since besides embodying the "engineering" or instrumental approach to economics, Kautilya is the classic proponent of political realism, of politics as the craft of obtaining and increasing power, without moralistic or idealistic illusions. Ethically, he is a consequentialist par excellence. His insight that material wealth is the linchpin of political power makes him the spiritual godfather of political economy. Max Weber, one of the founders of modern sociology and political science, is also a realist. Like Kautilya, he emphasizes the fundamental role of force—danda—in politics. Weber maintains the classic realist position that the state is grounded in violence, a monopoly of force that is granted to it by the governed, or dominated. The legitimization of this monopoly can be traditional, or charismatic (exercised by a prophet or demagogue), or legal, with appeal to a rational system of rules.[114] He tells us that politics is inherently riven by a tragic contradiction:

> He who lets himself in for politics, that is, for power and force as means, contracts with diabolical powers and for his action it is *not* true that good can follow only from good and evil only from evil, but that often the opposite is true. Anyone who fails to see this is, indeed, a political infant. We are placed in various life-spheres, *each of which is governed by different laws.*[115]

Our unease with Kautilya—and with politics and political economy—lies in that Kautilya is perhaps the first person in history to systematically lay out, and draw consequences from, the uncomfortable truths of the calculus of power. If political conduct is to be ethical, Weber maintains, there are two fundamental choices: one can maintain the purity of one's intentions and goals in an "ethic of ultimate ends," or one can recognize an "ethic of responsibility," where one holds oneself accountable for "the foreseeable results of one's actions."[116] This is the classic formulation of the tension between the utopian and the realist approaches in politics. The failed international politics of Woodrow Wilson and the League of Nations stands as the leading modern example of the weaknesses of the utopian approach. Weber maintains that politics is the preeminent realm where we must acknowledge that the ends can justify the means and that we may have to use dangerous or morally dubious means and weigh their consequences. The believer in an ethic of ultimate ends weighs his or her actions by the purity of intention and the worthiness of the goal, and is prone to ignore the practical consequences of his or her actions. Not only Weber, but other modern political thinkers like E. H. Carr conclude that the practice of politics is fundamentally tragic since it is bound up with fundamental ethical paradoxes.[117]

Kautilya's analysis, and the Hindu tradition in which it is rooted, are extremely helpful in clarifying these paradoxes. Kautilya appears to be something of a revolutionary in that he puts artha, the attainment of material wealth, ahead of dharma, spiritual good and morality, and kama, sensual pleasure, as the most important goal in life, since artha makes the other two possible. Dharma has many meanings and contexts; at the most general level it is the order, law, and truth of creation, and the knowledge, doctrine, and behavior that achieves that truth. But it also refers to the specific duties of specific positions and roles in society, and the specific ethics associated with carrying out those roles. Thus we have rajadharma, which is the set of duties and responsibilities associated with the role of a ruler—a *raja*. In the first book of the *Arthasastra*, Kautilya reaffirms Hindu tradition in repeating the specific duties and responsibilities associated with each of the four major Hindu castes (*varna*), and with each of the stages of life of an individual (the four *asramas*—the student, the householder, the dweller in the forest following middle age, and the wandering ascetic seeking enlightenment before death).[118] And there are some duties, Kautilya notes, which are valid for all: nonviolence (*ahimsa*), truthfulness, purity, freedom from envy, freedom from cruelty, and tolerance.[119]

All of these duties are dharma, but clearly there is conflict: nonviolence, for example, cannot always be reconciled with the king's obligation to use danda. In the Hindu tradition, specific duties appropriate to different social roles and contexts are known as *svadharma*, literally, one's own dharma.[120] *Samanya* dharma refers to universal, ethical duties, such as nonviolence, also mentioned by Kautilya, that are virtues in themselves, not linked to the specific goals of a specific social role.[121] Clearly, the practice of politics leads to situations where choices must be made between different dharmas.

The traditional Hindu answer to this dilemma is found in the *Bhagavad Gita*, where the hero Arjuna is faced with the prospect of performing his svadharma as a warrior, a Kshatriya, which involves engaging in a battle that will lead to immense slaughter, including that of his kinsmen. Arjuna ponders the duties of other dharmas, those of nonviolence and of not taking actions that lead to the death of his kin. Lord Krishna advises him that the order of the world will fall if individuals do not carry out their duty in specific situations, and that if he performs his svadharma without egotistical attachment to the fruits of his actions, he will be doing the only right thing, that which ultimately upholds the whole dharmic order of the universe.

The duty of the ruler, for Kautilya, is to uphold all of society by assuring the conditions for each person, in their respective caste and period of life, to carry out their dharma, which constitutes the well-being and good of each person and of all of society.[122] The ruler, in following his specific dharma (rajadharma), and in upholding the dharma of creation, must in the practice of politics pay attention to artha and danda first. It can be argued at least that in the broader scheme of things, Kautilya is not the amoral materialist he sometimes appears to be: he simply analyzes without illusions the nature of human political and social relations. He concludes, like Max Weber 2,300 years later, that if we want to be ethical in the conduct of politics, we cannot retreat into delusions of pure intentions and pure goals without taking note of the real world consequences of such utopianism. Just as with the warrior dharma of Arjuna in the *Bhagavad Gita*, fulfilling the kingly dharma as set out in the *Arthasastra* means inherently tragic ethical paradoxes and choices, including sometimes violating otherwise universal dharmic, ethical obligations. And indeed, in his essay *Politics as a Vocation*, Weber approvingly notes that "the Hindu order of life made each of the different occupations an object of a specific ethical code, a Dharma." The *Arthasastra*, he notes, continues the "Indian ethic's quite unbroken treatment of politics by following politics' own laws...even radically enhancing this royal art."[123]

Let us return to the British historian and political thinker E.H. Carr, who, like Max Weber, saw political life as inherently tragic in its moral paradoxes. In *The Twenty Years' Crisis*, he gives a classic account of the perennial tension between realism and utopianism in politics, and perhaps points to a way out of this quandary. Like Karl Polanyi, Carr wrote in the 1930s and 1940s and was concerned about the catastrophic failure of European statecraft that led to World War II. Like Polanyi, he examines the elements of the debacle. He concludes that Britain and the United States at least contributed to the collapse through a deluded neglect in the twenties and thirties of the "factor of power," of the realist analysis of international politics.[124]

Also like Polanyi, he traces some of the roots of the disaster to the pursuit of an unrealizable utopia of universal free trade, based on eighteenth- and nineteenth-century assumptions of Benthamite utilitarianism.[125] Woodrow Wilson "transplanted the nineteenth-century rationalist faith to the almost virgin soil of international politics . . . nearly all popular theories of international politics between the two world wars were reflections, seen in an American mirror, of nineteenth-century liberal thought."[126] The failure of a politics based on utopian delusions—what Carr called "Benthamism transplanted"—elicited in the 1930s the return with a vengeance of a cynical, power-oriented realism that plunged the world into war. Or, as Kangle, the leading modern Indian commentator and translator of Kautilya, concludes, Kautilya realized that it is a fatal error to confuse purely personal ethics with the moral order demanded by public affairs.[127]

The circumstances that Carr and Polanyi dealt with have changed less than we think: American approaches to politics and economics still dominate, and the dominant and popular theories still have roots in nineteenth-century liberalism, in an ideology of utility maximizers and universal free markets, and a neo-Wilsonian project to bring democracy, extremely selectively, to putatively benighted areas of the world. Sixty years later there is one historical irony: the proponents of these policies often pose as realists. In the economic sphere, the globalizing heirs of Bentham cast their critics as perhaps well-intentioned but ill-informed utopians; and the disastrous neo-Wilsonian project to bring democracy to Iraq by invasion was initially paraded as the first episode of a new American foreign policy of neorealism, grounded on the brute force of American military hegemony and the hegemon's unilateral self-proclaimed right to wage preemptive wars. And in 2008 the ideology of untrammeled economic liberalism, rationalized as a neo-Benthamite project of utility, plunged the world into an economic and social crisis that resurrected political reactions not seen since the 1930s.

Like Polanyi, Carr also critiques the attempt to disembed and separate the economic sphere from politics and power—in reality, the autonomous economy is a fiction, it is always a product of politically established conditions and rules. He asserts that "the military and economic weapons are merely different instruments of power."[128]

But he also maintains that a purely realist approach, based on the instrumental calculus of the manipulation of power, is equally untenable: power without a deeper ethical, as it were, "utopian," grounding loses legitimacy, and as a dominant principle in international relations, "makes any kind of international society impossible."[129] Realism, he notes, tends to emphasize the irresistible strength of existing forces and the inevitable character of existing tendencies, and to insist that the highest wisdom lies in accepting, and adapting oneself to, these forces and these tendencies. Such an attitude, though advocated in the name of "objective" thought, may no doubt be carried to the point where it results in the sterilization of thought and the negation of action.[130]

We certainly recognize an echo here of those who—even in the midst of a world economic crisis that globalization has spurred—repeat as a mantra that globalization in its current form is inevitable, unstoppable, that there is no alternative, and that those who protest and call for different global values and governance are utopians who might as well be trying to hold back the tide. Viable politics must strike a balance between the realist and the utopian, which necessarily exist on different, in some ways always incommensurable levels: "The state is built up out of these two conflicting aspects of human nature. Utopia and reality, the ideal and the institution, morality and power, are from the outset inextricably blended in it."[131]

Max Weber concludes his famous essay on politics with a similar reflection:

> Certainly all historical experience confirms the truth—that man would not have attained the possible unless time and time again he had reached out for the impossible. But to do that a man must be a leader, and not only a leader, but a hero as well, in a very sober sense of the word.[132]

There could be no better introduction to Ashoka, who, inheriting the empire grounded on Kautilya's realism, sought to transcend it.

CHAPTER 5

# The Gift of Dirt

In the autumn of 2000 a theater troupe from Manipur, a small strife-ridden state in northeast India, presented to modest audiences but rave reviews in several cities across America a play based on mythical incidents from the life of Ashoka. In the play, *The Final Beatitude*, Ashoka, as a child, witnesses the horrors of war, which only serve to harden his heart. When crowned king, Ashoka creates a personal prison where he delights in the torture and murder of innocents and monks. A moment comes when Ashoka too is faced with torture by Ghor, the monster whom he has appointed to administer this hell. Ashoka finally realizes the suffering he has inflicted. He recognizes the truth of Buddhism and embraces compassion and nonviolence in his personal life and kingly duties. The director of the play, Ratan Thiyam, said that the message of his work is very much a contemporary and personal one: ongoing ethnic unrest and human rights abuses, torture and murder by both rebels and the Indian army, having plagued his desperately poor home state for many years. The Manipur dirty war is only one of a myriad of little-known conflicts that have proliferated in the 1990s and 2000s as the world has become more closely bound together economically and technologically. "The more civilized we become," Thiyam observed, "the more things we have for creating violence." [1]

In the United States in the early years of the new millennium, Ashoka's example seems on occasion to speak with fresh urgency. What historical or cultural currents are at work today that make both Ashoka's mythical figure and historical personage—which in practice are difficult to entirely separate—of growing contemporary significance? We noted that Ashoka emerged at the end of nearly three centuries of transformation and turmoil in South Asian society—and indeed in the civilized societies of most of the European-Asian world—in a time of great philosophical and religious upheaval, the Axial Age. Based on a personal vision of universal transcendence rooted in Buddhism as well as in the vigorous philosophical debate of his day, Ashoka attempted to craft and put into practice a secular ethic of global, universal citizenship to which all people could adhere. Today we face the challenge of developing a global consciousness commensurate with the increasing physical interconnectedness of global society. Despite the distance of millennia, and the radically different material conditions of our lives, Ashoka, like few other figures in history, speaks to this challenge.

Before turning to the historical Ashoka, let us encounter Ashoka's mythical presence. Even a few hundred years after Ashoka's death, knowledge of the historical Ashoka had been lost, even the ability to read his rock and pillar inscriptions. But the influence of the mythical symbolism of Ashoka's life had already spread to much of Asia. Almost seven centuries after Ashoka's death, the Chinese pilgrim Faxian traveled to India to search for uncorrupted Buddhist texts and to visit the sites of Buddha's life. In the Ganges heartland, where Buddha's life and deeds took place, he encountered physical evidence of Ashoka's reign everywhere, but Ashoka was already a largely mythical figure. At times for Faxian the Ashokan artifacts appear to come from a civilization that literally appears extraterrestrial. He visits Ashoka's palace, then still standing in Pataliputra, and is so awestruck by its grandeur that he declares it has been "all built by spirits who piled up stones, constructed walls and gates, carved designs, engraved and inlaid, after no human fashion." [2] The ability to read Ashoka's rock and pillar inscriptions had been lost, and Faxian repeats translations of a pillar inscription that are patently false (probably recited to him by overly fanciful guides)—and repeated word for word by his more illustrious Chinese pilgrim successor, Xuanzang, two hundred years later. [3]

Faxian and Xuanzang recount myths recorded in the Buddhist canon, in Sanskrit and Pali. The major Sanskrit text that has come down to us is the *Asokavadana*, thought to have been written in the second century AD in northwest India. Later texts, such as the Tibetan Lama Tartantha's early seventeenth-century *History of Buddhism in India*, are based on the *Asokavadana* and now lost Sanskrit texts. [4] An *avadana*, Buddhist scholar John Strong tells us, "is a narrative of the religious deeds of an individual and is primarily intended to illustrate the workings of karma and the values of faith and devotion."[5] The other primary sources are the chronicles of the founding and history of Sri Lanka, the *Dipavamsa* (The island chronicle) and the *Mahavamsa* (The great chronicle), which come down to us from the great Buddhist monasteries in Sri Lanka in Anuradhapura. They both recount that Ashoka sent his son, Mahinda, as an envoy to Sri Lanka, converting the Sinhalese king Devanampiya Tissa to Buddhism, something that appears to be a historical fact, although there is some question whether Mahinda was Ashoka's brother rather than his son.[6] A *vamsa*, according to Strong, is a "lineage or chronicle" that seeks to establish the pedigree of a country or sect.[7] As such, the Sri Lankan chronicles are more nationalistic and tendentious in their account—the *Asokavadana* makes no mention, for example, of Mahinda.[8]

The *Asokavadana* was already translated into Chinese in AD 300, and became well known in translation in Japan, Korea, and central Asia. The *Mahavamsa* and *Dipavamsa* are to this day influential in Sri Lanka, since they are nothing less than the mythical national chronicle of 2,300 hundred years of uninterrupted history; in a very real sense, Sinhalese history and identity begins with the visit of Ashoka's son. But the vamsas and Theravada Buddhism rooted in Sri Lanka are also influential in much of Southeast Asia, including Thailand and Burma. Given the importance of Buddhism in the historical cultures of all these countries and regions, any discussion of the roots of "Asian Values" in an age of globalization would be remiss in not taking into account the historical and continuing importance of these texts.[9]

Ashoka first appears in the *Asokavadana* as a little boy, Jaya, who gives a handful of dirt to the Buddha, an act that, because of its sincerity (all the boy had to give was dirt), presages his reincarnation as a chakravartin, a righteous world-ruling king. The gift of a handful of earth in an earlier life proclaims the rule of a future king over the earth in a future life—and, we shall see, Ashoka's giving away of that kingdom before his death.[10] The notion of gift and giving—dana—is critical in these accounts, and it establishes a contrast with the traditional role of force and coercion—danda—that is so critical in Kautilya's ideal state. Yet since dirt is also impure, this gift "necessarily entails impure karmic consequences."[11] He is born a physically ugly person (just like Kautilya): "Now Ashoka's body [had bad skin; it] was rough and unpleasant to the touch and not at all liked by his father.... [Ashoka retorted] The very sight of me is hateful to the king."[12]

And, in the *Asokavadana* account, his reign will not be one of pure compassion, but like his skin, rough, with acts of both necessary and wanton brutality and coercion. Even in the hagiographic accounts of Ashoka's life, Kautilya lurks in the background.

## ASHOKA'S HELL

The *Asokavadana* is full of incidents of the cruelty of Ashoka, mainly before his conversion to Buddhism, but importantly, also following it. Perhaps the most famous is the story of Ashoka's Hell, which both Faxian and Xuanzang repeat in some detail. Faxian tells us that Ashoka's henchmen know they have found the man Ashoka is seeking when they see a fierce-looking fellow who likes to catch fish and animals of all kinds and kill them for pleasure. The *Asokavadana* recounts that his name was Girika, and that even as a boy he "reviled his mother and father, and beat up the other boys and girls. With nets and hooks, he caught and killed ants, flies mice and fish." [13] When Ashoka offers him his new job and his parents hesitate to grant him permission to leave, Girika promptly murders them both. Faxian tells us that Ashoka instructed his state torturer to camouflage the torture chambers as an enticing palace "with all kinds of flowers and fruits, with good pools for bathing, the whole so beautifully ornamented as to cause people to long to gaze upon it." [14] Ashoka instructs Girika to spare no one who ever enters the torture chamber, even Ashoka himself. The *Asokavadana* catalogs a gruesome list of the various tortures Girika plans to inflict upon Ashoka's victims, such as "pry[ing] open their mouths with an iron bar and pouring boiling copper down their throats." [15]

But in these mythical accounts, the torture chamber also becomes the place of Ashoka's conversion: a pious mendicant (named Samudra—"Ocean") miraculously withstands all of the tortures. Faxian and the *Asokavadana* tell us that when Samudra is thrown into a cauldron of boiling water (for effect, the *Asokavadana* adds human blood, marrow, urine, and excrement), the hot water cools down and in the middle of it sprouts a lotus on which the mendicant sits. When Ashoka hears of these miracles he enters the torture chamber; Samudra converts him to Buddhism and recounts the Buddha's forgotten prophecy that Ashoka's will reign as a righteous chakravartin over one of the earth's four continents. Girika reminds Ashoka of his order to let no one leave the torture chamber alive—and Ashoka responds, "Which one of us entered this place first?" Girika has to admit, it is he—and

Ashoka orders that he be burnt to death. And so, the *Asokavadana* concludes, "the beautiful jail was then torn down, and a guarantee of security extended to all beings." [16]

## ASHOKA THE FIERCE

Even before the construction of his hell, Ashoka exhibits in the early part of his reign an arbitrary cruelty worthy of a Nero or a Caligula. He orders his ministers to chop down all the flower and fruit trees in the kingdom but to preserve the thorn trees. They ask whether he hasn't confused what he wanted to order—shouldn't the thorn trees be eradicated and the flower and fruit trees preserved? "Ashoka became furious at this; he unsheathed his sword and cut off the heads of five hundred ministers." [17] He has five hundred young women in his harem burnt alive because his body "was rough skinned, and [they]...did not enjoy caressing him." [18] Thus, he is known as Candasoka—"Ashoka the Fierce."

After his conversion by the mendicant Samudra, Ashoka still on occasion indulges in acts of unmitigated cruelty. He does not spare Girika, his head torturer, from a gruesome death. He has eighteen thousand Jain heretics put to death. But still the heresy persists, and Ashoka declares he will give a gold coin for the head of each heretic that is brought to him. Ashoka's brother Vitasoka spends a night disguised as a commoner in the hearth of a cowherd, who mistakes him for a heretic mendicant and brings his head to Ashoka asking for a reward. Ashoka faints, and according to the *Asokavadana*, when he recovers consciousness, his ministers admonish him that "you should guarantee the security of all beings." Ashoka followed their advice and no one was ever condemned to death again.[19] Nevertheless, later in the mythical account of his life, in a tragedy reminiscent of Greek dramaturges, he orders his second wife, Queen Tisyaraksita (a variant of Tissarakha),[20] to be burnt alive, and the citizens of a rebel city, Taksasila (Taxila), to be put to death.

Queen Tisyaraksita attempts to seduce Ashoka's son, Kunala, whose mother is another of Ashoka's wives. Kunala is renowned for the beauty of his eyes. When he refuses Tisyaraksita's advances, she plots revenge. The opportunity occurs when Ashoka sends Kunala to quell an uprising in Taksasila. Ashoka becomes extremely ill, and Tisyaraksita is able to find a cure, by ordering Ashoka's doctors to bring anyone in the kingdom suffering from a similar illness directly to her. She finds such a man, and after killing him, discovers that the illness is caused by a large stomach worm that can be killed by ingesting an onion. When she cures Ashoka, he grants her wish to be given command of the kingdom for a week, and her first order is for officials in Taksasila to have Kunala's eyes plucked out. When Kunala returns, he pleads for mercy for Tisyaraksita, and the purity and truthfulness of his pleas causes the miraculous restoration of his sight. But Ashoka is implacable and has her killed along with the inhabitants of Taksasila.

The story of Kunala also illustrates the power of enlightenment and the transitoriness of physical desire, pain, and pleasure. In the *Asokavadana,* Kunala's blinding is the occasion of his spiritual liberation. When Xuanzang visits Taksasila in the seventh century AD, he finds that it is a pilgrimage site for the blind who come to pray for the restoration of their sight.[21] And over the centuries, the myth of Kunala has inspired blind poets in Buddhist Asia, including Japan.[22]

Although the blinding of Kunala is the last, most egregious act of rancor by Tisyaraksita, it is not the only one. The Ashoka of myth is portrayed as beset by the machinations of his chief wife. Following his conversion, Ashoka is particularly reverent of the Bodhi tree at Bodh Gaya (in the present-day state of Bihar), under which the Buddha first achieved enlightenment. Ashoka sends to the site of the Bodhi tree an offering of precious jewels. Tisyaraksita is consumed by jealousy and pays a sorceress to destroy "Bodhi, her rival." The sacred tree begins to wither, and Ashoka is so grief stricken that he exclaims that if Bodhi dies, he will too. Tisyaraksita says she will bring him pleasure if he no longer has Bodhi, and it is then that she finds out that Bodhi is the sacred tree, not a mistress. Recognizing her mistake, Tisyaraksita pleads with the sorceress to restore the tree, which she can do by watering it with a thousand pitchers of milk a day. Ashoka is so overjoyed that he vows to establish a great quinquennial festival to honor the *sangha,* the Buddhist community of believers.[23]

### THE ESSENCE OF DHARMA

More often, though, it is Ashoka himself who, following his conversion, finds novel ruses to bring enlightenment and the truth of dharma to his entourage. In the Hindu social order, every individual and caste had and has a specific dharma according to station and age. For Buddhists, Dharma is revealed through the Buddha's teachings: the Four Noble Truths about the nature and cause of suffering in life and the Eightfold Path that releases humans from suffering and leads to enlightenment. For Kautilya, dharma is very practical, hardheaded, linked to the real-world conundrums of politics and governance—and indeed, often subservient or identical in politics to economics and the primary pursuit of wealth, artha. We shall see that the dharma (or dhamma, in Pali) that the historical Ashoka sets down in his edicts is related to the Kautilyan and Buddhist dharmas, perhaps in a sense attempting to reconcile or transcend them. But accounts of the mythical Ashoka—which paradoxically may have had more lasting historical influence than Ashoka's actual edicts—emphasize the Buddhist Dharma (that is, the Buddha's teachings), using key episodes in Ashoka's life as examples.

For example, in the *Asokavadana*, Vitasoka is not a believer in Buddhism, and thinks that Buddhist monks are a rather corrupt lot, lazy and hedonistic. Ashoka pretends to sentence Vitasoka to death, and through a prearranged subterfuge, grants him at the urging of his ministers a one-week reprieve where he will reign as king before his execution. Despite having every conceivable power and pleasure at his disposition, Vitasoka is miserable and consumed by anxiety during his short reign. Ashoka then reveals the deception, and points out to Vitasoka:

> Can it be that the fear of death—in just one lifetime—kept you from all pleasures, even after you had obtained the privileges of a king? How then can you think that the Buddhist monks enjoy worldly pleasures—they who are afraid of death in hundreds of lifetimes and who see all the realms of rebirth and sufferings which go with them?[24]

Vitasoka recognizes the truth of the Buddhist Dharma.

One of the most important examples of Dharma in the mythical accounts of Ashoka is the story of Yasas, the abbot of Ashoka's favorite Buddhist monastery and a government minister. Yasas, though a very holy man, berates Ashoka for prostrating himself before every Buddhist monk he encounters. Some of the monks are of low-caste origin, Yasas observes, and it is not appropriate for the high-caste king to bow before them. Ashoka does not react initially, but sometime later orders each of his ministers to procure the head of a different animal and sell it in the marketplace. Yasas has the task of obtaining a human head and attempting to sell it. When Yasas returns from the market, Ashoka inquires how things went; Yasas replies that the other ministers were all able to sell the heads of various beasts, but the human head inspired disgust and was impossible even to give away. Ashoka inquires if it was the particular head that inspired disgust or the heads of all humans, to which Yasas replies all humans. And Ashoka then asks whether his own head would also be disgusting and forces Yasas to answer yes. And Ashoka replies:

> You, sir, are obsessed with matters of form and superiority, and because of this attachment, you seek to dissuade me from bowing down at the feet of monks...You...look at the caste and not at the inherent qualities of the monks. Haughty, deluded, and obsessed with caste, you harm yourself and others....for Dharma is a question of qualities, and qualities do not reflect caste.[25]

Good conduct, says Ashoka, is the essence of the human being, the body is a jar that when smashed at death leaves only its "dharmalogical pith or core of value," i.e., good actions (karma).[26] But ever the pragmatist even in myth, Ashoka does tell Yasas that caste discrimination is justified in social intercourse, but not in the more fundamental matter of the inner merit of individuals: "When you invite someone, or when it is time for a wedding, then you should investigate the matter of caste, but not at the time of Dharma."[27]

Nonetheless, the at least partial setting aside of the caste system—in fact any hierarchical class system—is a profoundly egalitarian, almost revolutionary doctrine, and it was reflected in the Dhamma edicts of the historical Ashoka.

ASHOKA THE RIGHTEOUS

Directly following his conversion by Samudra, Ashoka undertakes a massive sacred building campaign, taking the relics and ashes of the Buddha and distributing them in eighty-four thousand stupas that he has built all over the subcontinent. According to John Strong, the number eighty-four thousand is significant because "it is generally symbolic of totality, but corresponds more specifically to the traditional number of atoms in the body. Thus in building eighty-four thousand stupas over eighty-four thousand minute relics, Asoka is trying to reconstruct the Buddha's physical body on the face of his own realm."[28] Eighty-four thousand also represents the number of sections in the Buddha's teachings of the Dharma. So Ashoka's stupa building unites the physical and spiritual elements of the Buddha, and "cosmologize[s]" the physical expanse of his kingdom into an embodiment of the truth of the universe. The stupas are the "Dharma in stone." [29] Thus, Ashoka's avadana declares: "For the benefit of beings throughout the world the noble Maurya built stupas. He had been known as 'Ashoka the Fierce'; by this act he became 'Ashoka the Righteous [Dharmasoka].'" [30]

We can still see remnants of these stupas all over India, and the accounts of Faxian and Xuanzang are full of references to them. Xuanzang states that many of them are two hundred, even three hundred feet high. Even today, new archaeological discoveries are uncovering them. In the summer of 2006 the Orissa State Institute of Maritime and South East Asian Studies announced it had unearthed five large Ashokan stupas in a region in Orissa where Xuanzang wrote Ashoka had constructed them, including "a huge inscribed monolithic stupa along with other remnants of Buddhist establishments...on top of Panturi hill in Jajpur district." [31]

Later Ashoka undertakes a grand pilgrimage guided by the monk Upagupta to visit all the important sites of the Buddha's life, from Lumbini, the site of Buddha's birth, in present-day Nepal, to Kusingari, the place of his death and final nirvana. A large, finely sculpted pillar commemorating Ashoka's visit to Lumbini in 251 BC is still standing; we do not know, however, if this was the same visit that was guided by Upagupta.

THE SPIRIT OF THE GIFT

*Before while amassing all this wealth, I lived in constant fear of never finding a storeroom solid enough to keep it in. But now that I have spread it in alms upon the field of happiness I regard it as forever preserved!*
—Harsha, Emperor of India at the great quinquennial festival of AD 643 [32]

In the year AD 643, Xuanzang, having already spent thirteen years in travel to and around India, was the guest of Harsha, one of the greatest of all rulers in Indian history. Harsha tells Xuanzang that he has reigned over India for thirty years and confesses, "I was disturbed to see myself making no (sufficient) progress in virtue. Deeply grieved at the impotence of my efforts in the direction of good, I assembled vast quantities of wealth...and every five years I have distributed it." [33] The year 643 was the time for another such quinquennial "distribution of deliverance," and Xuanzang's biographer describes the festival, held on a plain near the confluence of the Ganges and Yamuna rivers, near present-day Allahabad. A crowd of five hundred thousand people awaits Harsha, as well as the rajas of eighteen vassal states. He has erected dozens of "thatched halls to contain vast quantities of costly objects, gold, silver, fine pearls, red glass, precious stones. . . . [and] several hundred sheds to house the silks and cottons." [34] He builds an immense dining hall and a hundred shelters; each holds a thousand persons. And then, over a period of weeks, he gives it all away.

First, ten thousand Buddhist monks receive each "a hundred gold pieces, a cotton garment, and various drinks and foodstuffs, as well as perfumes and flowers." Gifts are made to Brahmins and to representatives of non-Buddhist sects, including "Jain mendicants who had come from distant lands." [35] Then, "Alms were given to the poor, the orphans and those without family, lasting for a month. At the end of that time all the wealth accumulated in the royal coffers over a period of five years was entirely spent. Nothing remained to the king but the horses, elephants and weapons of war necessary to maintaining order in his realm." [36] According to Xuanzang's eyewitness account, Harsha, emperor of what was at that time probably the richest kingdom on Earth, then publicly divests himself of

> the clothes he was wearing, his earrings, his bracelets, the garland of his diadem, the pearls that adorned his throat and the carbuncle that blazed at the crest of his hair, all this Harsha gave in alms, keeping nothing back.....When the whole amount of his wealth was exhausted, he asked his sister to bring him a worn and common robe and, dressing himself in this, went to worship before the Buddhas. [37]

Harsha is filled with religious joy. His vassal kings then gather much of the wealth he has distributed, including his royal garments and jewels, and give it back to him. Xuanzang tells us that Harsha gives it away again, and the cycle is repeated several times.

Harsha's magnificent ritual was the reiteration of a ceremony initiated over nine hundred years before by Ashoka. While the Kautilyan state is built on force and wealth (danda and artha), Ashoka in both myth and history tries to transcend this by building his kingdom on righteousness, dharma. The accumulation of wealth is only justified by the goal of giving it away. An outstanding example that is historically documented and exercises even today an influence in Southeast Asia is the great quinquennial festival. According to the *Asokavadana*, Ashoka inaugurated the ceremony after the miraculous recovery of the Bodhi tree.

Ashoka holds the first quinquennial festival at his capital Pat-aliputra. He convokes three hundred thousand monks and gathers large quantities of precious gifts, food, drink and a hundred thousand pieces of gold to give away. Then his son Kunala (the festival predates his blinding by Tisyaraksita) holds up two fingers before the crowd, indicating that he will give double the amount Ashoka has offered, and the crowd roars with laughter. Ashoka then declares he will give away three hundred thousand pieces of gold and "bathe the Bodhi tree with three thousand pots of scented water." "Proclaim in my name," he shouts, "a great quinquennial festival!" Kunala holds up four fingers. Ashoka declares that, except for the state treasury, he will give to the community of Buddhist believers and monks "my king-ship, my harem, my state officials, my self, and Kunala. . . . proclaim in my name a great quinquennial festival!" [38]

It is intriguing, and significant for our later evaluation of Ashoka, that even in this potlatch of piety, Ashoka does not give away the core state treasury. It would seem that even in the mythical account of Ashoka's pious deeds, there remains an underpinning of the statecraft of Kautilya. Ashoka then bathes the Bodhi tree in milk and serves food and drink to the monks with his own hands. Finally, after giving away all except the treasury, Ashoka, with four hundred thousand pieces of gold, buys back from the Buddhist community "the earth, his harem, his cabinet, himself, and Kunala," bringing the great fes-tival to a close.[39]

The whole ritual is one of giving material wealth, then of one's self and identity, and at the end recovering it back in a spiritually re-newed state. It is a ritual of the renewal and reconsecration of political power, as well as of spiritual rejuvenation.[40] To gain and retain the world, one must be ready to renounce it. In the quinquennial festival of AD 643, Harsha, after symbolically giving away most of his king-dom several times, regains it for another five years. Ashoka's example also spread to China, where in the sixth century the emperor Liang Wu, according to Strong, "held several festivals of dana in which he made tremendous offerings to the sangha, and clothed himself in a monk's robe and preached to the assembly. Before long, however, his ministers would come . . . to ransom him back."[41]

This aspect of Buddhist kingship continues symbolically in mod-ern times in the traditional Buddhist initiation ceremonies for young boys, where parents give their sons to the monasteries for a limited amount of time, and subsequently they are given back to the world and return to their lay lives.[42] The model of kingship in Southeast Asia that Ashoka inspired—which continues to this day in Thailand—also involves the ritualistic retiring of the king periodically to monastic life and then the returning to worldly duties.[43]

The spirit of giving emerges as a key element in the mythical accounts of Ashoka's efforts to reinvent the sources of state authority. The legitimacy of state power and wealth is at least partly grounded on the willingness of its possessors not just to distribute it but ritually and symbolically to periodically give it away. This spirit of donation and charity is a striking contrast to the realpolitik of the Kautilyan state, not to speak of the modern capitalist world, where guaranteeing untrammeled exchange and profit has become the virtually legitimizing characteristic of state authority. Yet, in the quinquennial festivals by Ashoka and Harsha, the treasury remains intact and is used to buy back the chakravartin and his power. Accumulation of power and wealth is not absent in the mythical Ashokan kingship, but the contrast with the modern world lies in the spirit in which this power and wealth is then used and legitimized.

We are reminded in part of Adam's Smith's view in *The Theory of Moral Sentiments* of the role of Beneficence—of magnanimity and compassion—as one of three underpinnings of society along with Prudence and Justice. But the Beneficence of Smith appears rather wane and etiolated in comparison with the Buddhist mythical accounts of Ashoka's dana. For Smith, Beneficence is partly based on the natural sympathy and compassion he supposes to be part of human nature, reinforced by social approbation and by an internalized kind of superego.[44] Dana, in contrast, while emanating from the self-knowledge and enlightenment of the individual, draws its strength from being based in an order and truth that transcends the individual and any society per se: the Buddhist Dharma, which for believers is the truth of existence itself.

The attempt to base social order and authority on an individual, internalized sense of Justice and Beneficence, based on mutually perceived and accepted rational rules, has been called "modernity's wager."[45] It is the wager now of the entire planet in an age of secular market globalism. Over most of the past twenty-five centuries the ultimate ethical authority of the state has been rooted in the great Axial religions and moral traditions, where the social and political regime is partly rooted in a transcendent order. Even for much of modern times, state authority has invoked a social and ethical order that, even if on its face secular, derived much of its cohesion from religious, transcendent beliefs and traditions.

ASHOKA'S LAST GIFT AND DEATH

*With this gift, I do not seek the reward of rebirth . . . even less do I want the glory of kingship that is unsteady as a choppy sea. But because I gave it with great faith, I would obtain as the fruit of this gift something that cannot be stolen . . . and [is] safe from all agitation: sovereignty over the mind.*
—Ashoka in the *Asokavadana*[46]

In myth, Ashoka's life ends, as it was presaged in an earlier reincarnation, with the humblest of gifts, which, because it is all that he has, and is given in great faith, has the greatest of consequences. Immediately preceding his final illness, Ashoka makes an account of all he has given through the building of the eighty-four thousand stupas, his pilgrimages to the sites of the major events of the Buddha's life, and his donations in the great quinquennial festivals. It adds up to ninety-six *kotis* (a huge amount, probably 960 million gold pieces).[47] Ashoka has still fallen short of his goal of giving to the community of Buddhist believers as much as the legendary rich merchant Anathapindada, who gave the Buddha a hundred kotis. Ashoka falls ill but starts sending gifts of gold coins to the country's main monastery. His ministers are alarmed; citing the Kautilyan precept that "the power of kings lies in their state treasury," and they implore Kunala's son Sampadin to stop Ashoka's profligacy.[48] In effect there is a coup d'état, and Sampadin orders the treasury to ignore Ashoka's requests. Ashoka is still served on gold dishes, and he continues to give these to the monastery. His ministers and Sampadin forbid Ashoka to use gold dishes, which are replaced by silver, which he still gives away; the silver dishes are forbidden, and Ashoka is reduced to eating off humble clay plates.

Finally, Ashoka is for all practical purposes destitute and stripped of his powers. All that he has in his possession is half a myrobalan fruit.[49] He asks that it be taken to the monastery and offered to the monks, who grind it up and mix it in a soup. Ashoka then asks his prime minister, Radhagupta: who is lord of the earth? Radhagupta answers that it is Ashoka. Ashoka, according to Buddhist scholar and translator John Strong, regains his authority as ruler of his kingdom through the piety of this gift of all he has, little though it is—half a myrobalan. The gift echoes the gift of dirt in an earlier life.[50] Ashoka then makes his last wish and gift: "Except for the state treasury, I now present the whole earth, surrounded by the ocean, to the community of the Blessed One's disciples."[51] With this last gift, Ashoka seeks not to repeat his life and win in some future existence sovereignty over the earth again, but to obtain that which "cannot be stolen" and that which is "safe from all agitation...sovereignty over the mind."[52]

Ashoka dies, and his advisers are left in a quandary; although they possess the state treasury, Ashoka apparently has managed to trick them and succeed in giving away the entire land of the kingdom to the Buddhist community. They ask Radhagupta for a way out of this dilemma, and he tells them that Ashoka needed four kotis more of gold to complete his last wish; they can recover the kingdom if they pay the sangha the four kotis to support the spread of the Buddha's Dharma. And so "the ministers therefore gave four kotis of gold pieces for the Teaching in order to buy back the Earth, and they consecrated Sampadin as king."[53] Radhagupta, in a previous reincarnation, was the other little boy who was playing with the boy Jaya when the Buddha passed by and Jaya offered him a bowl of dirt.

The beauty and symmetry of this mythic account of Ashoka's deeds and life are both compelling and simple. Ashoka is portrayed as trying to show in his life that the essence of Dharma is simply good actions and good conduct, and that in judging people, ultimately nothing else is more important. His reign is described as infused increasingly not by the spirit of danda but by dana. But there are examples, too, that show for all his piety even after his conversion, he is only human and imperfect. On several occasions the old "Ashoka the Fierce" remains, and he is described as persecuting other sects, killing the largely blameless inhabitants of Taxila as vengeance for the blinding of Kunala, as well as showing no mercy to Tisyaraksita. Of importance too is the Kautilya-esque core of the myth: at all times, the state treasury is never put at risk. Ashoka does finally succeed posthumously in getting his ministers to donate four kotis of gold to the Buddhist community, but in return they regain the entire earth—certainly the best real-estate deal in either myth or history.

## THE END OF THE MAURYAS

One fine early morning, around 183 BC, the ninth king of the Mauryan dynasty, Brhadratha, reviewed his vast army, a practice that Kautilya had recommended.[54] We can imagine with some verisimilitude the spectacle: the colorful parade of elephant and horse cavalry, chariots, infantry armed with various kinds of bows and swords, protected in armor of iron mail, rhinoceros, and alligator skin, and even a camel corps. They may have totaled hundreds of thousands—though certainly fewer than Chandragupta's great conquering army that numbered more than six hundred thousand infantry, thirty thousand horse cavalry, nine thousand elephants, and at least eight thousand chariots.[55] At Brhadratha's side was his military chief of staff, Pushyamitra Sungha. Perhaps as Brhadratha turned from Pushyamitra to pass muster over what he thought were his loyal troops, Pushyamitra made his move, slaying the last Mauryan king, proclaiming himself emperor and beginning a new dynasty.[56]

Pushyamitra was the first of the Sunghas, who lasted only about a hundred years. Some Buddhist texts and more recent historians portray him as kind of Pinochet who led a harsh counterrevolution of the traditional higher castes of Brahmins and Kshatriyas against the relative egalitarianism of Buddhism and the Mauryas.[57] Modern historians believe that Buddhism continued to do well enough as a religion, although the Sunghas may have led a socially conservative backlash and supported a revival of caste and Vedic ritual.[58] After nearly 140 years of the Mauryas, Pushyamitra revived the ancient Hindu horse sacrifice. In this traditional assertion of dominance by Hindu rulers, a ritually sanctified horse would be set loose to wander for a year, accompanied by a band of the king's warriors. Princes on whose territory the horse would roam would be obliged to acknowledge homage or do battle; at the end of the year the king in a grand ceremony sacrificed the horse.[59]

The *Asokavadana* also concludes with Pushyamitra becoming king. It describes him as a Mauryan (rather than the first of the new Sungha dynasty) under the influence of "a Brahmin priest who was a mean and faithless man."[60] The priest tells Pushyamitra that he can obtain still more renown than Ashoka by destroying the eighty-four thousand stupas that Ashoka had erected. Pushyamitra puts to death the monks of the chief monastery Kukkutarama, the community to which Ashoka willed the half myrobalan seed and the entire earth. He vows to destroy the Buddhist religion but is put to death by a *yaksa*, a supernatural demon, before he can accomplish his goal.[61] All is transitory, the myth tells us, and the last of Ashoka's descendants try to destroy his work.

Nonetheless, the core of the myth retains a potent symbolism for our times: Ashoka proceeds from the rule of force and violence to the dominion accomplished through charity and the giving of both material means and of himself. With his last and greatest gifts he realizes that the most important and far-reaching conquest to be achieved is sovereignty over the mind since he has already possessed the earth.

Are we not in this new millennium faced with the same dilemma? We have conquered the earth by force and only painfully and inadequately recognize the need for greater charity on a crowded planet, rather than more acquisitiveness. At this point we do not need to conquer and dominate the earth again; rather we need to conquer ourselves. Surely our ascendancy will be short lived unless we assume sovereignty over our thoughts and desires and understand what we really want individually and as social beings. Astoundingly, the historical Ashoka speaks even more clearly to this challenge than the Ashoka of the myths.

# CHAPTER 6

# The Greatest Conquest

Let us return to the beginning of our inquiry, to that dramatic, quiet hill at Dhauli, overlooking a great plain in Orissa. On the morning of February 4, 1837, Markham Kittoe, a young lieutenant in the service of the British East India Company, began to scale the hill. The young lieutenant was looking for—or was supposed to be looking for—coal. The East India Company had sent him to Orissa to prospect for coal-fields, but, far from the eye of his employer, he spent a good part of his time searching for antiquities. In the report he sent back to Calcutta, he described what happened next:

> There is neither road nor path to this extraordinary path of antiquity. After climbing the rock through thorns and thickets, I came of a sudden on a small terrace open on three sides with a perpendicular scarp on the fourth or west front the face of which projects the front half of an elephant of elegant workmanship, four feet high; the whole is cut out of the solid rock. On the northern face beneath the terrace, the rock is chiseled smooth for a space of over fourteen feet by ten feet and the inscription, neatly cut, covers the whole space.[1]

Since the 1600s British travelers and agents had found similar in-scriptions on several large, monumental columns—some fifty feet high or more—in far removed sites all over the Ganges Valley in northern India. Some had speculated that the script was an adulter-ated form of early Greek, perhaps connected with Alexander the Great. Comparative linguist Sir William Jones—who first identified the common Indo-European parentage of Latin, classical Greek, and

Sanskrit—conjectured before he died in 1794 that the writing of the pillars was "Ethiopian and to have been imported a thousand years before Christ."² His reading of the pillars was even more off track than his Chinese predecessors Xuanzang and Faxian. They correctly identified the columns as having been erected by Ashoka, although it is clear that already by the fifth century AD, local guides had lost the ability to decipher the inscriptions.

In the fourteenth century the Muslim Sultan of Delhi, Firoz Shah, was so impressed when he came upon one of the mysterious columns in a village called Topra, that at tremendous expense he had it transported to Delhi (about 120 miles distant) "as a monument to future generations."³ Thousands of men dragged the column down to the Yamuna River on a specially constructed carriage of forty-two wheels, where it was transferred to a number of large boats lashed together for the journey downstream to be erected in the courtyard of the Sultan's palace. By Firoz Shah's time (1351–88) the memory of Ashoka had become so attenuated that Brahmin priests told him the mysterious inscribed pillars were the petrified walking sticks of the Pandavas, heroes of the Hindu epic Mahabharata, who, like the Titans of Greek mythology or the "giants in the earth" of the Old Testament, lived in a time when men grew over a hundred feet tall.

Five centuries later, in Calcutta, James Prinsep was working toward deciphering the enigmatic "column" script, which increasingly obsessed him. Prinsep had arrived in India in 1819 at the age of twenty as assistant assay master of the mint in Bengal, later taking the post of chief assay master. For several years he devoted virtually every spare moment to the riddle of the script. Over the years, a growing network of correspondents all over British India had sent him copies and rubbings of the mysterious writing from pillars and rocks; shortly after the discovery of the Orissa Dhauli rock inscriptions, a Captain Edward Smith sent him reproductions of inscriptions in the script carved on elaborate stone railings surrounding a massive, ancient Buddhist stupa at Sanchi.⁴

The Sanchi inscriptions helped Prinsep identify some of the consonants of the language (Prakrit) with specific characters, and within weeks he finally succeeded in deciphering the script of one of the two mysterious monumental columns that the British had found at Delhi—the very column that Firoz Shah had moved at great expense. The column proclaimed the edicts of a great king, who in the twenty-seventh year of his reign, commanded that "stone pillars be prepared and let this edict of religion [Dhamma] be engraven thereon, that may endure into the remotest ages." The edicts were remarkable, declaring in some detail the measures the king had taken, both administratively and through individual self-examination, to spread the "law of piety" among all his subjects, a law "whereby compassion, liberality, truth, purity, gentleness, and saintliness will thus grow among mankind."

It was the mythic great chronicle of Sri Lanka, the *Mahavamsa,* just translated in part by another correspondent of Prinsep, George Turnour, that allowed Prinsep in 1837 to identify the author of the pillar inscriptions. The name of the king inscribed on the column was Devanampiya Piyadasi; according to the *Mahavamsa,* the first ruler of the island kingdom to convert to Buddhism was called Piyadasi. The ancient Pali text said he was the contemporary of a great King of India and patron of Buddhism who was consecrated 218 years after the Buddha's death, a king also named Piyadasi but known as Ashoka. Piyadasi literally means "he of gentle visage." [5]

Early in 1838, another correspondent of Prinsep, hearing of his recent success in deciphering the long-lost script, sent him copies of a second series of rock edicts, 1,500 miles from Orissa on the west coast of India at a site called Girnar. The Girnar text appeared to be identical in most respects with that of Dhauli.

Thanks to Prinsep's breakthrough, the Dhauli and Girnar rock edicts subsequently could be translated. They were engraved in the thirteenth year of Ashoka's reign, and set forth a much more detailed account than the pillar inscriptions. They include a declaration of religious tolerance for all sects, as well as details of administration and principles of good government. The rock edicts also mention the names of five Greek kings, the successors to Alexander the Great and his empire, whose exact reigns were recorded in Greek sources; cross-dating with Greek historical accounts and comparison with the Pali chronicles thus made it possible to determine the dates of Ashoka's reign (268 or 269 to 232 BC). For Prinsep and others, the pillar and rock edicts immediately called to mind ten other edicts another prophet claimed to have received on stone tablets on Mount Sinai. In the ethical history of humanity, they arguably are of equal significance, if not of equal importance and influence.

Prinsep himself succumbed to a tragic end—rapidly descending into dementia in 1838, leaving for Britain in November of that year, declining into full insanity and dying a year later. His work and that of his correspondents, like Markham Kittoe and George Turnour, is one of the great archaeological adventures and linguistic accomplishments of all times, less known but equal certainly to the work of Champollion in deciphering ancient Egyptian hieroglyphics. There is a certain historical irony in the fact that it was of all entities the British East India Company—the most Kautilya-esque of undertakings—that unintentionally subsidized the deciphering of the edicts that embodied the historical effort to transcend a purely Kautilyan ethic.

The deciphering in 1837 of the long-forgotten script—which became known as Ashoki Brahmi—of the rock and pillar edicts marked the beginning of the rediscovery and recovery of the historical Ashoka. The first major event of Ashoka's reign that we can date with certainty occurs eight to nine years after his coronation—the great war against Kalinga.[6] It is Ashoka's voice speaking across time in the edicts themselves that tell us this story, not mentioned in any of the mythic accounts:

> When he had been consecrated eight years the Beloved of the Gods, the king Piyadassi, conquered Kalinga. A hundred and fifty thousand people were deported, a hundred thousand killed and many times that number perished....On conquering Kalinga the Beloved of the Gods felt remorse...the slaughter, death, and deportation of the people weighs heavily on his mind....This participation of all men in suffering, weighs heavily on the mind of the Beloved of the Gods.[7]

Moreover, the king proclaims, "one who does wrong should be forgiven as far as it is possible to forgive him.... For the Beloved of the Gods wishes that all beings should be unharmed, self-controlled, calm in mind, and gentle." The "foremost victory," the king continues, is what he calls "victory by *Dhamma*." The edict declares earlier that after Kalinga was annexed, the king "very earnestly practised *Dhamma*, desired *Dhamma*, and taught *Dhamma*."

The Dhamma of which Ashoka speaks is related to Buddhist and older Brahmin teachings of dharma, but Ashoka defines it in his various edicts and inscriptions as a secular ethic of nonviolence, charity, compassion, tolerance, social welfare, good governance, purity of heart, respect for parents and kin, protection of animal and plant life, and frugality. One of the earliest British experts on Buddhism, T. W. Rhys Davids, observed that in the edicts proclaiming Dhamma, there is not a word about Buddha, Buddhism, not to speak of the soul or God.[8] Some earlier translations of the edicts render Dhamma as "The

Law of Piety." [9] In more recent translations it is rendered as "truth." [10] Both are good English-language paraphrases, but since the term is polysemic, it has multiple, simultaneous meanings, and because Ashoka's use of it is idiosyncratic, it is probably best to cite it as *Dhamma*, which is the practice of leading contemporary Indian historians.

### THE LAW OF PIETY

Ashoka sets out his Dhamma in two major sets of edicts: fourteen major rock edicts in the fourteenth year of his reign (around 256–55 BC) and seven major pillar edicts issued in the twenty-seventh and twenty-eighth years of his rule (243–41 BC). Fragments of the fourteen rock edicts can be found at some ten sites all over South Asia, from present-day Afghanistan to southern India. As perhaps one might expect, given the chronology, the pillar edicts elaborate the principles set out in the rock edicts.

The first rock edict declares an end to the slaughter and sacrifice of animals for ritual purposes. Ashoka also proclaims that that formerly "in the [royal] kitchens...many hundreds of thousands of living animals were killed daily for meat...now only three animals are killed....Even these three animals will not be killed in the future."

Ashoka states in the second rock edict that he has established all over his kingdom two medical services, one for the care of men and the other for the care of animals. He also has endowed these medical services in neighboring foreign lands—in Ceylon (Sri Lanka), in the realm of "the Greek king named Antiochus" (who ruled over what is today Syria and the Near East) and even in the territory "of those kings who are neighbors of that Antiochus." In the same edict, Ashoka also states he has procured and planted medicinal herbs "useful to man or to beast," and roots and fruit "wherever they did not grow," that is, along with hospitals he also promoted the propagation of useful plants and trees both within and beyond his borders. [11] Along the kingdom's roads he had wells dug and trees planted—again to benefit both men and animals.

Ashoka tells us in the third rock edict that he establishes inspection tours every five years on the part of his officials and administrators to "instruct people in the *Dhamma*" as well as for other business. He gives an indication of some of the things Dhamma entails: being good to one's mother and father, friends, and relatives, being generous to Brahmin priests and religious hermits, not killing living beings, and frugal, simple living: "It is good not only to spend a little, but to own the minimum of property." There is a provision for a kind of public transparency: officials are to be instructed to record this edict regarding inspection tours and the elements of Dhamma, "making it both manifest to the public and explaining why."

Ashoka says his promotion of Dhamma has reversed a trend of increasing killing and injuring of living beings and of growing lack of respect for family and priests. In the fourth rock edict, he declares that not only he but his "sons, grandsons...and great grandsons will advance the practice of *Dhamma* until the end of the world." One must be virtuous and good to practice Dhamma, which is why it is good to promote it. "For this purpose [this] inscription has been engraved—that men should make progress in this matter, and not be satisfied with their shortcomings." The fourth rock edict is one of the places where we hear the personal voice of Ashoka speaking not only to the inhabitants of the Mauryan Empire in the third century BC, but also across time, to all people. It is this tone of urgent timelessness that, in the words of British historian John Keay, "sends a shiver down awe-struck spines," a directness that across the millennia gives Ashoka's edicts "even now such awesome immediacy." [12]

One of the most unusual innovations of Ashoka's rule, described in the fifth rock edict, was his creation of a new class of officials called "officers of *Dhamma*" whose task expressly is to promote good deeds, charity, and the progress of Dhamma throughout the empire. They are to work "among servants and nobles, Brahmins and wealthy householders, among the poor and the aged...for the welfare and happiness of those devoted to *Dhamma* and for the removal of their troubles." They are to promote "the welfare of prisoners" and "release...those that have children, are afflicted or aged." They are to support the administration of charities. Ashoka appears to be establishing the bureaucratic apparatus of an early welfare state. Ashoka makes no mention of Buddhist priests (*bhikkhus*) or lay people in promoting his Dhamma; it is above all a new government and social policy to be overseen by a new category of government officers. This is one of several clear indications that the Ashokan Dhamma is quite distinct from Buddhist teachings or doctrine. [13]

Ashoka makes known in the sixth rock edict his program for administrative reform: "In the past, the quick dispatch of business and the receipt of reports did not take place at all times." He promises to attend to public business quickly and to be accessible and well informed at all times. The officers of Dhamma are to report to him immediately at all times if there is any dispute or problem. Ashoka tells us he is not a workaholic, for "in hard work and the dispatch of business alone, I find no satisfaction." No, it is that "I consider...I must promote the welfare of the whole world, and hard work and the dispatch of business are the means of doing so.... whatever may be my great deeds, I have done them in order to discharge my debt to all beings."

The seventh rock edict is the first of two pleas for religious toleration. Ashoka "wishes that all [religious] sects may dwell in all places, for all seek self-control and purity of mind." Indeed, self-control and purity of mind also appear to be elements of Dhamma.

Ashoka announces in the eighth rock edict that he has replaced the traditional hunting and pleasure tours of the king with tours to spread Dhamma where he meets with priests and ascetics, bestows gifts and gold, meets with the aged and the people of the countryside, gives instruction on Dhamma and answers questions about it. Ashoka says he now "derives more pleasure from this than from any other enjoyments."

Ashoka comments on the ineffectiveness and superficiality of many traditional ceremonies popularly practiced to bring success in undertakings such as marriage, birth of children, and going on a journey (the ninth rock edict). It is the practice of Dhamma, he says, such as "regard for slaves and servants, respect for teachers, restrained behavior toward living beings...and similar practices" that is of true worth. Dhamma, he says, "is effective for all time, for even if the object is not attained in this life endless merit is produced for the life to come. But if the object is attained in this life, there is gain in both respects."

Ashoka reiterates in the tenth rock edict that his only goal is to promote Dhamma, in particular he sets no great store in fame or glory except to the extent that it is useful in promoting Dhamma. His efforts are "all done with a view to the after-life, that all men may escape from evil inclinations." But the path of Dhamma is a difficult one for all men "whether humble or highly placed, without extreme effort and without renouncing everything else, and it is particularly difficult for the highly placed."

There is no gift comparable to praise, sharing, and fellowship of Dhamma (the eleventh rock edict). He repeats core elements of its practice: "good behavior towards slave and servants, obedience to mother and father, generosity towards friends, acquaintances and relatives, and towards sramanas [ascetic holy men] and brahmans [priests], and abstention from killing living beings."

The twelfth rock edict is a proclamation of toleration for all religious and philosophical sects, and what this implies. The proclamation of toleration is in itself an extraordinary act for the third century BC but not totally unprecedented in ancient history since Cyrus the Great also issued an edict of religious toleration when he conquered Babylon. But Ashoka goes much further. He says all sects have an essential doctrine that he seeks to actively support through "gifts and various forms of recognition." He says it is his desire that "all sects should be well informed and should teach that which is good." Everywhere, Ashoka proclaims, the adherents of different religions should be told that he "does not consider gifts or honor to be as important as the progress of the essential doctrine of all sects." This is, for the time, a revolutionary statement since Ashoka seems to be saying that beneath the outward form all religions and beliefs have an essential core that aims for the good, and that it is his policy to support the progress of all sects because they aim essentially for the same. In the *Asokavadana*, the mythical Ashoka too tries to show that beneath differences of caste and status in life and beyond the transitoriness of human mortality the essence of dharma is good conduct; good conduct transcends social status and the ephemerality of human life itself and in this all men are to be judged equally.

Moreover, in the twelfth rock edict Ashoka emphasizes the importance of discussion and debate, of listening to and respecting different religious opinions: "This progress of the essential doctrine [of all religious beliefs] takes many forms, but its basis is the control of one's speech, so as not to extol one's own sect or disparage another's on unsuitable occasions." It is thus important that each person should honor the sect, or beliefs of others. To disparage another person's sect, or praise one's own with the sole goal of showing it in a more favorable light, harms one's "own sect even more seriously. Therefore, concord is to be commanded, so that men may hear one another's principles and obey them."

The Dhamma that he is promoting, Ashoka seems to be saying, both contains and strives to further the fundamental core values of existing religions and beliefs.[14] Ashoka concludes the twelfth rock edict by proclaiming that promoting the essential doctrine of all sects is the duty of the officers of the Dhamma, of the managers of state farms, and of "women's officers." Thus, he states that the practice of Dhamma extends to the treatment of animals in farms and to a category of officials, in charge of women's affairs, about whom unfortunately we do not know very much but who probably oversaw the royal harem and regulated prostitution.[15] The result of promoting concord and the progress of the essential doctrine of all sects "is the increased influence of one's own sect and glory to *Dhamma*."[16] Ashoka pleads for an ecumenism, in which all sects, beyond certain superficial rituals and ceremonies, can prosper and in concord promote spiritual advancement and good conduct.

One can hardly overemphasize the importance of what Ashoka sets forth in his edict of tolerance, particularly given the tension between different sects, like the traditional Brahmana beliefs and the Sramana sects. He has an overarching vision to transcend this discord; Ashoka not only sees respectful public debate among different beliefs as a key way to achieve progress in his ethical system of Dhamma, he also believes that debate will reveal the essential core commonality of what different religious sects aim for, and he sets down specific rules for conducting this debate.

Ashoka describes his great remorse for the Kalinga war in the thirteenth rock edict and declares that the greatest conquest is not physical conquest but the victory achieved through Dhamma. He urges his descendants to renounce a foreign policy of military conquests, or if absolutely unavoidable, that "in whatever victories they may gain [they] should be satisfied with patience and light punishment." In fact, the only true conquest is by Dhamma.

The fourteenth rock edict concludes that the edicts have been engraved throughout the empire—and that many more will be engraved—in abridged, medium-length and extended versions. It acknowledges that "there is considerable repetition because of the beauty of certain topics and in order that the people may conform to them," and that if there are inaccuracies it is due to the error of the engraver.

Overall Ashoka's rock edicts are a call for a moral, social, and administrative revolution through respect for all living beings, compassion for the less fortunate, religious tolerance, public works, public transparency and efficiency in government, and the establishment of an administrative corps of social welfare officials.

We could view Ashoka's establishment of hospitals abroad and supporting the sharing of beneficial plants as perhaps the first recorded example of foreign aid in history. The Canadian writer and historian George Woodcock detects a singularly modern ring to Ashoka's statements and suspects that his "envoys" [to the Hellenistic kingdoms and other foreign lands in the twelfth rock edict] were not ambassadors at all in the formal sense but rather a kind of ancient Peace Corps, consisting of men who would demonstrate their faith in many parts of the world by acts of service to other men, no matter what the land or language.[17]

While secular in tone, it is clear that his Dhamma is rooted in a belief in a transcendent order that lies beyond human life and society: he refers several times to the good consequences of the practice of Dhamma in this life and the next. Indeed, Ashoka tells us that the practice of Dhamma is a wager involving a leap of faith, stating in the ninth rock edict that Dhamma may or may not be effective in this life, but will produce merit in the lives to come. If we win the wager, we will be rewarded both in this existence and the next. We are reminded of Pascal's famous spiritual bet two millennia later, where the wager was transposed to the next life: if we believe in God, and that he or she exists, we win salvation after death; if we lose the wager and there is no God, we have really lost nothing that was not already lost. For Ashoka the individual reward of ethical behavior in this life appears to be more of an uncertain bet, whereas he has faith in its effectiveness after individual death. For Pascal uncertainty lies in what our faith may bring after death, while its effect—or lack of practical relevance—in this life is given.

Finally, and potentially most revolutionary, Ashoka proclaims a domestic and foreign policy of nonviolence, of renunciation of the use of force in favor of the ethical victory of Dhamma.

We also note that Ashoka is not an absolutist: the thrust of the edicts is a major move in the direction of nonviolence and respect for all beings, but in practice it cannot be achieved completely. The royal kitchens do not serve purely vegetarian fare, but mostly—with the goal of eventually renouncing killing even a single animal for food. (We are reminded perhaps of Saint Augustine's famous dictum, "God make me chaste, but not quite yet.") He proclaims and promotes religious toleration, warns against disparaging one another's beliefs, but bans religious rituals and festivals that sacrifice animals, and expresses his disdain for various superstitious ceremonies that detract from the pursuit of Dhamma.[18] The renunciation of conquest through force is not total—but the wish is expressed that it will be, and if in the future military victory is necessary, it is to be tempered with maximum compassion.

But we also find in the rock edicts elements of both the old "fierce Ashoka" and a priggish, puritanical, and misogynistic Ashoka. The renunciation in the eighth rock edict of the traditional kingly pleasure and hunting tours in favor of periodic countrywide circuits to preach Dhamma has a rather puritanical flavor. He accompanies his expression of distaste for "trivial and useless" popular ceremonies with the observation that "women especially" are involved in such superstitions. Most of all, the creation of officers of Dhamma whose charge is ubiquitous moral meddling—even with rights to snoop in the royal household—has an almost Orwellian undertone: "They are busy everywhere, here [in Pataliputra, the capital] and in all the women's residences, whether my own, those of my brothers and sisters, or those of relatives. Everywhere throughout my empire the officers of *Dhamma* are busy in everything." Ashoka also warns that an iron fist lurks beneath the velvet glove of Dhamma, which will crush disobedient subjects if they don't follow the rules. In the famous thirteenth rock edict, where he expresses his regret for the killing fields of Kalinga, he also adds that "the Beloved of the Gods conciliates the forest tribes of his empire, but he warns them that he has power even in his remorse, and he asks them to repent, lest they be killed."

In fact, Ashoka proclaimed his remorse for the Kalinga war everywhere in his empire except in Kalinga itself. He also did not publish his edict of religious toleration in Kalinga. The thirteenth rock edict, along with the eleventh and twelfth rock edicts, are not inscribed at Dhauli and in a second site, Jaugada, also within the conquered kingdom. Instead we find two edicts not found elsewhere, expressly addressed to local inhabitants and officials. The first separate rock edict is addressed to the officials and city magistrates at Tosali and Samapa, ancient cities that existed near modern Dhauli and Jaugada. Tosali, moreover, was one of the four major regional capitals of Ashoka's empire, having jurisdiction over Kalinga. Here, Ashoka warns his officials that they should "strive to practice impartiality," avoiding "jealousy, shortness of temper, harshness, rashness, obstinacy, idleness, or slackness. All men are my children," Ashoka proclaims, and "you are in charge of many thousands of living beings." Ashoka wants welfare and happiness for all men just as he would for his own children, but "you," Ashoka upbraids his officials, "do not realize how far this principle goes—possibly one man among you may realize it, but even he only in part and not entirely." Apparently there are major abuses of power going on: "Often a man suffers imprisonment or torture and then is released from prison, [all] without reason, and many other people suffer further." Ashoka orders the edict be read aloud in public at regular intervals, "even to a single person," if no one else is present.

Our image of Ashoka is brought down to Earth by his concluding statement that the purpose of the edict is to ensure that city magistrates do not imprison and torture people "without good reason," implying that there are justifiable grounds for state-sanctioned torture. Nonetheless, apart from exhortations, he proclaims specific measures of administrative review to prevent future abuses: "I shall send out on tour every five years an officer who is not severe or harsh; who having investigated this matter..., shall see that they carry out my instructions." Most revealing, and disturbing, is the indication that the problem of abuse of power is not just a regional phenomenon in Kalinga: at Ujjain in north central India, and Taxila in the northwest, similar tours of inspection are to take place, and in the case of Ujjain, at even shorter intervals of every three years.[19] Taxila may have been a source of continuing political trouble in Ashoka's life: the *Asokavadana* relates that he was sent there as a young prince to quell a revolt, and also had to send his son Kunala to deal with more unrest later in his reign.

The second separate rock edict found at Dhauli and Jaugada amounts to a proclamation to his officers urging the pacification of unconquered tribal and indigenous peoples on the empire's borders. This should be read in conjunction with the not-so-veiled threats in the thirteenth major rock edict to kill forest peoples if they do not conform. In addressing directly the frontier and tribal peoples on his empire's borders, he softens the message somewhat, proclaiming again that "all men are my children," and specifically:

> If the unconquered peoples on my borders ask what is my will, they should be made to understand that this is my will with regard to them—the king desires that they should have no trouble on his account, should trust in him, and should have in their dealings with him only happiness and no sorrow. They understand that the king will forgive them as far as they can be forgiven and that through him [i.e., following Ashoka] should follow *Dhamma* and gain this world and the next.

Ashoka says he will send special couriers and officers to his border officials to reinforce this message—for "you," he says to them directly, "are able to give the frontier people confidence, welfare, and happiness in this world and the next." As with the first separate rock edict, he orders that it be publicly read at least every four months, and optionally more frequently, "even to a single person."

So Ashoka was not always politically correct, as some commentators would have us believe.[20] It is quite clear that in particular his policy toward indigenous and tribal peoples, whether in the forests or on his frontiers, is paternalistic and colonial at best. With respect to these peoples, the spreading of Dhamma he enjoins to his officials almost recalls the role of Christianity as it accompanied the colonial expansion of Western powers in modern times. Torture, regulated in detail we recall in the *Arthasastra*, appears to remain as a state policy. There appears to have been even at the height of his reign systemic problems of abuse of power by his administration. The pervasive intrusiveness of his chosen officers of the Dhamma recalls the ubiquitous and stifling measures for internal spying recommended by Kautilya. These inconsistencies do not invalidate the overall greatness and uniqueness of Ashoka's attempted ethical revolution; they simply indicate that it was a work in progress. Ashoka's Dhamma reflects both a personal evolution and practical, political considerations, rooted in, and constrained by, the cultural and social conditions of his time. What remains almost miraculous is the extent to which he attempted to move one of the greatest empires in history toward transcending these limitations.

## "AS LONG AS THE SUN AND MOON ENDURE . . ."

*I have done all this so that among my sons and great grandsons and as long as the sun and moon endure, men may follow Dhamma. For by following it one gains this world and the next.*
—Ashoka, seventh pillar edict

Thirteen years later, in the twenty-seventh and twenty-eighth years of his reign, Ashoka issued a new set of proclamations on Dhamma, which he had inscribed on tall pillars, some over fifty feet high. To date, whole pillars or fragments have been discovered at eleven sites in different parts of India, mostly near Delhi or in the Ganges watershed but also in present-day Pakistan and on India's southeastern coast. The pillars themselves are marvels of ancient stone polishing and engineering—the one that Firoz Shah moved to Delhi is so finely polished that travelers through the nineteenth century thought it was cast metal of a quality so high that the technology had not since been equaled.[21] Early last century British art historians proclaimed that in style and technique the carvings on the Sarnath Pillar's capital were "unsurpassed...by anything of their kind in the ancient world."[22]

The seven major pillar edicts embody both an elaboration of the elements of the major rock edicts and a summing-up by Ashoka of the progress his Dhamma has made. In the first pillar edict Ashoka finds that although "it is hard to obtain happiness in this world and the next without extreme love of *Dhamma*, much vigilance, much fear of sin, and much energy...through my instructions, care for *Dhamma* and love of *Dhamma* have grown from day to day, and will continue to grow." "What is *Dhamma?*" he asks in the second pillar edict. "It is having few faults and many good deeds, mercy, charity, truthfulness, and purity. I have given the gift of insight in various forms," Ashoka continues, "and have conferred many benefits on man, animals, birds and fish, even to saving their lives." In the third pillar edict he emphasizes how easy it is not to notice one's wicked deeds and remember only one's good deeds. One should reflect that "cruelty, harshness, anger, pride, and envy" produce sin and one's downfall. Historian Romila Thapar detects a change in tone in these first three pillar edicts, one in which growing puritanism, rigidity, indeed even "the germ of fanaticism and megalomania" can be found.[23] There is more and more repetition of Dhamma, almost as a catechism, an emphasis on sin, an undertone of harshness and imperiousness.

In the fourth pillar edict Ashoka describes how he has given independent authority to a class of officials he calls rural officers (*rajukas*): "Just as one entrusts his child to an experienced nurse, and is confident that the experienced nurse is able to care for the child satisfactorily, so my *rajukas* have been appointed for the welfare and happiness of the country people." Obviously, Ashoka's bent toward paternalism only increased with age. But he also adds one of the most intriguing and possibly revolutionary elements of his Dhamma: "There should be uniformity in judicial procedure and punishment." One interpretation of this phrase is that it proclaimed what we would understand as the equal protection and application of the laws, the equivalent of the Fourteenth Amendment to the U.S. Constitution, basically meaning that the same punishments should apply to all regardless of caste or social standing.[24] This is a principle that did not exist in the Western world until the end of the eighteenth century. An argument can certainly be made for this sense since it would have been in the spirit of Dhamma.[25] There is a thrust in Ashoka's ethic toward equality, or least the spiritual equality of all people. But in practice the abolition of caste differences in judicial procedure and punishments would entail nothing less than a social revolution. Thus it is also argued that Ashoka here is only arguing for the application of a uniform penal and judicial code all over his empire, which would not infringe on the traditional caste distinctions in punishment.[26] This would still be an extraordinarily progressive measure for its time, amounting to a guarantee of due process of law. Ashoka also declares in the fourth pillar edict that men who are sentenced to death be given three days respite during which their relations may appeal for clemency. At the end of the fifth pillar edict he records that every year for the past twenty-five of his reign he has issued mass pardons of prisoners.

The fifth pillar edict is one of the most remarkable from a modern perspective, since it amounts to nothing less than an environmental protection law, listing all of the species of animals declared as protected and exempt from slaughter—including tortoises, bats, ants, ducks, geese, swans, doves, porcupines, squirrels, deer, lizards, rhinoceroses, and pigeons. In fact, all four-footed animals, "which are not eaten and of no utility," are to be protected. He promulgates what we would call measures for habitat protection, declaring that "forests must not be set on fire either wantonly or for the destruction of life," and that the chaff in fields "must not be set on fire along with the living things in it." On numerous fixed days other kinds of animals may not be destroyed and elephant forests and fish ponds are not to be harvested. On other fixed days various ritual mutilations and sacrifices of other animals are prohibited, as well as the branding of horses and oxen.

One of the most intriguing provisions of the fifth pillar edict is that "an animal must not be fed with another animal," a measure that could have stopped the spread of mad cow disease in our own time and that goes against the entire practice of using fish and animal feed in raising modern livestock. We are increasingly seeing the environmental and public health consequences of using the processed remains of animals to feed other animals—not to speak of the ethical implications of turning normally vegetarian mammals into carnivores, even cannibals.

This is only one example where an Ashokan injunction rooted in considerations of respect and nonviolence toward other sentient beings can have very practical environmental and social repercussions that only today we are becoming aware of. Another is the commandment to not burn the chaff in the fields so as not to kill the insects and animals that may be living in or off it. This is a practice that has enjoyed a revival in both India and the United States in recent years for different reasons. In India there have been widespread protests by landless villagers for decades against attempts to replace traditional agricultural crops with eucalyptus tree plantations, since poor populations traditionally had access to farmers' fields to use the chaff of food crops for fuel and fodder.[27] In the United States, concern with the high financial and environmental cost of input-intensive agriculture has fostered a movement toward sustainable agriculture over the past decade and a half. One of the primary features of sustainable agriculture is no-till cultivation, whereby soil erosion is markedly reduced by not removing chaff from the fields after harvesting and not ploughing deep furrows for sowing. The decaying chaff provides a natural source of fertilization as well as protection against erosion.

Ashoka repeats in the sixth pillar edict that he has had inscriptions of Dhamma engraved "for the welfare and happiness of the world," and that he "honor[s] all sects with various kinds of reverence."

The seventh pillar edict sums up Ashoka's efforts, combining impatience that more progress is not being made with a recognition that the changes he seeks cannot be legislated but must occur through a process of individual reflection and conversion. It begins with a note of authoritarian moralism: "How then could people be made to conform to *Dhamma*...? I shall make them hear proclamations of *Dhamma*, and instruct them with the knowledge of *Dhamma*....many instructions of *Dhamma* were ordered, and my administrators were appointed over many people; they will admonish them and explain *Dhamma* to them." He describes how he has had banyan trees planted on the roads of his empire "to give shade to beasts and men," as well as wells, mango-groves, and rest houses at regular intervals. He says other kings have instituted such public works, but that "I have done these things in order that my people conform to *Dhamma*." He repeats how his officers of Dhamma are busy everywhere "in many matters of public benefit," and how his officials "are busy with the distribution of charity both on my behalf and that of my queens."

Finally, Ashoka concludes that

> the advancement of *Dhamma* has been achieved through two means, leg-
> islation and persuasion. But of these two, legislation has been less effective,
> and persuasion more so. I have proclaimed through legislation for instance

> that certain species of animals are not to be killed, and other such ideas. But men have increased their adherence to *Dhamma* by being persuaded not to injure living beings and not to take life.

"Persuasion" here has also been translated as "meditation" or "quiet contemplation."[28] The key point is that Ashoka realizes that inner conviction, brought about through persuasion, or through meditation and reflection, in the long term is much more effective in realizing Dhamma than outward prescription and regulation. After all, it is the way he himself came to realize and formulate Dhamma.

## AN ETHICAL REVOLUTION

We find in these major rock and pillar edicts an attempt to promote a continent-wide social ethic and system of governance grounded in the common, core social values of South Asia 2,300 years ago. At the same time, almost everyone who studies the edicts comes away with the conclusion that they also embody something new and unprecedented in history. In the edicts Ashoka speaks not just to his own subjects but also to future generations and all humankind. These interpretations are not contradictory; they are complementary.

Certainly there is a sense that Ashoka, in important ways, attempted to transform statecraft and governance from the Kautilyan rule of force to the primacy of morality, "an administrative philosophy...which is based on the assumption that human nature is basically good."[29] In this view Ashoka clearly is one of the first avatars of a long lineage of utopians or idealists in politics, in distinct contrast to the realist school embodied by Kautilya. There is also an emphasis in the Ashoka of the edicts, as well as in the mythical Ashoka, on charity and gift giving—dana—in contrast to the primacy of acquiring and managing wealth, artha.

Ashoka's definitions of Dhamma, no doubt inspired by Buddhism, formulated a social ethic that drew on older common traditions rooted in the core values of existing religious sects. All of these sects—Buddhist, Jain, and Brahmin—are grounded in a worldview where concepts of dharma and karma are accepted. Although dharma means in various contexts law, truth, and duty, it is also a flexible concept that denotes socially appropriate behavior for particular individuals in specific situations. Ashoka clearly tries to give the concept a more secular, ecumenical meaning that would be accepted by all peoples and religious sects in his empire.

There are two interrelated aspects to Ashoka's Dhamma. First, we have an idealistic, universal ethic characterized by respect for the sanctity of all life and all beings, universal toleration and guarantees of equality in law, or at least uniform application of the law. Second, his Dhamma is an injunction for individuals to fulfill their practical duties in life, particularly regarding respect for parents, relatives, and religious figures.[30] Ashoka's Dhamma was not simply a watered down version of the Buddhist Dharma but a genuinely distinct attempt to foster an ethos of citizenship, cultural assimilation, and inclusion in his multicultural, multinational empire.

Ashoka's Dhamma can also be viewed as a practical code for promoting Adam Smith's three underpinning values of the social order, as set out in *The Theory of Moral Sentiments*: Justice, Prudence, and Beneficence. Ashoka's emphasis on uniform, due process of law, perhaps even of equal application of the same penalties to all people regardless of caste or class, as well as his edict of religious toleration, is the essence of justice. His personal engagement to quickly hear complaints and efficiently dispatch business, his compassion for the poor, the aged, and for prisoners, and his grants of clemency—all reinforce an ideal of Justice. The emphasis in his edicts on restraint, abstention from violent action, and on frugality, recalls Prudence, which for Smith combines understanding with self-command. His attention to charity and donations, the state support of all religious sects, and the preeminence of dana, is the practice of Beneficence.

Ashoka may have also seen his Dhamma as a practical solution to the challenge of inspiring a multiethnic, multinational empire with a common cause and purpose.[31] The Kautilyan analysis of the state is in most regards a technocratic one, clearly insufficient as an ideology to unite a vast multiethnic empire. Rational analysis of the acquisition and management of wealth and power is useful in building the economy and the state but alone cannot inspire unity or long-term loyalty. Dhamma provided a common political ideology, based on a secular reinterpretation of the shared transcendent values of the time. Ashoka's doctrine was also flexible enough not just to tolerate but also to include and support sects such as the Ajivikas, which did not share all the elements of these common values.

A reflection on Ashoka's great experiment raises the critical question of whether social ethics and governance can over the long term be rooted simply in negotiated or agreed-upon rational rules—the project of the Enlightenment—or whether the cultural glue that holds society together ultimately derives an important part of its perceived authority from a shared belief in transcendent values. For Ashoka, Dhamma is not religious in a conventional Western sense of belief in a monotheistic god. Rather, it is a belief in underlying principles governing existence beyond the shorter-term calculations of material advantage and power in Kautilyan statecraft.

Yet the *Arthasastra* is not only the description of an ideal state, it largely reflected the mores of the times, albeit through the lens of Kautilya's radically materialist interpretation. It is just as apparent, both in myth and from the edicts themselves, that Ashoka not only acquired power and expanded his empire through Kautilyan means, but after his conversion to the Dhamma, continued to compromise with Kautilyan realities. We recall that he threatens recalcitrant forest tribes with repression and death; he urges nonviolence—but not entirely, for example with respect to torture; and he proclaims that his descendents, if they must conquer, be satisfied with "light punishments" for the vanquished.

A surprising number of specific measures in the edicts have correlates in the *Arthasastra*. Indian historian R. K. Mookerji compiled a table of some thirty-five examples where there appears to be direct parallelisms.[32] A number of the terms for administrative officers in the edicts are the same or similar to those in the *Arthasastra*, although Ashoka's creation of special "officers of the *Dhamma*" was a radical innovation. Certain other terms are the same or similar, such as the words for the king's hunting and pleasure tours (which Kautilya views as healthy diversions, but Ashoka renounces); similar words for elephant-forests (both Kautilya and Ashoka urge conservation measures), and for ritual festivals in which animals are killed (which Kautilya regulates but Ashoka bans).

Ashoka's protected species in the fifth pillar edict correspond in part to the protected species Kautilya lists in the *Arthasastra*. Kautilya calls for the conservation and sustainable management of various kinds of forests, but Ashoka goes much further in that he expressly forbids the killing of all animals that are *useless* to humans. Unlike Kautilya, whose motivation is one of rational, sustainable use, Ashoka is what we would today call a deep ecologist, someone who proclaims the conservation of nature and other species based on a nonutilitarian respect for the being of other living things. His conservation ethic is rooted in belief in a transcendent ethical order, whereas Kautilya's is that of instrumental rationality.[33]

Ashoka's commitment in the sixth rock edict to do business and be accessible almost the entire day is closely parallel to the rigorous schedule of kingly duties we find in the *Arthasastra*.[34] Ashoka's reference in the fifth pillar edict to twenty-five annual pardons of prisoners corresponds to a recommendation in the *Arthasastra* that the king release the old, the sick, and the helpless from prisons on the royal birthday and that there be general pardons on special occasions such as the birth of a son, the installation of the crown prince, or the conquest of new territory.[35] Kautilya regulated "hate speech," punishing slander based on "body, character, learning, profession, and country" or physical handicaps.[36] Ashoka, in the thirteenth rock edict, urges "control of one's speech, so as not to extol one's own sect or disparage another's on unsuitable occasions." But Kautilya did not advocate religious tolerance and prescribed fines for feeding monks of heretical sects such as Buddhists.

One of the most repeated elements of Ashoka's Dhamma is respectful treatment of relatives, servants, and friends. The *Arthasastra* is full of specific measures concerning the rights of servants, slaves, and laborers, and duties of householders toward relatives and dependents. Finally, the top-down, rather paranoid element in Kautilya's system—the systematic and pervasive internal espionage and intelligence gathering—is also reflected in the Ashokan edicts, particularly in some of the later pillar edicts where Ashoka proclaims his agents are everywhere.

It is not entirely fair to characterize Kautilya as totally unethical and ruthless since he is really one of the first and most articulate proponents of the realist approach in politics: the ethical duty, the dharma, of the king is to focus on accumulation and management of wealth and power for the state to ensure the well-being of all. Kautilya also declared that "(Duties) common to all are: abstaining from injury (to living creatures), truthfulness, uprightness, freedom from malice, compassionateness, and forbearance."[37] In the words of R. P. Kangle, translator and scholar of the *Arthasastra*, "The fact is these ideals are meant for individuals. And Kautilya regards them as obligatory on individuals with as much sincerity as does Asoka. The only thing is that he does not agree that the conduct of public life should be guided by rules of individual morality."[38]

Nonetheless, Ashoka's revolution is one of public as well as of private morality, a daring attempt to move Kautilyan society toward transcending its grounding in an ethic of power, force, and wealth

to one evolving toward nonviolence, tolerance, and charity. This is
not to say that Kautilya does not advocate charity, forgiveness, and
forbearance from use of force in quite a number of specific cases, but
almost everything in Kautilya is based on instrumental calculation,
a careful weighing of the pragmatic consequences and costs of using
violence (danda) and deception in a situation as opposed to the advantages to be gained through more conciliatory means. It is quite clear
then that Ashoka, while maintaining the Kautilyan administrative
system, undertakes something radically new. The traditional dharma
of a king and a Kshatriya sanctioned violence and killing as a necessary duty. While Kautilya's system introduced the novelty of empha-
sizing the importance—indeed at times the preeminence—of wealth
and economic management in the kingly dharma, it also reiterated
and reinforced the need for the ruthless use of force, and willingness
to kill as indispensable elements of statecraft and governance. Ashoka's Dhamma appears to be an almost miraculous attempt by a ruler to
undertake a path of transcending the preeminence of danda and artha
in a daring *political* ethic of nonviolence, tolerance, and compassion.

There are a number of elements in Ashoka's policies that strike
us some 2,300 years later as more progressive than some aspects of
political discourse in the United States of the past thirty years. Certainly Ashoka had no reservations about establishing a state-supported
system of medical treatment centers, and the idea of government-
sponsored veterinary hospitals as a social obligation for other sentient
creatures is something not even the most left-wing Democrat would
suggest. Ashoka, while not abolishing the death penalty, seems to have
had more reservations about its use than some U.S. state governors.
His special expression of compassion for prisoners is one that contrasts
markedly with social attitudes in the early 2000s in the United States.
And we could do worse than changing foreign aid to focus on public
health and ecology, starting with endowing hospitals for humans and
animals, and propagating useful and beneficial plants.[39]

The ban on feeding animals with remains of other animals is one
that makes eminent ethical and practical sense, which again we could
only hope for in a society with markedly different values. The idea
that a head of state should also urge at least partial vegetarianism on
the grounds of empathy for other living creatures is again one we
can hardly imagine. There is clearly a notion of public good and the
role of the state to make expenditures and donations through public works, in marked contrast to the mantra of privatization that has

dominated much economic and political thinking over the past de-cades. (Let us hope we are seeing what could be characterized as a neo-Ashokan turning point in American politics with the social and public works programs of Barack Obama.) And Ashoka's public works are combined with specific injunctions on improving the efficiency and transparency of public administration.

DECLINE AND FALL

What are the historical lessons of Ashoka's extraordinary political ex-periment? Was it naïve and overly idealistic, destined to disintegrate in the face of the practical realities of power and politics? Some of the commentary on the subsequent decline of the Mauryan Empire casts Ashoka as an archaic third-century-BC Jimmy Carter or Gorbachev, a well-intentioned ruler whose legacy was fatally compromised by lack of political realism, misplaced idealism, or by a decadent, des-potic bureaucratic system.

Ashoka's reign did embody both the high point of the Mauryan dynasty, and the beginning of a political decline that culminated eighty-three years after his death with the murder of Brhadratha, the last Maurya. Ashoka may have begun to lose power in the later years of his reign—at the very least, Ashoka had problems with his queen and family—and there was a struggle for succession after his death. Some have argued that Ashoka's Dhamma was directly responsible for this decline and fall: his policy of nonviolence is alleged to have been a totally impractical one that encouraged both internal and external foes. Above all, Ashoka's policies of religious tolerance, equality be-fore the law, and abolition of animal sacrifices are alleged to have pro-foundly alienated the priestly caste of Brahmins, who, it is argued, lost many of their privileges as well as major sources of income[40] because of Ashoka's reforms.[41] It was only inevitable that a counterrevolution would follow.

It is also argued that the Mauryan Empire—and its Kautilyan ad-ministration—was a highly centralized, inherently despotic state, one that was overly dependent on strong political leadership on the part of the emperor. The heavy-handed nature of the regime became more apparent in the later years of Ashoka's reign—attested by the growing tone of impatience and authoritarianism in the major pillar edicts. Ashoka's omnipresent "officers of *Dhamma*," while promoting social welfare, were entrusted with the investigative and spying powers of a police state.

A more recent analysis by Romila Thapar argues that the Mauryan state at its core in Magadha may have been centralized along Kautilyan lines, but that over much of its area sovereignty and administration were more diffuse; in effect the empire may have been overextended to begin with and thus destined for a relatively short life.[42] Ashoka's successors were weak rulers—a "progeny of pygmies," in the words of one historian[43]—and increased the inherent instability of the system. The administration, though centralized in its core area of Magadha, was not effective in preventing abuses by local officials in outlying areas that could foster revolt.

The expenditures needed to support the bureaucratic Mauryan system may have also inevitably carried the seeds of economic decline, which set in and accelerated following Ashoka's death. According to Richard Lannoy, the first three Mauryan kings including Ashoka promoted a great expansion of agricultural production and trade that was principally managed through state enterprises and administrative services, as described in the *Arthasastra*. But once the expansion was consolidated, the "more static village economy could not long support a top-heavy bureaucracy...state control was gradually decentralized...the high productivity rate of state enterprises rapidly declined.....production always declined in inverse ratio to the increase in population in the village settlements."[44] There is some evidence of inflationary pressures in the later Mauryan years as evidenced by increasingly debased Mauryan coins.[45] In fact, Lannoy argues that the Mauryan rise and decline has been repeated several times in Indian history, where "successive empires enjoyed no more than brief periods of prosperity before the closed economy of village settlements they inevitably patronized halted all further growth."[46]

Thapar maintains that the decline "cannot be satisfactorily explained by quoting military inactivity, brahman resentment, popular uprisings, or economic pressure."[47] She ascribes an inevitable disintegration to two factors.[48] First, the dynasty was doomed by a lack of any real sense of national unity or consciousness among the diverse peoples of the empire, exacerbated by regional economic inequalities and cultural, religious, and linguistic differences. Ashoka's Dhamma was an enlightened attempt to propagate a national, unifying ethos, but it failed. Second, Ashoka's immediate legacy was doomed by a top-heavy command and control bureaucracy where power was concentrated in the hands of the ruler; it was not capable, in practice, of maintaining control, particularly in areas outside Magadha, but it was heavy handed enough to alienate important constituencies. Another leading historian argues that the failure of the Mauryan bureaucracy was rooted both in the "technological obstacles to [national] integration" and its enormous cost.[49] In the final analysis, in the words of Arnold Toynbee, "the Mauryan bureaucratic regime probably could, and did, largely defeat the Emperor's intentions."[50]

All of these arguments seem plausible but not entirely convincing. In reality, we do not have enough hard historical evidence to analyze with certainty the Mauryan decline. One can point to other empires of the ancient world that, despite apparently having more problems and challenges than those we find in Mauryan India, enjoyed much longer-lived political and economic sustainability: Egypt and Rome are two obvious examples. Kautilya, controversial as he is, did set forth with great lucidity what was for his time in many respects a progressive model of administrative rationality and equity, especially when compared with the excesses of imperial Rome or some elements of the pre–Civil War and even the modern United States.

Moreover, there is historical evidence—from the accounts of the Seleucid Greek ambassador Megasthenes, for example—of the prosperity, good governance, and relative equity that already characterized the regime of Ashoka's grandfather Chandragupta Maurya. A number of Ashoka's progressive innovations lasted for many centuries, as confirmed in accounts of later travelers. Faxian, for example, in the early fifth century AD, observed in the Ganges basin heartland the presence in major cities of "free hospitals, and hither come all poor or helpless patients, orphans, widowers, and cripples. They are well taken care of, a doctor attends them, food and medicine being supplied according to their needs. They are all made quite comfortable, and when they are cured they go away."[51] While, from the perspective of longer-lived empires like Rome, the Mauryan Empire was relatively short-lived, it nevertheless lasted just about as long—140 years—as British rule in India did more than two millennia later.

What is more certain, however, is that the longer-term legacy of Ashoka continues and indeed grows in our own time. It is a legacy that is more complex in its implications than we might first think, one where mythical and historical influences reverberate mostly for good, but also, not without evil.

# CHAPTER 7

# Ashoka's Legacy
## Conundrum and Challenge

*In our own time, I have heard Asoka heralded as a champion of Buddhist socialism, as a founder of Indian nationalism, as an advocate of animal rights, as the prophet of pacifism. Likewise he has been lambasted as a hypocrite, a totalitarian Big Brother, a maker of monastic landlordism. . . . it is likely that there is some truth in each [view] . . . taken together they testify once again to the ongoing development and the ever-changing nature of the image of Asoka.*
—John Strong[1]

Ashoka's shorter-term goal of a unifying ethic for his empire was perhaps foreordained to eventual failure. But like all the great ethical teachers of humanity, he consciously left a message for all times, and here paradoxically he has succeeded. Certainly Ashoka's attempt to put into practice over a huge empire an ethos of nonviolence and pacifism—imperfect in practice, and not always applied though it was—is one of the most astonishing events in history.

It is no exaggeration to view Ashoka as a forerunner of a number of modern concepts of human rights. He proclaims the right to due process, equal protection of the laws, and religious toleration. He establishes administrative mechanisms to investigate and rectify violations of rights,[2] and seeks to improve conditions in prisons, expressing special concern for due process for prisoners condemned to death.

Although the concept of environmentalism is in one sense a very recent one, it is also not an exaggeration to see Ashoka as a forerunner of environmentalist values.[3] We have seen that Ashoka can be viewed as a precursor of the fundamentalist environmentalism of the "deep ecology" school, which holds the protection of other living species as an absolute value in itself, not as a utilitarian, instrumental means to achieve "sustainable management" for human use. Modern Indian environmental activists cite Ashoka's protection of forests and animals in their battles to save the country's endangered ecosystems.[4] The beauty and simplicity of the Ashokan Dhamma is that the principles of protection of human rights and environmental values all flow from a secular application of the Buddhist/Jain principles of nonviolence, ahimsa and respect for all sentient beings.

Although we have no historical record of the influence of Ashoka's Dhamma missions to the West, they may have played a role in the diffusion of biodiversity, since he states in the second rock edict that "medicinal herbs" and "roots and fruit" have been planted beyond his borders where previously they did not grow. The spread, for example, of trees and plants such as frankincense, amomum, and nardum to the Near East and eastern Mediterranean may have originated with these missions.[5] Ashoka's efforts to protect and propagate as a gift to all mankind medicinal herbs and plants have been cited by Indian activists fighting against attempts of multinational agricultural and biotechnology corporations to patent native Indian trees and plants for private profit.[6]

In the remainder of this chapter we shall examine other, more complex aspects of Ashoka's legacy: the resurrection of Ashokan symbols and secular values in the birth of modern India; his key role in the propagation of Buddhism as a world religion; the invocation of Ashoka in the spirit of a secular Buddhist dhamma in the liberation movement of India's untouchables; and his intriguing, and in some respects troubling, political legacy in Sri Lanka and Southeast Asia. Finally, we examine the legacy of the religious and cultural reaction that followed the apogee of Ashoka's rule and the propagation of his Dhamma. Overall, the figure of Ashoka emerges as a multifaceted one, both a challenge and a conundrum.

## THE PERSISTENCE OF MEMORY

It is somewhat uncanny that, after more than 2,300 years, the leaders of the newly independent Indian state chose Ashokan symbols to embody the hopes of their nation. Not only was the wheel on the Sarnath column chosen to be on the flag, but the Sarnath capital itself, with its carved lions atop a plinth supported by a lotus flower, was chosen as the state seal. So in India today we find the capital of Ashoka's Sarnath pillar on everything from bank notes and coins to the letterhead for diplomatic correspondence. The wheel, or Chakra, we noted in chapter 1, had been a sun symbol in the Indian subcontinent and ancient Mesopotamia dating back to prehistoric times. In the Buddhist epoch of Ashoka it also symbolized Dharma, the wheel of Dharma being the wheel of truth and law. It was the Buddha's first sermon at Sarnath, near Varanasi, on the Four Noble Truths (life is suffering, desiring is the cause of suffering, ceasing of desire is the end of suffering, and there is an eightfold path to achieve this cessation) that "set the wheel of *Dharma*," the great wheel of truth and liberation, into motion. Earlier versions of the Indian flag had the Gandhian symbol of the spinning wheel with a spindle and string appearing parallel on the side, in the center of the tricolor. Nehru thought that this would look asymmetrical, and argued to keep the wheel, an ancient, polysemic symbol. But which wheel? At India's Constituent Assembly in 1947, Jawaharlal Nehru announced before the delegates the reasoning behind the final choice:

> We have associated with this Flag of ours not only this emblem, but in a sense the name of Asoka, one of the most significant names not only in India's history but in world history....the Asokan period in Indian history was essentially an international period of Indian history....It was a period in which India's ambassadors went abroad to far countries and went abroad not in the way of an Empire and imperialism but as ambassadors of peace and culture and good will.[7]

The modern legacy of Ashoka in Asia appears in other surprising contexts. For example, anthropologist Charles Keyes has written of the continued tradition in northern Thailand of linking Buddhist shrines and pilgrimage sites with relics of the Buddha, which, according to legend, were brought to Thailand by the emissaries of Ashoka in the third century BC.[8] Anthropologist S. J. Tambiah has examined modern politics in Thailand and Sri Lanka in the context of the Ashokan mythical-historical influence, and has found the Ashokan legacy very much alive.

That Ashoka is a living historical influence even in the everyday politics of Southeast Asia should not be surprising or seem far-fetched. An analogy is the historical and mythical influence of a figure such as Charlemagne in the modern politics of Europe. If a hypothetical researcher ignorant of Christianity were conducting a study of politics in contemporary Germany and Italy, our researcher would note the existence of "Christian Democratic" political parties, and encounter

literature asserting that former communist and socialist parties rein-
carnate some of the values of the Catholic Church in a secular form.
He or she would realize that to understand modern European politics, one would have to know something about the political and social history of Christianity and the critical unifying role of long-ago
emperors such as Charlemagne and Constantine—Ashoka has often
been compared to both of them. Our researcher would also encounter debates over the role of the church in society, and references even
to Charlemagne's Holy Roman Empire, which united most of present-day France, Germany, northern Italy, and the Benelux countries
as a predecessor of the European Union. He or she would hear of a
European Union "Charlemagne" prize and even read a weekly column "Charlemagne" on prominent European political figures in the
*Economist* magazine.

Ashoka is a pivotal figure in the historical spread of Buddhism.
The mythical accounts of Ashoka's life in the *Asokavadana* and Sri
Lankan chronicles also had a critical influence on the religious as well
as political cultures of much of Southeast and East Asia. "Asoka has
been the model for rulers all over the Buddhist world," observes Oxford professor Richard Gombrich:

> Within the next thousand years a least five kings of Sri Lanka prohibited
> the killing of animals. In Burma, Asoka's example has constantly been in-
> voked by kings, and Prime Minister U Nu, modeling himself on Asoka,
> had innumerable small stupas put up. The great Khmer ruler Jayavarman
> VII (1181–after 1215) ...in his inscriptions expressed Asokan sentiments on
> the material and spiritual well-being of his subjects and announced that he
> had had hospitals built. In eleventh-century Thailand, King Rama Kham-
> haeng ordered that for urgent business he should be disturbed even on the
> toilet....Of course no one before the nineteenth century had access to the
> inscriptions, or even knew they existed: they based themselves on Buddhist
> literary sources.[9]

In the thirteenth century Ashoka is cited in Mongolian chronicles
as a model for kingship.[10] The Sri Lankan chronicles describe how in
the middle of his reign Ashoka convoked a great Buddhist council, the
third since the death of the Buddha, where the leading theologians
and monks of his kingdom attempted to resolve a growing schism between orthodox and heterodox Buddhist practitioners. According to
the chronicles, under Ashoka's benevolent rule Buddhism flourished

in India but also attracted many to the monkhood who sought a life of relative ease and were not rigorous in their observation of Buddhist rites. The Third Buddhist Council, under Ashoka's aegis, resulted in the expulsion of eighty thousand heretics.[11] However, since the third council is not mentioned in other sources, nor in Ashoka's edicts, there is some doubt as to whether it actually took place.[12] The *Mahavamsa* (The great chronicle) describes how at the end of the third council, missionary monks were sent out to the far corners of Ashoka's kingdom. The *Mahavamsa* also directly links the theological purge at the third council with the subsequent trip of Ashoka's son, Mahinda, to Sri Lanka to convert the Sri Lankan king, Devanampiya Tissa.[13] "Obviously," Ashokan scholar John Strong observes, "the whole thrust of this account is to associate the great king Asoka with the specific sect of the Theravadins favored by the authors of the *Mahavamsa* and, by implication, by the island of Sri Lanka in general."[14]

Since Ashoka's time, Buddhism evolved into two major currents, the Hinayana, or "lesser vehicle"—of which the surviving school is Theravada (literally, the "school of the elders"), prevalent in Sri Lanka, Thailand, Burma, Vietnam, Cambodia, and Laos—and the Mahayana, literally the "greater vehicle," which prevailed in China, Korea, Tibet, and Japan. Though a great deal has been written about the differences between Mahayana and Theravada, it has been said that "the Mahayana schools, pre-occupied...with metaphysical and mythological questions, were largely indifferent to social structure," while "the Theravadin *Sangha* retained its belief in the value of a *socially-structured* Buddhism."[15] The Mahayana schools appealed to a broader popular mass since they represented, and in a sense worshipped, the Buddha as an image together with a proliferating number of Boddhisattvas, while the Hinayana schools, including the Theravadins, for a long time indicated his presence "merely by a footprint, a throne, a tree, [or] an umbrella."[16] It is thought that the imagery associated with Greek religion, which was already present in the Maurya Empire, had an important influence on the iconographic evolution of Mahayana Buddhism.[17] Toynbee has compared this iconographic influence to a radiating cultural wave, where ultimately, "as we travel back over the wake of this wave, a Japanese portrayal of the Buddha melts into a Greek portrayal of Apollo by insensible degrees."[18]

The Theravadins emphasized ritual and rites—and thus the importance of Buddhist practice in the monastic life—much more than the Mahayana sects, which offered a more liberal vision of Buddhism accessible to lay practitioners. Thus Ashoka's role embodies a bit of a historical paradox: while propagating a secular ethic of Dhamma accessible to all sects and nationalities, he presided—at least according to the Sri Lankan chronicles—over a theological purge that strengthened a ritualistic Buddhism less directly accessible to lay persons. All Buddhists invoke Ashoka as an embodiment of how Buddhist values are given political and social expression, but it is the Theravada tradition that has invoked the strongest historical-mythical continuity.

Whether Ashoka really did preside over a third Buddhist council is one of several areas where the mythical and possible historical Ashoka are inextricably confounded. Ashoka did issue a separate "schism edict" toward the end of his reign, calling for unity in the Buddhist community and threatening monks and nuns who cause dissension with ostracism. This is one of four so-called minor rock edicts, quite different in tone from the major rock and pillar edicts, that records Ashoka's personal involvement with Buddhism. In the other minor rock edicts, Ashoka commemorates his pilgrimage to the birthplace of the Buddha at Lumbini (in present-day Nepal), exempting the town from most taxes; records his visit to a stupa; and declares his "faith in the Buddha, the *Dhamma* and the *Samgha* [here Dhamma means the Buddhist creed, and Samgha, the Buddhist community]." [19] The personal profession of faith in the Buddha and his teachings found in this last minor rock edict—known as the Bhabra Inscription—seems to establish a clear link between the secular ethic of Ashoka's Dhamma in the major rock and pillar edicts and Ashoka's personal religious conversion and belief in a transcendent reality associated with Buddha's message.

## TO RECONSTRUCT THE WORLD

The 1947 Constituent Assembly, where Nehru chose the Ashokan wheel as the central motif in the Indian flag, was the equivalent for modern India of the U.S. Constitutional Convention in 1789. It was altogether fitting that it nominated none other than Bhimrao Ramji Ambedkar—who had done more than any other to resurrect the memory of a secular, egalitarian Ashokan Buddhist state—to chair the drafting committee that produced India's constitution as an independent state. One of the great leaders of the Indian independence movement, Ambedkar (1891–1956), converted to Buddhism shortly before his death, seeing it as a path for the social liberation of India's tens of millions of outcastes, oppressed by the orthodox Hindu doctrines of social hierarchy and discrimination. Ambedkar himself was of outcaste origin and returned to India to politically organize the untouchables after studying law in London and receiving a PhD from Columbia University in New York. He was a cohort of Gandhi and negotiated a historic pact with the great Indian leader in 1932 that ensured significant quotas of seats for untouchables in the provincial councils and national assembly of an independent India.[20] In India he was hailed as the "modern Manu," a sobriquet in which there is great historical irony, since Manu is the mythical author of the Brahmin/ Hindu laws—*Manusmriti*, "Institutes of Manu"—set down around the second and third centuries AD. The *Manusmriti* codified the caste system and the harshest discrimination against those outside it, who were considered impure.[21]

In 1947 India had a population of about 400 million, of which at least 50 million were outcastes, *Untouchables*—also known as Dalits, or Harijans—Gandhi's term, which meant "children of God." American journalist John Gunther described their situation in 1939 by comparing it to the plight of American blacks in the South, only worse.

Ambedkar himself was beaten as a boy when he attempted to drink from public fountains, and some of his teachers in primary school refused to touch his exercise books for fear of being polluted.[22] When he returned from his foreign studies with a PhD from Columbia to take up a civil service position for which he was grossly overqualified, his own employees treated him like a leper: fearing pollution from physical contact, they would throw papers and documents on his desk rather than hand them to him.[23] Already in 1927, as part of a campaign to allow Bombay's untouchables access to public water facilities (a law allowing this had been passed but there was much local resistance), Ambedkar led a group of activists to stage a ceremony where they publicly burned the *Manusmriti*. In the words of the British Buddhist author Sangharakshita, who knew Ambedkar in his later years, "It was one of the great iconoclastic acts of history...Ambedkar's burning of the Manusmriti has been likened, by some of his admirers, to Luther's burning of the Pope's Bull of Excommunication."[24] He gradually came to the conviction that a secular interpretation of Buddhist Dharma (or Dhamma, as Ambedkar always referred to it) could be the ideology of liberation for arguably the most oppressed people on Earth.

Ambedkar interprets the Buddha's Dharma in a very neo-Ashokan sense, as a secular, universal morality of equity, social equality, and compassion. For Ambedkar, the Buddhist dhamma was the only religious doctrine that was fully reconcilable with modern science, together with political values of liberty and egalitarianism.[25] In contrast, he describes Brahmin dharma as retaining even in the twentieth century an emphasis on ritual, and at its core, social discrimination: "The official gospel of Hinduism is inequality."[26]

Ambedkar's interpretation of Buddhism was a radical one; it took a revisionist approach to a number of widely accepted traditional Buddhist teachings, most notably the Four Noble Truths, which most Buddhists would argue are the core of the Buddha's message. He maintained they were not part of the Buddha's original tenets, along with subsequent distinctions such as Mahayana and Hinayana. In effect he advocated a "Neo-Buddhism," or Navayana.[27] Like Ashoka's Dhamma itself, one can perhaps best reconcile Ambedkar's radical reinterpretation of Buddhism as Ambedkar's Dhamma, rather than the Buddha's, a secular ethic inspired by, and rooted in Buddhism, but quite distinct from it.

Ambedkar's public conversion to Buddhism was one of the most dramatic events in modern Indian history, and it resonated intentionally with echoes of Ashoka. In September 1956, Ambedkar announced that he would convert to Buddhism on October 14 in a public ceremony together with other untouchables. October 14 that year in India was the festival of Dussehra, which honors the return of Lord Rama from his victory in the island of (Sri) Lanka over the demon king Ravana. Ambedkar and his followers rededicated the holiday to celebrate Ashoka's victory at Kalinga, and his subsequent remorse and conversion to Buddhism.[28]

The choice of place was not accidental either: the ceremony was held in Nagpur, the then capital of Madhya Pradesh State. Nagpur had been the ancient center of a non–Indo-Aryan tribal people, the Nagas, who had fought many battles with the Indo-Aryans, subsequently converting to Buddhism. Ambedkar's choice of time and place was a very conscious effort to awaken in his followers a reconstructed historical identity in which they could take pride.[29]

In the days leading up to the event, hundreds of thousands of untouchables traveled to Nagpur from all over India. In a simple, moving, and powerful ceremony, Ambedkar led some four hundred thousand outcastes to renounce Hinduism and be reborn in the Buddhist dhamma. Ambedkar died seven weeks later. Following

Ambedkar's example, millions of untouchable Indians converted to Buddhism (four million alone by February 1957), a Buddhism that embodies a universal, nondiscriminatory ethic inspired by Ashoka.[30]

ASHOKA'S LEGACY BETRAYED: BUDDHIST
NATIONALISM IN SRI LANKA

There is no place on Earth where the historical continuity of Ashoka's legacy is more present than a tree on a platform surrounded by a golden railing in the northern Sri Lankan town of Anuradhapura. It is a Bodhi tree[31] planted as a sapling by Ashoka's daughter; she brought it as a cutting from the branches of the original Bodhi tree at Bodh Gaya in India. The whole enclosure is surrounded by colorful prayer flags and is visited by hundreds, and on some days, thousands of pilgrims and devotees. The great chronicle of Sri Lanka, the *Mahavamsa*, describes how Ashoka sent his son, Mahinda, as an emissary to King Devanampiya Tissa of Anuradhapura and converted him to Buddhism; Mahinda's sister, Sanghamitta, a Buddhist nun, shortly followed, bringing the Bodhi cutting and several other relics. Following the conversion of Tissa, Anuradhapura flowered into the capital of a great civilization that lasted over a millennium until it was abandoned in the year 1063. At one time it was reputed to be the largest monastic city of the ancient world. The Bodhi at Anuradhapura is the oldest historically authenticated tree in the world, for it has been watched over by an uninterrupted series of guardians for some 2,300 years. In fact, the original Bodhi tree at Bodh Gaya in India died, and the tree that is now there has actually grown from a cutting from Anuradhapura.

One fine day in May 1985, armed, masked terrorists invaded the ancient city and in the immediate vicinity of the sacred Bodhi tree gunned down over 150 people. The terrorists were ethnic Tamils, who constitute about 18 percent of the Sri Lankan population. Their act was a response to escalating ethnic violence directed at them in preceding years by the dominant Sinhalese majority, including riots in the capital Colombo in 1983 in which between 350 and 2,000 Tamils were murdered. In those riots, writes anthropologist Stanley Tambiah, "We cannot leave out of account the role of some militant Buddhist monks in inciting crowd action, sometimes as active witnesses and orators."[32]

Sri Lanka, described by Marco Polo as "the most perfect island in the world," has become since the 1980s a tragic conflagration of eth-

nic conflict and civil war, evoking comparisons with Northern Ire-
land or more recently, Bosnia. Over sixty-five thousand people have
died and seven hundred thousand have been displaced. Two hundred
thousand Sri Lankan Tamils are living as refugees in southern India.
At root is the inability of the majority, ethnic Sinhalese population
to forge a political culture and modern state that can accommodate
a multiethnic society—the very kind of society that Ashoka tried to
promote. A significant part of the tragedy lies in the negative role of
modern Buddhism in Sri Lanka—the country on Earth that most
directly links its historical legacy and modern identity to Ashoka—in
promoting a narrow, ethnic-based nationalism instead of a tolerant,
secular culture.

One can seek the answer to this sad paradox in the general imperfection of human nature and society (Christianity too preaches love
but has a long and bloody history of provoking sectarian conflict and
genocidal violence). But, Tambiah observes, it is in the *Mahavamsa*
itself where we can find an even more pertinent clue. The outstanding
hero of the *Mahavamsa* is Duthagamani, who, in the second century
BC, only a hundred years after Mahinda's visit, led a campaign to
recapture Anuradhapura from the occupation of Tamils from south
India who were under the command of the Tamil king Elara. Like
Ashoka after the battle of Kalinga, or Arjuna before the great battlefield of Kurukshetra in the *Bhagavad Gita*, Duthagamani experiences
moral scruples and doubts over the slaughter of thousands of Tamils associated with his campaign to unify Sri Lanka. Eight Buddhist
saints reassure the victorious king that among the thousands of dead
he has killed only one and a half real human beings—one who was a
full believer in Buddhist doctrine and the other (who counts as half
a human) who was a novice. All the rest do not count since they are
"unbelievers and men of evil life." [33]

The *Mahavamsa*, much like the Old Testament and Torah of the
Jewish tradition with respect to Palestine, establishes a potent historical myth of the hegemonic destiny of the Sinhalese to rule, with religious sanctification, the island of Sri Lanka—with tragic and bloody
consequences in modern times as the myth has been revived and po-
liticized. [34]

From the late nineteenth through the twentieth century, Sri
Lankan Buddhism underwent a revival and partial secularization, one
where leading Buddhist intellectual monks evoked the image of a
utopian past in which the ancient Sinhalese kings were chakravartins

and *dharmarajas*, after the Ashokan model—righteous kings who set the wheel of Dharma in motion and realized some of the elements of "a welfare state and a social and economic egalitarianism in a non-competitive agricultural society of villagers." [35] But the narrow and distorted interpretation of this history on the part of major twentieth-century monk-intellectuals also fostered a politics of identity that is all too familiar. Anagraika Dharmapala (1864–1933), who is widely regarded as the founder and most eloquent proponent of the Sinhalese Buddhist revival, blamed, in a most un-Ashokan spirit, Christians, Muslims, and Hindus for all the problems that have beset the Sinhalese since their days of glory.

The inevitable crisis in a multiethnic society that such attitudes would provoke came to a head after World War II through a number of major political interventions that deeply infringed on the shrinking social and economic space left to the Tamils. So it was not only not an accident but also virtually inevitable that these social currents would culminate in the massacre of scores of innocent people by Tamil insurgents near the sacred Bodhi tree. The rest of the story is somewhat better known: in the mid-1980s the Tamil–Sinhalese conflict erupted into a full-fledged civil war, culminating with the Sri Lankan government agreeing in 1987 to Indian intervention and military occupation—by eventually as many as ninety thousand troops—of the Tamil areas of the island. Significant elements of the Buddhist clergy opposed the 1987 peace accords. Since the late 1980s there have been several subsequent truces and renewals of hostilities. The most recent resurgence of fighting began in 2006 and continued to rage through early 2009, when the Sri Lankan army pushed a final campaign to recapture insurgent-controlled territory.

There are uncanny echoes of other contemporary crises in the Sri Lankan tragedy. One cannot help but see analogies with the Israeli–Palestinian conflict, where a historical right of return has been invoked, sanctified by an ancient religious chronicle giving a single ethnic group a mythological entitlement to disputed lands. Or the Serbs' claims to Albanian-populated Kosovo, the ancient Serbian homeland where the oldest and most holy Serbian Orthodox monasteries are located. The fundamental failure is rooted in the fatal conceit of linking the universal ethic of Buddhism and Ashokan Dhamma (as set out in both myth and history) with the nationalistic mission of a particular ethnic group, in this case the Sinhalese. The ancient Sri Lankan chronicles can be read to fuel such an agenda, but no more arguably that the Old Testament and Torah can be cited to justify the contemporary resettlement of Palestinians or the New Testament to justify the ethnic cleansing of Albanian Muslims in Kosovo.

More thought provoking is how much of the discourse of Buddhist revival politics in Sri Lanka echoes the criticisms of many movements in revolt against the values and incursions of global economic integration, market fundamentalism, and consumerism. Stanley Tambiah summarizes the whole modern political and social project of this "political Buddhism":

> While many of the "truths" of doctrinal Buddhism at the level of the individual…fade in urgency, a collectivist conception of Buddhist "nationalism," and Buddhist "democracy"—even Buddhist "socialism…progressively suffuses and becomes the dominant public consciousness…refer[ing] back to certain canonical suttas [sutras—texts, scriptures] dealing with ideal righteous rulers in the form of cakkavatti [chakravarti]…it criticizes present-day party politics and present-day hankering after West-inspired materialist, consumerist, and capitalistic self-seeking goals and purposes and proposes in their place a simpler, harmonious "Buddhist way of life" in a "Buddhist democracy."[36]

What is discomfiting is that much that rings true as a critique of contemporary society can be combined with politics that is socially destructive, even genocidal in its consequences. The widespread popular appeal of earlier twentieth-century ideologies of communism and national socialism lay precisely in the fact that much of their critique of market capitalism and their ethical/emotional ideals were perceived and felt as true for decades by large numbers of people—as distorted or ugly as these ideals appear with the hindsight of history. The justified countermovements to global economic integration and its crises are prone to similar dangers and distortions: one need only look at one of the major global countercurrents, an increasingly potent identity politics based on virulent ethnic tribalism and fundamentalist religious revivals.

In evaluating the Ashokan legacy, then, it is not Buddhism per se, at least as an organized religion and tradition, that embodies the uniqueness of his political experiment. Tambiah formulates the question as follows: "Was it Buddhism that made it possible for the Asokan state to become such a unique experiment in political civility and rationality, or was it something else, such as a secularly derived theory or interpretation of politics and diplomacy?"[37] One answer is that the administrative system and politics of Kautilya—with all its faults—constituted the real glue that held the empire together at least for a time, though its flaws entailed perhaps an inevitable decline.

Perhaps the lesson to be gained is that of balance: idealistic, religious, moralistic ideologies can easily be distorted to promote socially destructive programs if they are not tempered by a healthy Kautilyan realist skepticism about human motivation and political interaction. The Ashokan and the Kautilyan approaches are not opposed; they are complementary and part of a continuum. If we view them as archetypes, we must face the world of the twenty-first century with Ashokan ideals *and* Kautilyan realism and somehow find a balance between the two.

## THE ORDER OF THE WORLD

Above all, Ashoka's greatest legacy was the practical attempt in the public sphere to introduce (all his flaws notwithstanding) a higher ethic of nonviolence and respect for all beings in the practice of politics. He gave a new answer to the most fundamental political and social questions: what is ethical, what is effective, what is duty, what is dharma?

Ashoka did not have the last word. His immediate legacy was challenged less than a century later by a political and cultural reaction that reasserted more traditional Brahmanic values. Following the overthrow of the Mauryan dynasty in the second century BC, over the next four hundred years many of the most important classical texts of Hinduism—the laws of Manu, and the great epics of the Mahabharata and the Ramayana—were revised and set down in the forms that have come down to us today. They reflect a more conservative, Brahmanical view of society and dharma.[38] The most famous section of the Mahabharata, the *Bhagavad Gita*, sets forth an interpretation of dharma and social duty that in some respects is very much at odds with Ashoka's Dhamma.

Ashoka was the culmination of a period in Indian history in which the older Brahmin order, grounded in the rigid caste system and the central role of ritualistic animal sacrifice, was increasingly challenged by groups of wandering *sramana* holy men.[39] The older Brahmin, Vedic order was characterized by the centrality of elaborate ritual sacrifice in religious and social life. "Large numbers of animals were required for grand sacrifices. The number ranged from seventeen to

260 and even more, depending on the nature of the ritual and the capacity of the sacrificer or patron of sacrifice."[40] In fact, in the earliest *Vedas*, ritual sacrifice is the most important element of dharma, necessary for upholding the entire social and cosmic order.[41] The sramanas were ascetics and gurus who advocated instead a spiritual, interior process of psychological discipline and sacrifice; many "developed yogic techniques in order to actualize the inner forces, and advocated a new dharma of ethical life."[42] Nonviolence, a more flexible view of caste, denial of the efficacy of rituals and animal sacrifice, and respect for all sentient beings were at the heart of their ethical revolution that challenged the established order. In his policy of Dhamma, Ashoka provided state recognition and patronage for these movements, such as Buddhism and Jainism, but also for conservative Brahmin sects and even for groups that Buddhists viewed as antagonists, e.g., the Ajivikas.

In the *Bhagavad Gita* we find a reassertion of the older ethic but in a new form. In the *Gita* the hero Arjuna stands before a great battle, which he knows will lead to immense slaughter; the situation is compounded by the fact that on both sides of the battle many are his kinsmen. Following Kalinga, Ashoka renounced warfare and violence, adopting a policy of conquest through nonviolence. But in the *Gita*, Lord Krishna tells Arjuna that "nothing is higher for a Kshatriya than a righteous war" and that not to fight and kill would be a sin.[43] Twice Krishna tells him that "better one's own duty [dharma], although imperfect, than the duty of another, well performed."[44] The laws of Manu state exactly the same proposition: "It is better to do one's own duty badly than another's well."[45] The code of Manu—which Ambedkar publicly burned as a symbolic declaration of the liberation of untouchables from traditional oppression—was also set down in the period following the overthrow of the Mauryan dynasty, from around 180 BC through the first two centuries AD. Besides reaffirming the traditional roles and duties of caste, in the *Manusmriti*, as in the other post-Ashokan Hindu legal writings,

> there is an uncompromising insistence on the regular performance of Vedic sacrifice. Although they take nonviolence (ahimsa) as a virtue in individual life, they do not apply to killing in sacrifice. Manu, for example, quotes the practice of ancient sages, priests, and tribes in support of the killing of superior animals and birds for sacrifice and thereby for the sustenance of life. In this sense, for him, those who kill in sacrifice are not slaughterers.[46]

We realize thus how threatening Ashoka's extension of nonviolence may have been, since by elevating it from a limited personal context to the organizing principle of society he threatened the status and livelihood of the two dominant castes of Brahmins (priests, whose livelihood depended on animal sacrifices) and Kshatriyas (warriors).

In the *Gita* the reaffirmation of the old order is bolstered by a new interpretation of dharmic duty. Whatever the individual action, even killing, it is not the ultimate cause of what occurs; and dutiful actions are dharma if performed in a spirit of nonattachment to the consequences. Krishna reveals to Arjuna that "even without Thee, none of these warriors, arrayed here in the hostile armies, will live." The Lord, as "world-destroying Time," has already killed those who will die, their souls are destined to be reborn in new forms. Moreover, Krishna urges, dharmic duty—in this case the warrior's duty to fight and kill—should itself be performed in the spirit of sacrifice and personal nonattachment to the benefits or results. In fact all the old rites of sacrifice should not be relinquished, but "even these acts are [still] to be performed, giving up attachment and the fruits." [47]

The *Gita* is the best-known and most often cited text of Hindu literature and has enjoyed a twentieth-century renaissance as one of the pivotal sacred texts of humanity. Gandhi himself read it as a manual of nonviolence, but this requires a metaphorical interpretation of the great battle that is the culmination of the *Gita* and Mahabharata. For Gandhi the battlefield where Arjuna stood was a metaphor for the forces struggling within the human soul and body; for other modern Hindu reformers it is the entire world as a moral battleground or even the fight for Indian independence.[48] But literally read, the *Gita* could be used as justification for mass murder as easily as for nonviolence. "Kill and be not distressed by fear. Fight!" Krishna urges Arjuna.[49] Thus, one of India's leading early twentieth-century anticolonialist nationalists, Balwantrao Gangadhar Tilak (1856–1920) incited revolutionary nationalist terrorism appealing to the moral code of the *Gita*. In an 1897 speech, he said, "We have a right even to kill our own guru and our kinsmen.... get out of the Penal Code, enter into the lofty atmosphere of the Shrimat Bhagavad Gita and then consider the actions of great men." [50] This very speech incited a young Brahmin follower a few days later to assassinate a British official.[51] In 1948, Nathuram V. Godse, member of a fanatical nationalist Brahmin paramilitary group, believed he was acting out his dharma in harmony with the message of the *Gita* by assassinating Mohandas Gandhi.[52]

In one sense it is unfair to hold the *Gita* responsible for fundamentalist acts of violence—or rather, if we do so, then we must also hold the Bible, the Koran, and Sri Lankan Buddhist Chronicles, as well as other great religious texts, responsible for all the acts of violence perpetrated in their name. But it is possible to see the *Gita* as an ideological counterthrust to Ashoka's universalizing Dhamma of nonviolence: "While Ashoka stands for a common human virtue, Arjuna stands for...an eternal way of life-style or system....Ashoka's dharma is universal and monolithic; Gita's dharma is particular and differentiated. Ashoka's dharma is dynamic and revolutionary; Gita's dharma is counterrevolutionary and conservative."[53] In fact, some commentators have written that recent Indian history can be understood in light of the tension between the Dhamma of Ashoka and the dharma of Arjuna; Ambedkar delineated this dichotomy in an extreme form. Although the modern Indian state sought inspiration from the secular, universal ethic of Ashoka, and chose Ashokan symbols as its emblems, Hindu fundamentalism and nationalism "take the Arjuna model seriously and take up swords," and even—or especially—at the outset of the twenty-first century, seek to purge Indian society of other religions and to instate an imagined reconstruction of the original Brahmin order.[54]

The contrast between Ashokan universalism and Brahmanic fundamentalism—which can cite, or miscite, the *Gita* as a sacred text—recalls and evokes the tension between the universal ideals of the Enlightenment and modern and postmodern religious and nationalistic fundamentalism in the West. In India, in fact, these two models of contrasting social tensions—one indigenously rooted and over two millennia old, the other a contemporary reaction to modernity and globalization—coincide and overlap, a historical and cultural palimpsest.

## YUDHISHTHIRA'S DILEMMA

The drama of dharma and the questioning of the Ashokan ideal is carried out on a much grander scale in the great epic of the Mahabharata, of which the *Bhagavad Gita* is only a small part. The Mahabharata is the longest epic poem in world literature, eight times the combined length of the Iliad and the Odyssey.[55] In the Mahabharata, Arjuna, the hero of the *Gita*, is one of five brothers, the Pandavas, who after a period of exile wage an apocalyptic war against their cousins, the Kauravas. The eldest of the Pandavas, and former king, is Yudhishthira, who wagered and lost the kingdom to the Kauravas in a single throw of dice. He agreed to go with his brothers and their common wife, Draupadi, into exile for thirteen years, after which they were to receive back the kingdom. Despite the promptings of Draupadi and some of his brothers for quicker revenge, Yudhishthira keeps his promise. Nevertheless, an all-destructive war ensues when the Kauravas, at the end of the agreed-on exile, refuse to keep their part of the bargain. Although the Pandavas are victorious, the massacre on both sides is horrendous. Archaeologists believe that the actual physical location of the battlefield, Kurukshetra, just happens to lie within the limits of the modern city of Delhi.

Yudhishthira is the main protagonist and a troubled hero since he is constantly is at odds with the dictates of kingly and warrior dharma, troubled by Ashoka-like scruples over the morality of violence and war. He, like Ashoka, is a dharmaraja, a righteous king, but is constantly beset by criticism from his wife and brothers for his ethical scruples. One scholar has asserted that the figure of Yudhishthira is modeled on Ashoka, and the various debates on dharma that fill the epic reflect the mixed legacy of Ashoka in the period following the overthrow of the Mauryas.[56]

When the Pandavas are exiled in the forest, Draupadi chides Yudhishthira for his ethical, dharmic commitment to be true to the promise of remaining in exile for thirteen years. She says he must act, rather than wait out the period of exile. "In this world a man never obtains virtue with Law (dharma) and gentleness, or patience or uprightness, or tenderness....," she says, and condemns the order of a world, and God himself, in which only force and power seem to matter. "As one breaks wood with wood, stone with stone, iron with iron, the inert with the insentient, so the blessed God....hurts creatures with creatures....the capricious blessed Lord plays with the creatures like a child with his toys." Either "God is tainted by the evil he has done" or "mere power is the cause of everything, and I bemoan powerless folk."[57] Yudhishthira replies that he follows dharma not because of its rewards, "but in order not to transgress the traditions and to look to the conduct of the strict." "The man who doubts the Law (dharma) ends up an animal," he states. "He who doubts the law (dharma) finds in nothing else a standard and ends setting himself up as the standard" and "the whole world would sink into bottomless darkness.... [men] would live like cattle." He has a transcendent faith in the justness of dharma, even if individually and immediately it bears no personal reward.

It would be hard to find a more eloquent statement of the problem of ethics, evil, and God: Draupadi's skepticism and Yudhishthira's reply are as timely today as the day they were written. We are reminded of Ivan Karamazov's famous dictum in Dostoyevsky's novel *The Brothers Karamazov*: "If there is no God, everything is permitted." Yudhishthira's transcendent faith in the dharma reminds us of Ashoka, where he expresses his faith, for example in the ninth rock edict, that Dhamma will bring benefit if not for certain in this world, certainly in the next world.

Yudhishthira's younger brother Bhima joins the debate, with even harsher words shouting, "You are Law (dharma), and crying Law (dharma)! You emaciate yourself with your vows; but is it possible, king, that despair has prompted you to the life of a eunuch?" Bhima argues that artha, translated here as Profit, is "the source of Law (dharma) and Pleasure (kama)" and that Yudhishthira's overly narrow and moralistic interpretation of dharma is leading them to disaster. Bhima's advice and worldview is quite Kautilyan: the duty of the king is to win back his kingdom through whatever means possible: "No king has ever conquered earth by being solely law-minded, nor have they thus won prosperity and fortune. It is by using a sweet tongue with the many lowly people whose minds are greedy that one gains a kingdom with trickery as a fowler gains his meal...you must with your strong arms cut down the enemies by resorting to trickery." [58] But Yudhishthira remains firm, saying he has sworn to an agreement. Though the dharma of the king and warrior (Kshatriya) imposes certain ethical norms that Yudhisthira feels he must follow, he also condemns the violence and bloodshed this dharma entails: "There is nothing more evil than the Kshatriya's *dharma*." [59]

Later in the epic, after the Pandavas have defeated the Kauravas, and most of the Pandava allies also have been massacred, Yudhishthira asks his brothers and his uncle, Vidura, to judge the order of importance of the three values of dharma, artha, and kama. Vidura gives the conventional answer that dharma is first, and it is an orthodox dharma that he means, since besides traditional moral virtues of truthfulness, compassion, and self-restraint, he mentions the performance of ritual sacrifices and the study of the Vedic scriptures. Arjuna takes the Kautilyan position, arguing that artha is supreme: "Without Profit or Wealth (artha) both Virtue (dharma) and (the objects of) Desire (kama) cannot be won."[60]

The two youngest brothers, Nakul and Sahadev, who are twins, see the three as interconnected: they acknowledge the importance of artha but argue that "there can be no Wealth in one that is destitute of Virtue." Therefore, "one should first practice Virtue (dharma); next acquire Wealth (artha) without sacrificing Virtue (dharma), and then seek the gratification of Desire." Bhima takes a novel position different from the one he espoused earlier: it is kama on which the order of the world is based, for without Desire one cannot wish or strive for either Wealth or Virtue. In a sense Vidura, Arjuna, and Bhima are respectively espousing rather modern viewpoints: the ethical or religious, the economistic, and the Freudian.[61]

Yudhishthira, however, rejects all opinions as false philosophy and appears to combine a Buddhist emphasis on achieving personal liberation (Nirvana) with an almost Ajivika–like fatalism: "No one in this world can act as he pleases. I act precisely as I am made (by a superior power) to act." He who has withdrawn himself from the trivarga, the triple aggregate of artha, kama, and dharma, "may succeed in winning Emancipation (nirvana), it seems therefore that Emancipation is productive of the highest good."[62] In the words of a leading British scholar of Hinduism:

> These are words of bitter disillusion, and it is strange that the King of dharma itself should reject dharma in favor of meek submission to an incomprehensible fate and the quest for Nirvana which puts a stop to all dharma as to all contingent things....he is not at ease in a world where the traditional dharma so obviously conflicts with the dictates of conscience and compassion....what he protests against time and time again is the dharma particular to the warrior class particularly as it applies to kings.[63]

Like Ashoka after Kalinga, Yudhishthira has won a great war but at a horrific cost. Virtually all his kinsmen have been slaughtered and the kingdom he has won has been desolated. Pained by remorse, he wants to renounce the kingship and retire as a hermit, but Krishna tells him that he must renounce his desire to give up attachment to the world, he must reign in the same spirit of nonattachment that Krishna urged Arjuna to adopt in going into battle in the *Gita*, to be in this world, but not of it.

We of course have no way of knowing for sure, but as Ashoka was near the end of his life a convinced Buddhist, this very well could have been the spirit in which he continued to reign while spreading his message of toleration and nonviolence.

The Ashokan experiment in nonviolence and toleration evoked something of a philosophical and social counterrevolution that was embodied in the perspective of the *Bhagavad Gita*. But post-Ashokan Hinduism also incorporated a recognition of Ashokan values and of the Ashokan dilemma—as embodied in the Ashoka-like deliberations of Yudhishthira in the Mahabharata.[64]

There is no easy or clear answer to Yudhishthira's quandary, which is the dilemma of politics itself. Looking at Ashoka, Kautilya, and both Arjuna and Yudhishthira in the Mahabharata, we seem to have three answers to the question of what balance of values should predominate in politics and society: Ashoka's message, for all his imperfections, is nonetheless a striving toward universal nonviolence and tolerance; Kautilya, the realist, sees the acquisition and rational management of material wealth, of the earth inhabited and worked upon by humans, as the preeminent social and political virtue. The message of the *Gita* and of Yudhishthira's dilemma in the Mahabharata is that of socially defined duty: each must fulfill his or her role and task, even if it entails violence or killing, and better to carry out one's true duty poorly than another person's duty well. For Yudhishthira the fulfillment of his kingly dharma is a soul-wracking torment, which he nevertheless fulfills in an exemplary fashion. In each case the answer is in effect a definition of dharma, of the values and duties that uphold society and that are perceived as being rooted in the natural world and in the transcendent order of the universe.

In the first decade of the twenty-first century, the age of economic globalization, on what values or priorities does the course of the world rest? How are we to uphold our world?

# CHAPTER 8

# To Uphold the World

In 1562 Michel de Montaigne, a lawyer and landowner whom we now remember as the greatest essayist of French literature, traveled to the seaport of Rouen. On its face, his journey might seem a strange one; he undertook an arduous trip to see a twelve-year-old boy he had never met. But the boy was the new French king, Charles the Ninth, who had arrived in Rouen following its bloody recapture from Protestant Huguenot rule. It was a time of terrible civil strife between Catholics and Protestants, accompanied by sickening atrocities on both sides. It was also the time of Europe's global expansion to the New World and to the coasts of Africa and Asia. In the seaport there was a great and curious attraction: a French ship had just returned from a new land, Antarctic France, corresponding today to eastern Brazil. The ship brought back three Brazilian Indians. At the dawn of the modern age and of the economic integration of the planet, let us revisit Montaigne's account of this uncanny encounter: "The King talked with them," he wrote, "for some time; they were shown our way of living, our magnificence, and the sights of a fine city." Then Montaigne himself asked "what they thought about all this, and what they had found most remarkable."[1] They mentioned three things, of which Montaigne remembered two:

> They said that in the first place they found it very strange that so many tall, bearded men, all strong and well-armed, who were around the King....should be willing to obey a child, rather than choose one of their own numbers to command them. Secondly—they have a way in their language of speaking of men as halves of one another—that they had noticed

among us some men gorged to the full with things of every sort while their other halves were beggars at their doors, emaciated with hunger and poverty. They found it strange that these poverty-stricken halves should suffer such injustice, and that they did not take the others by the throat or set fire to their houses.[2]

The encounter of the boy-king of France with three Brazilian Indians in Rouen in 1562 is emblematic of our world today. Over the past three decades, many of the mighty of the world, rather than following the blind authority of a child, genuflected before the mystical, unstoppable authority of the market, or of a putative economic globalization that cannot be stopped or influenced. The city of Rouen, with its splendor and oversatiated richer inhabitants alongside desperate poverty and hunger is still with us. It has become the entire planet, with its richer inhabitants in the global nodes and cities of the Network Society "gorged to the full with things of every sort" while billions still eke out a meager survival. And we see the rise of violent fundamentalist countermovements, feeding on the need for alternative identities and a collective sense of aggrieved injustice, calling for suicidal terror "to take the others by the throat or set fire to their houses." Until recently we heard that it is only more of the market and more economic globalization that will improve the situation; year after year, the leaders of the G8 and of the WTO proclaimed their sympathy with the sentiments of the globalization protesters while bemoaning the protesters' peculiar blindness to the putatively obvious solution—more of the same. Now, in the aftermath of the near collapse of global markets, more of the same will not work.

The great French Renaissance humanist did not share the belief in the unmitigated meliorative effects of global economic integration that even today is so widespread among the powerful. As he gazed upon the indigenous Brazilians at Rouen, he reflected, "poor fellows,... not knowing how costly a knowledge of this country's corruptions will one day be to their happiness and repose, and that from intercourse with us will come their ruin."[3] As indeed it did.

What kind of global ethic can we envisage to hold together a planetary society? And in what would such an ethic be grounded when, in the words of George Soros, "no external authority remains undisputed... the only possible source is internal."[4] Can we envisage the equivalent of a Dhamma for the twenty-first century, one that, unlike Ashoka's, would emerge from a bottom-up process of global self-organization, rather than through clumsy top-down impositions? Ashoka's project failed as much as anything from its top-down bureaucratic approach, an approach embedded in the very nature of the times and of the empire he inherited.

In the summer of 2001, a hundred thousand "anti"-globalization protesters raged in Genoa at the G8 summit, forcing the heads of state of the world's most powerful countries to meet under siege conditions. The need for a deciphering of globalization's dilemmas had never been greater, and it catapulted a rather turgid work of political theory authored by an imprisoned Italian Marxist theoretician and an American literature professor into the prime time of global media. *Empire*, by Michael Hardt and Antonio Negri,[5] became the subject of major articles in the *New York Times*, *Le Monde*, and other European newspapers, and in the United States, shortly after Genoa, one of the authors was interviewed on the *Tonight* program of the literati, PBS's *Charlie Rose* talk show.

Called "the *Communist Manifesto* for our time,"[6] much of the analysis draws explicitly or implicitly on Debord and Castells. *Empire* is Hardt and Negri's term for the new form of supra or transnational sovereignty, one based on an economically driven, globally encompassing "*decentered* and *deterritorializing* apparatus of rule," managing "hybrid identities, flexible hierarchies and plural exchanges through modulating networks of command."[7] This characterization is strikingly similar to Castells's conceptualization of the global Network Society. The "ether" of media, information flows and images, is the "glue that holds together" the global constitution of Empire,[8] and this analysis of Hardt and Negri is similar to that of Castells's characterization of "the culture of Real Virtuality."

Just as in the Spectacle and the Network Society, the "suspension of history" is an important component of Empire's power, i.e., "fix[ing] the existing state of affairs for history."[9] Such a world tends toward a soft postmodern totalitarianism in which there is no island of social or cultural life that is not subject to the instrumental logic and domination of Empire. There is no longer any transcendence, any escape; there is no "outside" of Empire, it is a world of total immanence and domination of a single logic, of a global, deterritorialized, network of production and consumption.

Empire produces what Hardt and Negri call "the multitude," the constitution through emerging global networks of billions of people as a potentially different kind of political actor. The interesting insight is that the deracinating, deterritorializing, global reach of Empire creates an emergent counterpolitical force in all of us, in so far as we all constitute "the multitude" in our unmediated involvement, production, and consumption in the networks of the global system. The current global economic crisis may accelerate its development. To recall Karl Polanyi's analysis, the dynamic of the "double movement," the reaction against the domination and disruption of embedded social values by the politically engineered domination of the market, is now global.

Castells articulates what the political project of the "multitude" might be. The opposition to—and within—the Network Society is founded on a dialectic of the "web and the self," of social countermovements basing themselves on the quest for, or reconquest of, identity, whether as historical, ethnic, religious identity,[10] or on identity founded in participation in projects of change in social values—for example, feminism and environmentalism. Identity-based movements base their program in transcendence of the Network Society and the global Web, be it in the reappropriation of history, religious identity, or a project of value-based social transformation.

But the analyses of global countermovements by Hardt and Negri, Castells, and others, while illuminating in some aspects, leave us with the realization that these movements are still seeking coherent agendas. There is no convincing, unifying system of belief apart from a growing reaction to the perceived social and political inequities of the emerging global order. We sense the inadequacy of the ethos and political agenda these analyses set out as an alternative. A great burden is put on the quest of a postmodern self for identity or subjective freedom—either alone or in collective projects. The global empire of instrumental reason and its planetary web of images and media have left only decontextualized tatters of cultures and history from which identities are improvised as fragile and ever-changeable collages.

In an uncanny way, Ashoka's attempt to reconcile the empire of his day with a reappropriation of the values of life, tolerance (inclusion), and respect for all living things speaks more directly to certain social and spiritual needs of our time. Ashoka has been there before us, and he can aid us in evaluating a number of contemporary proposals for a global ethic.

There is nothing forced or incongruous in such an approach, if we believe that human societies in the past, with all the differences in technological development, and across millennia of the evolution and fall of different social orders, have faced at critical moments similar or, at least to a degree, analogous crises. Arnold Toynbee has characterized this approach as the "philosophical contemporaneity of all civilizations." [11] In fact, Thucydides anticipated Toynbee in the notion of the "philosophical contemporaneity" of cultures by more than twenty-four centuries. "The past," Thucydides wrote, is "an aid to the interpretation of the future, which in the course of human things must resemble if it does not reflect it.... I have written my work, not as an essay which is to win the applause of the moment, but as a possession for all time." [12] Ashoka wrote, "I have done all this so that among my sons and great grandsons and as long as the sun and moon endure, men may follow *Dhamma*." [13]

Figures like Thucydides, Montaigne, and Ashoka offer not only the "philosophical contemporaneity" of human societies, but also invite us to open up the present to other alternatives through the recovery of history. They consciously spoke to the future with the knowledge, or at least the presentiment, that the experience and insight of their worlds and times would create a space of freedom for men and women millennia after their deaths.

There are other contemporary, more practical efforts to formulate common ethical principles of a global social consensus. One of particular interest, where the authors have invoked in their analyses both Ashoka and Kautilya, is the so-called "capabilities approach" articulated by Nobel economics laureate Amartya Sen and University of Chicago philosopher Martha Nussbaum. It is an approach that seeks to redefine the economic goals that dominate contemporary political and social discourse in terms that echo classical Western humanism. Concretely, Sen's approach "concentrates on the capabilities of people to do things—and the freedom to lead lives—that they have reason to value." [14] Education and health care, freedom of choice, and informed consent and participation in decisions that affect people's lives are important substantive values in the "capabilities approach," not just means to the end of greater economic efficiency or growth. A practical outcome of the capabilities approach has been articulated by the United Nations Development Program (UNDP) in its Human Development Index. The index is based on statistical studies of basic education, health, income, and other social welfare indicators that comprise the annual *United Nations Human Development Report*. The Human Development Index gives a more socially oriented account of comparative welfare in different countries than the more purely economic indicators of other international institutions, such as the International Monetary Fund and World Bank.[15]

Martha Nussbaum has elaborated the capabilities approach into what she suggests could be "the philosophical underpinning for an account of basic constitutional principles that would be respected and implemented by the governments of all nations, as a bare minimum of what respect for human dignity requires."[16] This would be the moral equivalent of an Ashokan Dhamma for the twenty-first century. While her immediate concern is articulating a common ground for the social and economic rights of women, she sets out criteria that she hopes constitute an "overlapping consensus" of people from different cultures and beliefs that nevertheless would be a common global ethic. The underlying proposition again is *"each person's capability* based on a *principle of each person as end."*[17] Nussbaum has formulated a list of ten "Central Human Functional Capabilities,"[18] based on years of study and cross-cultural discussions. These capabilities include being able to live a life of normal length; bodily health; bodily integrity (freedom of movement and freedom from physical assault); capacity to think and capacity to use and express the imagination (capacities built by adequate education); and capacity to express emotions and attachment (which requires freedom from fear and abuse). The core capabilities also entail freedom to plan one's life; freedom for social affiliation; capacity to control one's immediate physical and political environment; opportunity for recreation; and the opportunity to relate to nature and other species.

If we are considering the elements of a global ethic, one problem with the capabilities approach is that it is not rooted in any common, overarching belief, or even any commonly accepted concept of society—it is centered on the individual as an end in herself or himself, with appropriate constraints on infringing on the capabilities of others. In fact, Nussbaum invokes Ashoka for this latter principle of "moral constraint," citing the twelfth rock edict, where Ashoka exhorts his subjects to honor all religious sects and not to disparage the religious beliefs of others.[19] But Ashoka's Dhamma, while secular, emanated from both a cultural worldview encompassing transcendent values and from Ashoka's personal conversion to a new interpretation of those values. For example, with Nussbaum the relation to the natural environment is stated in terms of the individual-centered right to live in relation to nature and other species; it is a self-centered view of the function of all other life as an object of satisfaction or fulfillment for individual human beings. Ashoka's concern for species is rooted in a transcendently anchored belief in nonviolence and care for all sentient beings.

In addition, the "overlapping consensus" that the list of ten central human capabilities aspires to embody is a fragile one. One would certainly hope that some sort of concern for the natural environment would be a matter of evolving global consensus, but among the participants in Nussbaum's project it was not. She observes that the "ability to live in a fruitful relationship with animals and the world of nature" was not on her original list and was added mainly through pressure of the Scandinavian participants who could not conceive of a truly human life without this element.[20]

Let us return to the concluding paragraph of *Empire*, which points to what is missing in the analyses of the discontents of globalization—including, paradoxically, that of Empire itself. The authors invoke Saint Francis of Assisi, "who in opposition to nascent capitalism refused every instrumental discipline."[21] Saint Francis's refusal was anchored in a core belief in the holiness of all life—not just human life—emanating from a reinterpretation of a shared Christian religious and cultural tradition. Francis of Assisi underwent a profound personal conversion from his previous way of life as the playboy son of a rich merchant; he then sought to spread the message of his conversion, a message of respect for all living beings, and of nonviolence. But who apart from Ashoka has ever attempted to promulgate such an ethos in practical terms on a political, multinational level?

We find in both the life of Francis of Assisi and in Ashoka's Dhamma three elements that are lacking in contemporary analyses, such as Empire, the Network Society, or even the most progressive of welfare economists: a grounding in transcendence, a nonanthropocentric respect for all life and the environment, and a way to the realization of this ethic through personal reflection that amounts to a radical existential transformation, a conversion. The question of whether a secular, ethical, and political order can survive based purely on reason or enlightened self-interest has been called "modernity's wager," and the history of the twentieth-century is not very encouraging as to its future.

## MODERNITY'S PROBLEMATIC WAGER

Modernity's wager, as Boston University professor of religion Adam Seligman has expounded in a book by the same title, is that of the liberal, democratic secular state: a bet that authority based on common, universally shared principles of reason (backed by the force of the state) is enough to hold society together. The source of this authority is reason itself, as found in every individual.[22] Yet such a society is also one of self-actualizing selves pursuing their individual interests, one that builds a world where everything is exchangeable and negotiable.

The self as a center of authority cannot hold in such a world and community cannot be maintained. Authority must be in part constituted and legitimized outside the self; community also is constituted by commonly recognized authority. In a globalized economic society, the quest for a social identity, if it does not regress into ethnic tribalism or religious fundamentalism, becomes a search for recognition; but since there is no truly common ground for recognition, apart from the enveloping ether of images and media in the Spectacle, recognition itself degenerates into a solipsistic clamoring of isolated individuals or groups for acclaim.[23] Without a universal anchor for authority, individual or group affirmation risks degenerating into a quest for pure power and the self-interested manipulation of others. Recall the view of society that follows from Draupadi's skepticism of her husband Yudhishthira's invocation of his duty under dharma in the Mahabharata: "Mere power is the cause of everything, and I bemoan powerless folk."[24]

Thus, the relation of authority to the self is the critical nexus, and Seligman postulates three models. The first is the modern secular, civil self, with social authority rooted in reason shared by all humans—the Enlightenment Project. The second is a phenomenon we have already discussed, the quest for authority rooted in "primordial" identities of nation, race, tribe, gender, or religious fundamentalism. The third is transcendently rooted authority, which entered the history of humanity in the Axial Age between 500 BC and AD 600 with the foundation of the world's great universal religious and ethical traditions. Here, rulers and collectivities are perceived as being accountable to a higher order.[25]

Vaclav Havel is among those who have written most eloquently of the contemporary need for a "non-material order...above us but also in us and among us," that can ground individual and collective responsibility. The Kautilya-esque "reduction of life to the pursuit of immediate material gain without regard for its general consequences," in Havel's words, has led to the oblivion of being and history. This shortsightedness has exacerbated—and is an underlying cause of—what he sees as the fundamental problem of our time: "lack of accountability to and responsibility for the world."[26]

The analysis of Hans Küng is similar: he calls, above all, for an ethic of planetary responsibility in place of the "ethic of success," a new global ethic based on "concern for the future and reverence for nature."[27] Havel observes that the more the technological forces of globalization bring us together, the more aware many become of their residual differences. In our globalized world bereft of transcendence, our situation is like that of prisoners in a common planetary penitentiary "in which the inmates get on each other's nerves far more than if they see each other only occasionally."[28]

The necessity for a grounding in the transcendent does not necessarily mean the belief in a personal God in the Western sense, as Ashoka's Dhamma shows. Indeed many have characterized Buddhism as a fundamentally atheistic belief system. But it does imply an orientation beyond the present, the imminent and the purely human, a sense of humankind's place in an order and cosmos, the meaning and purpose of which is not short-term use and gratification. As Küng writes: "Only the bond to an infinite offers freedom in the face of all that is finite."[29]

We find Castells less enlightening when he announces that we have entered the stage of history where Nature has ceased to exist except as another cultural category. The times are gone forever, he maintains, when Nature dominated Culture and Society. He asserts we are now entering the domain of a totally and triumphantly human-centered and human-dominated world, where Culture only refers to Culture. His analysis of environmental movements as a project of global human identity as a biological species, forming a "global green culture" as a "human hypertext," is a cogent one—as far as it goes. For Castells, "the meaning of the environmental movement [is] to reconstruct Nature as an ideal cultural form."[30] But accelerating global warming, massive species extinctions, and fishery collapses are not matters of debate over ideal cultural forms, they are increasingly threatening consequences of our living as if Nature were only a cultural form.

Francis of Assisi and Ashoka refer us back to the obvious—which globalized economic civilization relegates to oblivion—that we inhabit a world of other sentient beings, the welfare of whom we should respect and care for as an absolute end in itself, as a foundational principle of individual and social behavior. Such an attitude of reverence for life carries with it the principle of nonviolence toward all living beings.

## THE GLOBAL HOUSEHOLD

For many years in the early eleventh century AD a monk named Romauld wandered along ancient Roman roads through thick forests in the Apennine Mountains in central Italy. Near the end of his life he founded a hermitage in a hauntingly beautiful place called Campo Amabile ("lovely meadow") in dense mountain woods at an elevation of 3,500 feet. Romauld died in 1027, and was soon canonized. Saint Romauld is remembered for innovating a form of monastic life that combined Eastern, Byzantine, and Anchorite traditions with Western, Roman Cenobite practice. Anchorites are monks who seek salvation in solitude and reflection as hermits, and Cenobites are monks who live in community. Nearly a thousand years later, this forest and place is still much the same (Campo Amabile has been foreshortened to Camaldoli): it is one of the last patches of intact, primary forest in the Apennines, managed and conserved for many centuries by the spiritual heirs of Romauld, the monks of Camaldoli. In effect, these monks developed one of the first forestry codes in the Western world, every year planting thousands of seedlings. Rules for the care of the forest were part of the "Rule of Ermetical Life" that the monks followed as a daily routine. In the 1980s the forest was incorporated by the Italian government as part of a new national park, and the Holy Hermitage of Camaldoli is a favorite weekend retreat for meetings of the Italian Green Party.[31]

Camaldoli is only one of numerous examples of the Christian church in its role as a steward of creation rather than as an ideological bulwark of anthropocentric economic exploitation—as has sometimes been argued. The example of Francis of Assisi is the best known, but we can find many others dating back to the Middle Ages. For example, in 1328 in Northern Germany the new Bishop of Bamberg had to swear to a special oath before he could be inaugurated: that he would place the forests of his bishopric under his protection and forbid any new forest clearings. His successors through the end of the fourteenth century had to make the same pledge.[32]

Such traditions resonate in a renewal of Christian thought that has taken up the issues of economic globalization and its discontents both in theory and in practice. Hans Küng's writings are one example; the worldwide campaign for developing country debt relief at the turn of the millennium—the so-called Jubilee 2000 Campaign—another.[33] Most importantly, in contemporary Christian thought we find a number of principles that provide critical alternatives for how to think about the globalized world of the new millennium. These key concepts can be summarized as follows: First, the notion of the economy as *oikos*, as God's household, with the connotation of the economy as livelihood, rather than accumulation of wealth and ever-growing exchange. Second, the premise of the *plenitude* of creation as the basis of policy, rather than scarcity, which is the founding assumption of modern economic analysis. Third, the concept of nature and the environment as *creation*, rather than as reified raw material or stuff to be used, transformed, or managed for human utility. Fourth, the notion of *stewardship*, with connotations of trusteeship and planetary responsibility, as our role on this earth.[34] One does not have to believe in Christianity, or even in a personal God, to recognize the cogency of these concepts, though they all follow from the premise of the relationship of humankind to that which is transcendent, yet present, in our human world.

The Greek word *oikos* means household, and is the root term in both economy and ecology. Oikos also appears throughout the New Testament, particularly in the term *oikonomia tou theou*, literally, the economy of God. The early Christian notion of oikos was very much rooted in Hellenistic traditions, particularly Aristotle's conception of economy—oikonomia—as the management of the household. There are natural limits, according to Aristotle, for this kind of economic activity, the goal of which is acquiring those goods necessary for livelihood. Trading and moneymaking as goals in themselves, beyond what are necessary for the needs and livelihood of a household, community, or state, are "unnatural," since they intrinsically have no limits, and rather than focusing on livelihood lead to men exploiting one another.[35] Christianity introduces transcendence into this scheme, both in the sense of nature and human household management being part of God's creation, and the presence of God in this Creation. Aristotle's analysis has been invoked by a number of contemporary thinkers as a call to reflect on the social limits that should apply to markets and purely economic values.

It might be ventured that the antiglobalization protesters are call-

ing for a return of Aristotle's perspective—people above profits. Although the slogan is simplistic, it expresses a core truth. Daniel Bell,
surveying American society in the 1970s in *The Cultural Contradictions
of Capitalism*, reframed Aristotle's original insight as the need for a
"Public Household," a return of public values to the economy where
"the controlling idea is that of *needs.*"[36] In fact, Bell called for a re-
definition of self and society as "the only basis on which [society] can
survive," based on three conjoining actions: the reaffirmation and
recovery of the past, "for only if we know the past can we be aware
of the obligation to our posterity; the recognition of the limits of resources and the priority of *needs*, individual and social, over unlimited
appetite and wants; and agreement on a conception of equity which
gives all persons a sense of fairness and inclusion in the society."[37]
Published in 1976, Bell's call for limits on the domination of a certain
kind of "economism," for the restoration of a public oikos, is more
urgent today then ever. We can hear an echo of Ashoka in his program: awareness of the obligation to posterity, recognition of limits
and control over unlimited appetite and wants, and a conception of
justice, fairness, and inclusion.

Another critical aspect of oikos is its emphasis on the integrity of
the local unit or household; the planet as oikos is made up of local
communities and households whose sociological and ecological integrity is safeguarded. "*Oikos*," according to Union Theological Sem-
inary theologian Larry Rasmussen, "is at odds with the particular
kind of globalism of the present globalized economy, even an ecologically sensitized global economy. Such global thinking has disregard
for local community loyalties and needs."[38] In practical terms this is
reflected in the principle of *subsidiarity*, that is, carrying out social,
economic and political functions at the most appropriate, most local
organizational level, closest to those who are affected by a particular decision or action. It is a principle that is part of Catholic social
thought as well as European Union law.[39]

Contemporary Christian critiques of economic globalization posit
that God's economy—the Earth as oikos—is based on abundance and
plenitude rather than scarcity. Where there is faith in the Christian
community, there is always more than enough to share with others.
The modern economy is based not only on the assumption of scarcity, but also on producing new forms of scarcity—and thus the need
for more consumption—through advertising and the media, as well
as through socially constructed inequality. According to theologian

Donal Meeks and others, the New Testament, by questioning the fundamental presuppositions of capitalist society, is profoundly subversive of the current globalized economic order.[40] Also associated with oikos is the notion of nature, the environment, and humankind together as *creation*. We do not and cannot own the earth, we are sojourners on it, as Leviticus 25:23 reminds us—"the earth and all existence are the gift of the Creator." There is a marked contrast again with the economistic conception of nature as resources or, in a more ecologically fashionable vein, natural capital and ecosystem services, all for instrumental use by humankind. Since Creation is the abundance of God's grace, the fruits it yields to human labor are to be shared, not hoarded. There are numerous passages in the Old Testament to this effect—in the seventh year land is to be left fallow "that the poor of your people may eat; and what they leave, the beasts of the field may eat. In like manner you shall do with your vineyard and your olive grove."[41] One is reminded of Ashoka's somewhat different injunction not to burn or consume the chaff in the fields, out of concern for the living things that are in it or depend on it. The people of Israel are also enjoined at harvest time to leave sheaves in the field, and grapes and olives in the vineyards and olive groves for "the stranger, the fatherless, the widow."[42] And of course most extraordinary is the Old Testament call for a Jubilee year every half century: "And you consecrate the fiftieth year, and proclaim liberty throughout all the land to all its inhabitants."[43] In the year of the Jubilee, debts are forgiven, slaves are freed, and land is to be redistributed to original owners who have been forced to sell.[44]

Finally, associated with the gift and plenitude of creation, and of economy as management of oikos, is the role of humankind as steward, literally oikonomos, "economist." The role of the oikonomos in the New Testament is interesting to contrast with the modern notion of an economist. The oikonomos is literally the person who knows and administers the rules for the oikos, the household; the oikonomos was often a household servant, or even a slave. The translation of oikonomos in the King James version of the New Testament is steward, and in the revised standard version, manager. According to one etymological interpretation, steward is derived from the Middle-English *stigweard*, the keeper of the pigsties.[45] Steward carries a connotation of care in the service of another or of others, of trusteeship and responsibility (swine were the most valuable household resource in Saxon England). In contemporary Christian theology the Biblical notion of stewardship is contrasted with the too often exploitative approach of modern economic life. "It means broad responsibility for the world we affect, including the deep and far-reaching impact on nature," writes Rasmussen.[46]

If we return to the Christian principles of economy as household stewardship or trusteeship of the plenitude of Creation, there emerges a principle of global responsibility. But it would seem that such a sense of responsibility would have to be grounded in a "transcendent anchor" of which Vaclav Havel has spoken. The Christian tradition is clearly one such anchor; the South Asian beliefs of 2,300 years ago, shared by Hinduism, Jainism, and Buddhism, in a dharmic order of the universe was another. It is a question of what humans together sustainably can perceive as a source of authority, and the semisolipsistic postmodern self is too fragile to be such a ground or source. Modernity's wager of a shared utilitarian reason of enlightened self-interest or a common rational project of social improvement has also proven to be a shaky bet at best.[47] Havel observes that "politicians at international forums may reiterate a thousand times that the basis of the new world order must be universal respect for human rights, but it will mean nothing as long as this imperative does not derive from the respect of the miracle of Being, the miracle of the universe, the miracle of nature, the miracle of our own existence."[48]

What form of social reason might leave more openness for the transcendence of which Havel and others speak?

## THE SEARCH FOR PARADIGMS AS A HINDRANCE TO UNDERSTANDING

*I would suggest a little more "reverence for life," a little less straitjacketing of the future, a little more allowance for the unexpected.... [L]arge-scale change...when it happens...is bound to be an unpredictable and nonrepeatable event.*
—Albert O. Hirschman[49]

Albert Hirschman is an unusual development economist. Thirty years ago he warned of the dangers of "compulsive and mindless theorizing" that characterizes economics and other social sciences, facilitated by increasing use of computers.[50] He suggested that much of this theorizing was rooted in the hegemonic need of our culture to understand, explain, control, and dominate a multifaceted, complex social and natural reality that will always be beyond total understanding

and control. Writing in 1969, he warned that the developing countries had become objects of historical domination, "fair game for the
model builders and paradigm molders, to an intolerable degree." [51]
He urged a respect and recovery of history, history that recognizes
the uniqueness and unpredictability of human events. Prediction and
control are difficult to impossible because of "the *open-endedness* of
history that is the despair of the paradigm-obsessed social scientist." [52]
The shock, depth, and unexpectedness of the 2008 global economic
crisis has confirmed the urgency of Hirschman's call for a more modest, less hubristic cognitive style.

Yale political scientist James Scott has written of the abuses of
"high modernist ideology," the social and environmental disasters that
a hubristic faith in paradigmatic knowledge and control has wrought
through state-sanctioned schemes of administration and failed development. In the hands of the modern state these schemes of making society and nature "legible" for control and standardization fail through
their ignorance of the complexity and heterogeneity of local social
and ecological systems. [53] Scott urges more respect for local knowledge
and tradition and uses the classical Greek term *Metis* to characterize
this practical knowledge, which is not amenable to systematization or
summarizing in universal rules. Metis is the "cunning" or "cunning
intelligence" that Odysseus uses to survive his extraordinary journey
and eventually reach home. It is also the local knowledge and practice
that most traditional rural communities have acquired through the
ages, a knowledge that has been systematically ignored, at tremendous cost, by large-scale economic development schemes. Echoing
Hirschman (whom he quotes), Scott urges a political and social cognitive modesty, in which political and economic action "*begins* from
a premise of incomplete knowledge," of "the radical contingency of
the future." [54]

He suggests four basic principles that should inform development
planning to avoid the miscarriages of "imperial knowledge," and, one
might add, the principles are valid for social and political action in
general. First, social interventions and change should be based on
*small steps*; second, these steps should not be irrevocable, we should
*favor reversibility*; third, we should build in *flexibility* and the *capacity
to deal with surprises*, which almost inevitably occur; and fourth, we
should proceed with *provisions for future improvisation*, planning on
human inventiveness. [55] In practice, such principles would foster a
greater awareness and sense of responsibility for what surrounds us.

The problem is not the absence of universal, global solutions, it's looking for them in the first place—and then structuring institutions around universal global discourses and treating the world as a Procrustean bed to impose them. We see today the collapse of the credibility of a certain way of thinking and acting in the world, a call for a gentler, less arrogant and more attuned approach to social knowledge and action. It is an approach that more fully recognizes noneconomic values in human behavior and has more respect for local knowledge and the autonomy of others; it recognizes the irreducible heterogeneity of existence, which we ignore at our peril. It starts, as Albert Hirschman put it, with "a little more 'reverence for life,' a little less straitjacketing of the future, a little more allowance for the unexpected." [56]

The more modest cognitive style and practice urged by all of these thinkers are not new themes in Western history. In fact philosopher Stephen Toulmin has argued that there are two origins of Modernity: the first was in sixteenth-century Renaissance humanism embodied by Montaigne and Erasmus, characterized by a gentle skepticism and humility concerning human reason and power, coupled with tremendous openness to the world, to other cultures, and to fascination of the particulars of creation, be they natural or human. This humanist phase was replaced by a quest for certainty in both reason and faith in the seventeenth century, the age of Descartes, Bacon, and the Counter Reformation. It was also a narrowing of perspective and a retreat from openness to the world.

The seventeenth century was a period of greater political, economic, and social instability—of which the hecatomb of the Thirty Years War was an outstanding example—that prompted a cultural search for intellectual and political authority, hierarchy, and stability. [57] Seventeenth-century rationalism sought certainty in the abstract and universal, a quest for certainty and predictability that did violence at times to the reality of the specific and the local. [58]

In the ruins of modernity's wager, a postmodern skeptical humanism would be the posture most suited to our situation, an attitude of "skeptical toleration" and "epistemological modesty" and openness to the outside, to the past, to the transcendent in all forms, including the future. [59]

Hirschman, Scott, and above all Montaigne call us back to what is unique, specific, and irreducible in human events and in all that exists, and to the humanist skepticism of what Adam Seligman has called "the false universalism of Jacobean modernity," which is only the other, secular side of the fundamentalist coin.[60] We recall Czeslaw Milosz's *plaidoyer* for the spirit of poetry, which in mindfulness of the particular is the antidote to the transactional logic of the global market. This mindfulness is the path to the recovery of being, Milosz says, and it is a form of "reverence, even piety." It is a mindfulness that "respects the reality outside the ego."[61]

Mindfulness and reverence for being involve the recognition and reappropriation of history, since history embodies the uniqueness, the nonreducible heterogeneity of events, not only shared commonalities and patterns. There is no need for history if the world and human events are totally knowable and predictable, amenable to global management and control, since the past would have nothing irreducible or unique to teach us. Lessons once learned would be static and abstract rules valid for all societies, with no need to account for the heterogeneity of specific cultures and times, and for fundamental change. This indeed is the project of some branches of the social sciences, particularly some schools of economics.

Mindfulness of being and history is also an attitude of responsibility for and accountability to the world, an antidote to the pathologically short attention span of the global market Network Society. One of the more original proposals to call us to back to mindfulness and history is The Clock of the Long Now, a project to construct a giant mechanical ten-thousand-year clock—larger than Stonehenge—in the desert of the American Southwest.[62] The originators of the project—which would include a ten-thousand-year library and a foundation—are Stewart Brand, the creator of the *Whole Earth Catalog* in the late 1960s, and several world-renowned computer experts, such as Daniel Hillis (who played a key role in the development of supercomputers) and Esther Dyson. In Brand's words, "accepting responsibility for the health of the whole planet, we are gradually realizing, also means responsibility for the whole future. The worst of destructive selfishness is not *Me!* but *Me! Right now!* The generous opposite could be phrased as *All of us for all time*—presumably including nonhumans."[63]

Their concern mirrors that of Havel and many others, namely that the short-term lack of mindfulness of our economistic civilization is profoundly irresponsible; to uphold the world we must be anchored in that which is transcendent in the most fundamental sense, in that which is outside the present and ourselves.

In considering the project of The Clock of the Long Now there is also a certain irony, since Ashoka's 2,300-year-old edicts bear the same message of responsibility and mindfulness, for the benefit of all. It would be an interesting wager to see, two millennia hence, whether Ashoka's rock edicts, or The Clock of the Long Now, or both, will still be present to plead with humankind for universal responsibility.

We live in what many have called the cusp of a second "Axial Age," where the old Gods are dead and what will replace them is still being born. Nonetheless, there would appear to be two sources for an emerging sense of the transcendent that could have global credence. The first is certain common elements in the religious traditions of all civilizations. The second is a growing worldwide ecological consciousness, which goes beyond environmental management as an adjunct to conventional notions of management or economics, useful as these approaches are.

The Christian framework of oikos, reverence for creation's plenitude, and stewardship, provides one convincing framework, an approach that is cogent beyond the world of Christianity, since oikos, creation, and stewardship are ecumenical concepts that are not necessarily dependent on belief in Jesus Christ or even in a personal God. In its basic elements, this framework expresses and promotes in different terms fundamental elements of Ashoka's Dhamma. In fact here at least we find confirmed another one of Ashoka's precepts, the belief, stated several times in the twelfth rock edict, in the "essential doctrine" of all religions and sects. The ultimate role of Ashoka's Dhamma was to promote this essential doctrine.

Havel has said that a common ground for transcendence in our age would begin with finding "a new and genuinely universal articulation of that global human experience...one that connects us with the mythologies and religions of all cultures and opens for us a way to understand their values. *It must expand simply as an environment in which we may all engage in a common quest for the general good.*" [64] Toynbee recognized a similar need—and opportunity. He pointed out that the non-Western cultures of the world have realized that Western culture and history have become a part of the culture and history of every other society on Earth. We now have to realize that the West cannot escape the past of non-Western cultures becoming a part of its own cultural future. But we cannot say what this future will be like, and what elements of world religions and cultures will remain as the ground for a new sense of transcendence. Havel speculates that a renewed belief in transcendence will not be based on a new cult, dogma, or religion in the conventional sense. This would only be another fundamentalism in a postmodern terrain of competing fundamentalisms. Rather, "it will more likely be multi-leveled and multi-cultural, *with a new political ethos, spirit or style, and ultimately will give rise to a new civil behavior.*" [65] Ashoka's Dhamma was also very much an attempt to formulate what we could call basic rules of citizenship in a multiethnic, multinational empire. But citizenship is anchored in shared common values.

The civil rights movement in the United States provides a revealing example of how the struggle to reclaim voting rights for African Americans in the South was grounded in such shared values, in this case an ethic of universal justice. The nonviolent political approach Martin Luther King adopted had deep historical, international roots. He was particularly influenced by Gandhi, and by Henry David Thoreau's essay on civil disobedience. King visited India for a month to better understand Gandhi's legacy and methods.

Gandhi in turn was a cosmopolitan figure, influenced by an unusual cross-fertilization of Eastern and Western values. His mother was a Jain, and that was clearly one factor in his formulation of a nonviolent creed; but much of his thinking on nonviolence was also influenced by Western sources, which in turn had drawn on ancient Indian thought. He spent part of his early adult years studying in London and practicing as a lawyer in South Africa. His introduction to classical Hindu scriptures was through his contact with the vegetarian movement in England, and he read Henry David Thoreau's essay on civil disobedience when he was in jail in South Africa. He cited Thoreau in his early publications, urging a nonviolent passive resistance to achieve Indian independence. [66] Yet Thoreau's essay in turn had been inspired by the translation into English of Hindu scriptures such as the Upanishads, which he and other New England Transcendentalists read and discussed in the 1840s.

Ancient Indian sages, Thoreau, Gandhi, and Martin Luther King, were all engaged in a philosophical and political dialogue that transcended their separation in time and space, a dialogue that continues today. The nonviolent protest of the U.S. civil rights marchers in turn had an important historical reverberation around the planet; the nonviolent popular uprisings in Eastern Europe in 1989 were in part inspired by its methods, as well as the democracy protesters in Tiananmen Square. The doctrine of ahimsa is truly an example of the philosophical contemporaneity of civilizations.

King wanted to remedy wrongs that violated the rights of African Americans under the U.S. Constitution, but his political ethos and approach were grounded in something that went beyond that particular struggle: one might call it a sense of universal responsibility, global justice, global citizenship. Thus it was totally consistent that in the last months of his life he turned his attention to the injustice of poverty in the United States and to criticism of the Vietnam War. In the United States over the past three decades our political leaders seem to have lost much of that sense of global responsibility, justice, and citizenship that King and the civil rights movement awakened. The rather hard, ruthless ethic of economic globalization promised material benefits to many, but in practice both within nations, and among them, it undermined the values that King tried to awaken in his compatriots. In the era of growing global economic integration, the Kautilyan priorities of artha in the social sphere and danda in international politics resurged with a vengeance, particularly in the world's most powerful state. We now see that the same global markets that many worship as a cargo cult of everlasting growth can also drag us all down together, in a frightening spiral of economic and political disruption and ecological destruction. In such a time, the need for a new global ethic is urgent.

This is why Ashoka's example is important, and in a sense, why especially today we need to reflect on what he attempted. Here is the example of the ruler of the greatest nation on Earth at the time who, with all the caveats, faults, and compromises we have analyzed, nonetheless tried to formulate and put into practice a vision of global citizenship, nonviolence—not just toward humans but also toward other sentient beings—responsibility, and justice.

The shared values of nonviolent civil disobedience movements provide one example that nevertheless gives hope that there is an evolving global heritage of certain basic social values that would correspond to Adam Smith's triad of Justice, Prudence, and Beneficence—values that for their time were embodied in Ashoka's Dhamma. We recall Smith's admonition that justice is the most important and essential of this ethical triad, without which no society can long sustain itself.

Concerning the universal appeal of justice, Toynbee recounts a revealing anecdote. When Napoleon's army invaded Egypt at the end of the eighteenth century, the Islamic Egyptian historian Al-Gabarti recorded the events of the occupation. The French staged a scientific and technical exposition in Cairo. Al-Gabarti was there, and indeed was impressed, as the French intended. But, Toynbee recounts, he was even more impressed and provoked to deeper reflection by French behavior in several other incidents. French soldiers looted local houses and assaulted the residents; Napoleon ordered the soldiers to be executed. The head of the French occupation army, General Kléber, was assassinated by a Muslim fundamentalist, and the French held a lengthy trial. The accused was represented by an attorney, and evidence was entered in the proceedings for both sides. Much more than the technical gadgets and scientific knowledge the French displayed, Al-Gabarti admired what he saw as a society that attempted to have impartial standards of justice. He found the trial so extraordinary and thought-provoking that he "incorporat[ed] a dossier of the trial in his narrative,"[67] reproducing the transcripts verbatim. Al-Gabarti confessed that he did not think that Islamic society in Egypt at the time could have been capable of such relative fairness in analogous cases. The parallels and contrasts between this situation and U.S. involvement in Iraq, and the kind of justice administered at Abu Ghraib and Guantánamo Bay, are both obvious and thought provoking.

In the long term we may gravely overestimate the material accomplishments of Western civilization, particularly its technical and economic achievements, which beyond certain necessities are often elaborations of the trivial and nonessential in human life. Al-Gabarti reminds us of what is important, that the extent to which Western values have become "universal" is linked to the fact that they correspond to aspirations, or even existing values, in all societies. One of the major fallacies and self-deceptions of our time is to imagine that the social and governmental practice of these values—for example, Justice, Prudence, and Beneficence—are Western inventions. As we have seen in the case of Ashoka and, indeed, that of Kautilya, too, in some respects these values were better developed in South Asia nearly two millennia before the flowering of what we think of as modern Western civilization.

VENERATION, PARTICIPATION, MINDFULNESS

Octavio Paz, the great Mexican Nobel Prize–winning writer, was the Mexican ambassador to India for a number of years, an experience that informed his attempts at the end of his life to understand the era of economic globalization in a truly global historical context. His last work before his death in 1998 was a short intellectual biography, *Itin-*

*erary.*[68] The book is a meditation on the lack of Justice, Prudence, and Beneficence in the world of the global market. Our society lacks virtue, he wrote, in the antique classical sense of self-mastery and control—something akin to Smith's Prudence, and Ashoka's wish that "all beings should be unharmed, self-controlled (the thirteenth rock edict) and that "it is good to spend little" and "own the minimum of property" (the third rock edict). Market-driven consumerism, Paz writes, has led us to the point where "we can no longer control our appetites," leaving us "ready to be dominated by someone else." Our consumerist "hedonism is not a philosophy of pleasure but an abdication of free will that would have scandalized both the gentle Epicurus and the frantic Marquis de Sade."[69]

Paz, like Havel, evokes the need for a social and individual anchor in a belief in transcendence, since from the moment of birth and first consciousness "we feel we are a fragment detached from something more vast and intimate."[70] There is a need to participate in this totality, which in religions takes place through good works and sacraments. He is not advocating the "transformation of religious experience into political idolatry," which often ends in a bloodbath. But he reaches a conclusion similar to Seligman in *Modernity's Wager*: religion must remain separate from politics, but it is one way of participating in transcendence that can "reveal our lack and help us rediscover and recuperate certain values."[71]

For Paz, participation in totality is based on veneration: "We venerate the world around us, and at another level, that veneration spreads to all things and living beings, to stones and trees and animals and humans. Fraternity is an aspect of participation and both are expressions of veneration. Without veneration there can be no participation or fraternity."[72] The ecological movement, Paz concludes, insofar as it is a call to different social values, "expresses our thirst for totality and our yearning to participate." Like Milosz, he sees it as an example of the recovery of the potential to venerate in modern society, and the potential to venerate "is the only one that can open the doors to fraternity with people and nature."[73] There is an uncanny commonality or core theme in Paz's "itinerary" that we also found in Ashoka's Dhamma.

Beyond immediate responses to local problems, something truly unprecedented has been occurring over the past two decades: the worldwide growth of a new, increasingly widely shared ethic, one that is "biocentric," linked to a nonanthropocentric sense of what transcends the immediate human situation. It is not a new value—as Ashoka, Francis of Assisi, and many others in the past demonstrate. Harvard biologist E. O. Wilson has written of "biophilia" as a value that is almost genetically programmed in our species, if we can free ourselves of contemporary economic and social values that have suppressed and discouraged this most essential of human propensities. But it is for the first time increasingly shared on a global scale.

## THE "ESSENTIAL DOCTRINE" AND REVERENCE FOR LIFE

*The great fault of all ethics hitherto has been that they believed themselves to have to deal only with the relations of man to man. In reality, however, the question is what is his attitude to the world and all life that comes within his reach. A man is ethical only when life, as such, is sacred to him, that of plants and animals as well as that of his fellow man.*
—Albert Schweitzer[74]

When Albert Hirschman spoke of a cognitive style that would have "a little more 'reverence for life,'" he invoked a phrase associated with the thought of the great Alsatian thinker, missionary, and physician, Albert Schweitzer. Reverence for life is a perspective that, if systematically thought through and applied, would transform current practice in every area of social and political activity.

In his autobiography Schweitzer describes how he came to a period of doubt and confusion, since the tradition of Western philosophy did not seem to offer a coherent or convincing notion of the ethical in the twentieth century. All the treatises he read "could be said never to have concerned [themselves] with the problem of the connection between civilization and attitude toward the world."[75] In political and philosophical thought "the modern concept of progress had become to it such a matter of course that it had felt no need for coming to hear clear ideas about it."[76] In 1915 he was already beginning to work as a missionary in French Equatorial Africa, what is today Cameroon. He undertook a long journey going upstream on a barge on a river. Lost in thought, on the third day he describes how the barge had to make its way through a herd of hippopotamuses, and then "there flashed through my mind, unforeseen and unsought, the phrase 'Reverence for Life.'"[77]

In hindsight it appears as a simple insight, but its crux is that "anchor in transcendence" of which Havel has written. For Schweitzer "the ethic of the relation of man to man is not something apart...it is only a particular relation that comes from a universal one." It is only "ethical acceptance of the world and of life...which enables us to distinguish between what is essential in civilization and what is not."[78] Reverence for life became, one could say, his "essential doctrine."

The problems brought by the relentless penetration of the logic of economics and technology into every sphere of life will not be solved by more economics and technology. A way forward will come from mindfulness and reverence for the world and life, from an acceptance—and social practice—of values beyond and outside the interventions of instrumental reason, but that could guide and limit these interventions in a different spirit.

In the Jewish Kabalistic tradition we find the concept of *tikkun*, which literally means to repair or fix the world. Tikkun involves collaborating with God to heal and transform the world; every individual is thought to have a special tikkun, a particular role or mission in accomplishing this. Tikkun recalls some aspects of dharma, the concept of each person having a specific role or duty within an encompassing order that upholds the world. Tikkun has also been compared to the Buddhist notion of mindfulness.

The ancient Egyptians had *maat*, a concept similar in some respects to dharma. Maat meant order, morality, individual duty, self-control, and also artistic symmetry and balance. Maat was grounded in the cosmic order, and was personified in the pharaoh. "To break an artistic canon, to infringe pharaoh's law, to sin against god; all were a denial of *maat*."[79] When justice, social order, prosperity, and compassion prevailed in the land, there was an abundance of maat. The opposite of maat, historian Paul Johnson tells us, "was not change, but covetousness, associated with deceit and violence....The man who lives by *maat* will live for ever, but the covetous has no tomb."[80] We are reminded of Ashoka's dictum that "*Dhamma* is effective for all time, for even if its object is not attained in this life, endless merit is produced in the life to come" (the ninth rock edict).

If one were to venture a definition of the core of Ashoka's "essential doctrine," indeed of his whole Dhamma, it would be reverence for life. It is a principle that goes beyond the realm of just treatment by human beings of one another: reverence for life means upholding the world—embracing, but also anchored outside of, purely human-centered action.

## THE TRAGEDY OF ASHOKA

So as we near the end of our own itinerary in this book, we recall one more lesson that Ashoka has left us, the lesson of his imperfection and failure, one might say of his tragedy. It is not just that elements of the old, "fierce Ashoka" remained after his conversion to the way of Dhamma, or that he issued threats—inconsistent with the policy of nonviolence he espoused—to tribal and border peoples. He was human, and no state can totally renounce the use of force at least in maintaining internal order. The lesson is more that we can only do justice to Ashoka's ethical and political project if we view it in the Kautilyan context, of the Weberian "tragedy of politics": we cannot ignore the fact that part of the basis of politics is violence, power, and force. In politics, Weber said, "it is *not* true that good can only follow from good and evil from evil, but...often the opposite." [81] This understanding is the basis too of Reinhold Niebuhr's question, couched as a statement, to James Bryant Conant, the president of Harvard, immediately after World War II: "How much evil we must do in order to do good?" [82]

Disconnected from this context, Ashoka's legacy has encountered two forms of distortion. One is the appropriation of his myth for nationalistic or fundamentalist politics of identity, as has occurred in Sri Lanka. The other is the disembodiment of the Ashokan legacy, its reduction into a set of hortatory principles disconnected from the drama of dharma and the tragedy of politics. To limit our purview of Ashoka to the principles of his edicts would be a bit like citing the memorable phrases of the speeches of Abraham Lincoln without considering the immensely tragic choices he confronted in the Civil War.

The critical issue is not the desirability of Ashoka's principles, which at a certain level of generality is easy to acknowledge. How to put these principles into practice in a society, and Ashoka's success and failure in doing so, is the deeper issue, bound up with the context of Kautilyan–Mauryan governance.

The greatness of Ashoka lies not only in his conversion to the policy of Dhamma following Kalinga, but in his heroic effort to reconcile the underlying, tragic tensions between the dharma of the king and warrior, which prioritizes force and violence, danda; the revolutionary materialism of Kautilya and his espousal of artha in statecraft; and a universal dharma of nonviolence.

Ashoka sought and fought to reconcile and transcend what in his time and for most of human history has been irreconcilable. Viewed in this light, he is a tragic figure. Dharma, and Ashoka's particular version of dharma, the Dhamma of his edicts, is indeed literally that which upholds the world. It means following distinct duties and actions based on an understanding of the transcendent order of the world and each person's role in a particular place and time in it. Ancient Indian thought explored the complexities, dilemmas, and perhaps necessary contradictions of this fundamental dilemma of social organization, particularly the conflict between social, political duty and the imperative of a higher universal moral law. This was Yudhishthira's dilemma. Ashoka believed that ultimately it would be possible to reconcile in practice social, political duty and a universal ethic of respect for all life and nonviolence. He wagered on transcending the tragedy of politics. For his time he was wrong. Much of the failure was rooted in the cumbersome, top-down nature of governance that may have been the only mode possible for a large subcontinental area at the time.

We are still confronting Yudhishthira's quandary, but on a planetary scale: how to reconcile the current forms of global economic and political organization with a universal ethic of justice.[83] Justice, too, is one of the fundamental meanings of dharma.

Around the world we see the proliferation of what Polanyi called the "double movement," of movements based on resistance identities or project identities, to use Castells's terms. Many of these movements at the local or international level are grounded in perceptions of some form of local or global injustice. In a global system, the question of global justice looms larger and larger. Even terrorist organizations secure what legitimacy they can attain with their supporters through shared perceptions of some form of injustice (usually with some limited grounding in reality, but at the same time pervaded by nihilistic violence). The growing nonviolent movements of social and intellectual discontent, amalgamated as "antiglobalization" protests, are not only protests against specific, local problems. Many are also calls for justice in the broadest, most inclusive sense.

We have yet to find a satisfactory articulation of this common ground, but we are reaching out for it, just as the people of the original Axial Age sought out a new consciousness of individual, social, and religious identity in a burst of new philosophies and ideologies. In the era of economic globalization and the net, observers like Hardt and Negri and Castells could be right: the *means* may now be available for a bottom-up, self-organizing "politics of enlightenment," for the realization, as a worldwide political project, of the "essential doctrine" that is the core of Ashoka's Dhamma—a global system grounded in reverence for life, nonviolence, toleration, inclusion, benevolence, self-control, and justice.

The vision thus stated sounds utopian, but we have Ashoka to remind us that long ago a great leader of the world's most power-ful empire dared to try to put into practice what for his times must have seemed even more utopian. We will need Kautilyan realism as well as Ashokan idealism to achieve such a project. The great Indian poet Tagore said, when the twentieth century was still young, that Ashoka's "thought had been standing on the wayside for all these ages longing to find a refuge in the mind of every man." This moment may now be arriving.[84]

Emperor Ashoka is one of the great figures of Indian history, whose life and achievements still have much to teach us today. This is clearly acknowledged by India's adoption, on achieving independence, of the lion capital of the pillar at Sarnath bearing an Ashokan edict as its national emblem.

Ashoka, who had earlier been a cruel and ruthless ruler, learned from his own experience the futility of war and violence. The sight of the slaughter that resulted from the Kalinga war brought about a complete transformation in his attitude to power and the value of life. Consequently, when he heard the Buddha's teachings on compassion, he became convinced that the path of nonviolence and service to others was the way to lead a meaningful life. Of course, many individuals down the ages may have come to a similar conclusion with regard to their own personal conduct. However, what distinguishes Emperor Ashoka is that he not only decided to reshape the attitude, conduct, and policy of Indian society according to universal ethical principles, but he also had the power and the ability to do so. The various pillars and rocks bearing the emperor's edifying edicts are remarkable and surviving indications of his efforts to educate his subjects and encourage the practice of compassion.

Adopting Buddhist principles as his own and making significant efforts to support Buddhist institutions within India, Ashoka also dispatched emissaries abroad, notably sending his son and daughter to Sri Lanka, to spread the Buddha's words. Nevertheless, under his reign an era of tolerant religious pluralism flourished.

It is often suggested that the idea of democracy has its roots in the West, but by insisting that citizens be treated as equals, protected under law, and that he and those who served him should regard the promotion of the people's welfare as their highest duty, Emperor Ashoka seems to have anticipated some of democracy's key ideals.

One of the most important aspects of Ashoka's transformation, and one that is important for us today, is his promotion of ahimsa, or nonviolence. He encouraged kindness in human relations, and also forbade the arbitrary slaughter and cruel treatment of animals. He fostered positive international relations and set his weaker neighbors' minds at ease. Vivid experience had taught him, as it should teach us, that while violence may seem effective in the short term, in the long run adverse consequences nearly always outweigh those achievements.

We live in a time when wars are being fought, yet I take heart from the conviction that there is today a greater appreciation of peace throughout the world, greater respect for human rights and much concern over damage to the environment. In this new millennium, when our world is increasingly interdependent, we must find ways to resolve our problems and conflicts through nonviolence. *To Uphold the World* should serve as a source of great inspiration. There are those who regard nonviolence as a sign of weakness; Ashoka's life surely reveals it as a sign of strength and maturity.

I find it moving to know that is was during a visit to the sacred land of India that Bruce Rich came to the very site at Dhauli (in eastern India) where Ashoka changed his mind, and that he was stirred to research and write this book. It is my hope and prayer that readers today may be inspired by this tale of a powerful ruler, who was such a great force for good throughout ancient India, to find ways to contribute to making the world in which we live a more just and peaceful place.

HIS HOLINESS THE DALAI LAMA
September 2007

ACKNOWLEDGMENTS

I am deeply grateful to Amartya Sen for his moral support and extremely generous contribution of his time in reading drafts of the manuscript and contributing the foreword. His work and reflections on economics and ethics, as well as writings on Indian history, are an inspiration for increasing numbers of people around the globe concerned with the challenges of ethics, economics, and globalization. I am profoundly grateful to His Holiness the Dalai Lama and his Office for the moving afterword his Holiness has contributed. Many thanks go to Romila Thapar for granting permission to use her translation of Ashoka's edicts, as well as sharing comments on part of the manuscript. I have relied substantially (but not entirely) on her interpretations of ancient Indian history and Ashoka, but of course am responsible for all errors of fact and interpretation.

A number of people were extremely generous in their time in reading earlier drafts of the manuscript and providing comments, particularly professors Leo Ribuffo, Dan Babai, and Tamara Gutner of George Washington, Harvard, and American universities, respectively. Deep thanks go to numerous friends and colleagues who have read parts of the manuscript and offered their encouragement. Special thanks go to my agent, Elaine Markson, whose patience and persistence in supporting this project over several years have been a tremendous boost. Special kudos go to Joanna Green at Beacon Press for her professionalism and editing skills in preparing the American edition of *To Uphold the World*. My thanks to John Strong at Bates College and Princeton University Press for permission to use excerpts from his translation of the *Asokavadana*, and to Motilal Banarsidass Publishers for permission to use extracts from R. P. Kangle's translation of Kautilya's *Arthasastra*.

I shall always feel profound gratitude to have had the privilege of knowing the late Smitu Kothari, founder of Inter-Cultural Resources, Delhi. Smitu reviewed portions of this book and helped with its publication in India. His life and work are an inspiration for activists and thinkers around the world and embodied the values of compassion and justice exemplified long ago in the Dhamma of Ashoka.

Foreword

1. H. G. Wells, *The Outline of History: Being a Plain History of Life and Mankind* (London: Cassel, 1920, 1940), 389.

2. It was Ashoka's grandfather Chandragupta who was the real empire builder, but Ashoka completed the task through conquering Kalinga (roughly modern Orissa)—a conquest that proved to be the decisive turning point in his life, when, revolted by the cruelty of war and conquest, he turned into a dedicated pacifist, keen on establishing a tolerant welfare state and on spreading the message of nonviolence of Buddhism within the country and abroad.

3. John Rawls, *A Theory of Justice* (Cambridge, MA: Harvard University Press, 1971).

4. I have tried to address this issue, among others, in my recent book *The Idea of Justice* (Cambridge, MA: Harvard University Press, 2009).

Chapter 1: Past Present

1. Chris Giles, "Poll Reveals Backlash in Wealthy Countries against Globalization," *Financial Times,* July 23, 2007.

2. "Church of England leaders criticize markets," *International Herald Tribune,* September 25, 2008; Sam Jones, "Don't Blame the Bankers—Deregulation and Spending Caused It Too, Says Williams: Archbishop Delivers Attack on Impact of Globalisation," *Guardian,* March 9, 2009.

3. Richard Owen, "Pope Says World Financial System 'Built on Sand,'" *Times Online* (London), October 6, 2008.

4. George Soros, *The Age of Fallibility: Consequences of the War on Terror* (New York: Public Affairs, 2006), 102.

5. Hans Küng, *A Global Ethic for Global Politics and Economics* (New York: Oxford University Press, 1998), 204.

6. Aramaic was the Semitic language of Syria, Palestine, and Lebanon more than two millennia ago. It was the lingua franca of the Persian Empire, widely spo-

ken from the Mediterranean to what is present-day Pakistan, and is thought to have been the mother tongue of Jesus Christ.

7. Alain Finkielkraut, *In the Name of Humanity: Reflections on the Twentieth Century* (New York: Columbia University Press, 2000), 108, 112.

8. Aristotle, *The Politics*, trans. T. A. Sinclair (London: Penguin Books, 1962), 84–85.

9. R. P. Kangle, trans., *The Kauṭilya Arthaśāstra, Part II: An English Translation with Critical and Explanatory Notes* (Delhi: Motilal Banarsidass, 1992), 1.7.2. The Kangle translation and accompanying materials of Kautilya's *Arthasastra* is in three volumes: the first volume is the original Sanskrit text, the second volume is the translation proper, and the third volume is a book-length critical essay and exegesis by Kangle. In subsequent citations, the book, chapter, and verse from the translation (i.e., from volume 2), are given.

10. The three goals are known as the *trivarga*. A fourth goal, *moksa*, spiritual release or enlightenment, became more prominent in later times; it is a final spiritual goal, and is set above or over the three worldly goals of artha, kama, and dharma. See Richard Lannoy, *The Speaking Tree: A Study of Indian Culture and Society* (Oxford, England: Oxford University Press, 1971), 302–3, 346.

11. Heinrich Zimmer, *Philosophies of India*, ed. Joseph Campbell (Princeton, NJ: Princeton University Press, 1969).

12. Kangle, *Kauṭilya Arthaśāstra, Part II*, 1.7.6.

13. Max Weber, "Politics as a Vocation," in *From Max Weber: Essays in Sociology*, trans. and ed. H. H. Gerth and C. Wright Mills (New York: Oxford University Press, 1958), 124.

14. Zimmer, *Philosophies of India*, 93.

15. E. H. Carr, *The Twenty Years' Crisis, 1919–1939: An Introduction to the Study of International Relations* (New York: Harper & Row, 1964).

16. Küng, *Global Ethic*, 204.

17. Amartya Sen, *On Ethics and Economics* (Oxford, England: Blackwell, 1988), 2–7.

18. Amartya Sen, "Adam Smith's Market Never Stood Alone," *Financial Times*, March 11, 2009.

19. This is particularly the case in the Theravada Buddhist countries of Southeast Asia. See Stanley J. Tambiah, *World Conqueror and World Renouncer: A Study of Buddhism and Polity against a Historical Background* (Cambridge, England: Cambridge University Press, 1976), 520–21.

20. John S. Strong, *The Legend of King Aśoka: A Study and Translation of the Aśokāvadāna* (Princeton, NJ: Princeton University Press, 1983), 39.

21. Jainism arose in India in the sixth century BC at about the same time as Buddhism. Like Buddhism it was an egalitarian reform movement of traditional Hindu Brahmanic beliefs, with a focus on reverence for life and nonviolence (ahimsa) as the basis of Jain ethics. The founder of the Jains, Vardhamma (Mahavira) was thirty-five years older than Siddharta Gautama, the Buddha. Today there are about 3.3 million Jains in India.

22. Radha Kumud Mookerji, *Chandragupta Maurya and His Times* (Delhi: Motilal

Banarsidass, 1966), 16–21; Purushottam Lal Bhargava, *Chandragupta Maurya: A Gem of Indian History* (New Delhi: D.K. Printworld, 1996), 118–22.

23. Friedhelm Hardy, *The Religious Culture of India* (Cambridge: Cambridge University Press, 1994), 391.

24. Abraham Eraly, *Gem in the Lotus: The Seeding of Indian Civilization* (New Delhi: Penguin Books India, 2000), 342.

25. Stewart Brand, *The Clock of the Long Now: Time and Responsibility* (New York: Basic Books, 1999), 82–92.

26. James Fallows, "File Not Found: Why a Stone Tablet Is Still Better Than a Hard Drive," *Atlantic,* September 2005, 142.

27. John Keay, *India: A History* (New York: Atlantic Monthly Press, 2000), 130.

28. K. V. Soundara Rajan, *Junagadh* (New Delhi: Archaeological Survey of India, 1985), 30.

29. Keay, *India: A History,* 131.

30. Robert Thurman, *Inner Revolution: Life, Liberty, and the Pursuit of Real Happiness* (New York: Riverhead Books, 1998), 117.

31. C. Satapathy, "Did India Give the World Its First Customs Tariff?" *Economic and Political Weekly* 34, no. 8 (February 20, 1999).

32. George Woodcock, *The Greeks in India* (London: Faber & Faber, 1966), 48.

33. J. A. B. van Buitenen, trans., *Two Plays of Ancient India: "The Little Clay Cart"; "The Minister's Seal"* (New York: Columbia University Press, 1968), 206.

34. Karl Jaspers, *The Origin and Goal of History* (New Haven: Yale University Press, 1968), 153.

35. In the words of Romila Thapar, "The first millennium BC witnessed a seemingly spontaneous burst of new ideologies in areas that subsequently became nuclear regions for major civilizations. The impression is one of a chain of apparently similar developments linking the then known world. . . . The almost simultaneous and sustained period of speculative thought throughout this area resulted from the juxtaposition of a number of seminal regions and their interconnections or from internal developments within each society that broke the relative quiescence of the earlier bronze age cultures." Romila Thapar, "Ethics, Religion, and Social Protest in the First Millennium B.C. in Northern India," in *Cultural Pasts: Essays in Early Indian History* (New Delhi: Oxford University Press, 2000), 856.

36. Jaspers, *Origin and Goal,* 3.

37. Ibid., 2.

38. Karen Armstrong, *The Battle for God* (New York: Ballantine Books, 2000), xiii–xv.

39. Karen Armstrong, "A Conversation with Karen Armstrong," interview by Jonathan Kirsch, in *"The Battle for God*: A Reader's Guide," appendix to *The Battle for God* (see n. 38).

40. Strong, *Legend of King Aśoka,* 44–49.

41. Dharma (or Dhamma, in the vernacular Prakrit and Pali languages spoken in Ashoka's time; Prakrit and Pali evolved from Sanskrit in much the same way French and Italian evolved from Latin).

42. Benjamin Rowland, *The Art and Architecture of India* (New York: Penguin Books, 1984), 67–70.

43. Ibid., 70.

Chapter 2: The Age of Transcendence

1. Around 1500 BC, so-called Indo-Aryan pastoral peoples are thought to have migrated to the subcontinent in successive waves from central Asia, merging with the existing peoples and creating a rich religious oral culture. Their myths and rituals were preserved in the *Vedas* (meaning "knowledge"), the earliest of which were composed in the second millennium BC but not written down until the first and second centuries AD. Ritual and animal sacrifice were important components of their way of life, as well as the observation of a religiously sanctioned separation of social groups into various castes, of which the four principal ones were the priests (Brahmins); warriors (Kshatriyas); producers: farmers, artisans, and merchants (Vaisyas); and laborers (Sudras). The castes corresponded to a strict hierarchy, involved prescriptions against intermarriage, and proliferated over time into hundreds of subcastes, many of which eventually became hereditary and linked to very specific occupations. There has been controversy in India in recent years concerning the Indo-Aryan migration theory, often linked to contemporary currents of identity politics. For more detailed scholarly historical accounts, see Romila Thapar, *Early India: From the Origins to AD 1300* (Berkeley: University of California Press, 2002), and Stanley Wolpert, *A New History of India* (New York: Oxford University Press, 1997). On the Indo-Aryan migration debate, see Edwin Bryant, *The Quest for the Origins of Vedic Culture: The Indo-Aryan Migration Debate* (New York: Oxford University Press, 2001).

2. D. N. Jha, *Early India: A Concise History* (New Delhi: Manohar, 2004), 81.

3. Thapar, *Early India,* 155.

4. Ibid., 157.

5. Jha, *Early India,* 114.

6. Eraly, *Gem in the Lotus,* 335 (see chap. 1, no. 24).

7. For an interesting discussion of possible correspondences between Ashoka's Dhamma, particularly his policy of religious toleration, and the Achaemenids, especially Cyrus the Great, see F. Scialpi, "The Ethics of Aśoka and the Religious Inspiration of the Achaemenids," *East and West* (Istituto Italiano per il Medio Ed Estremo Oriente) 34, nos. 1–3 (September 1984): 55–74.

8. Dr. Darius Jahanian, "The First Declaration of Human Rights," Circle of Ancient Iranian Studies, www.cais-soas.com/CAIS/Culture/human_rights.htm; "Cyrus the Great's Cylinder, Transliteration & Translation of the Text," Circle of Ancient Iranian Studies, www.cais-soas.com/CAIS/History/Irak/hakha-maneshian/Cyrus-the-great/cyrus_cylinder_complete.htm#R.

9. James B. Pritchard, *Ancient Near Eastern Texts Relating to the Old Testament* (Princeton, NJ: Princeton University Press, 1950), 316.

10. Thapar, *Early India,* 144.

11. Romila Thapar, "Aśokan India and the Gupta Age," in *A Cultural History of India,* ed. A.L. Basham (Delhi: Oxford University Press, 1975), 40.

12. Jha, *Early India,* 71.

13. Karen Armstrong, *The Great Transformation: On the Beginning of Our Religious Traditions* (New York: Knopf, 2006), 200.

14. Thomas McEvilley, *The Shape of Ancient Thought: Comparative Studies in Greek and Indian Philosophies* (New York: Allworth Press, 2002), 321.

15. Armstrong, *Great Transformation,* xvii, 211–20.

16. Thapar, "Renunciation: The Making of a Counter-Culture," 881–82 (see chap. 1, n. 35).

17. Ibid., 881.

18. Eraly, *Gem in the Lotus,* 176–77.

19. Ibid.

20. A.L. Basham, *The Wonder That Was India* (Calcutta: Rupa, 1986), 298.

21. Alain Danielou, *A Brief History of India* (Rochester, VT: Inner Traditions International, 2003), 91.

22. Amartya Sen, *The Argumentative Indian: Writings on Indian History, Culture, and Identity* (London: Allen Lane, 2005), 23.

23. Eraly, *Gem in the Lotus,* 310.

24. Ibid.

25. Mookerji, *Chandragupta Maurya and His Times,* 5 (see chap. 1, n. 22).

26. Ibid., 13–15.

27. R.P. Kangle, trans., *The Kauṭīlya Arthaśāstra, Part II,* 15.1.73, 515 (see chap. 1, n. 9).

28. Eraly, *Gem in the Lotus,* 74, 307.

29. Ibid., 307; Mookerji, *Chandragupta Maurya and His Times,* 229.

30. The unpopularity of the last Nanda king seems to be one point on which all the classical historians and the Buddhist, Jain, and later Brahman texts agree.

31. Mookerji, *Chandragupta Maurya and His Times,* 230.

32. Eraly, *Gem in the Lotus,* 309.

33. Ibid.

34. Mookerji, *Chandragupta Maurya and His Times,* 233.

35. Ibid., 231.

36. Ibid.

37. Ibid., 233–34.

38. The most successful conservative movements are often revolutionary and unsettling in their means: We might think of the novel tactics of the rise of the American conservative movement from the 1970s onward, or the revolutionary social changes wrought by contemporary economic globalization, which ironically appear to be bringing us to a place where corporate power is nearly as untrammeled as it was a hundred years ago.

39. Kangle, *The Kauṭīlya Arthaśāstra, Part II*, 1.19.34.

40. Ibid., 2.4.23.

41. Thapar, "Aśokan India," 41 (see note 11).

42. L. N. Rangarajan, trans. and ed., *Kautilya: The Arthasastra* (New Delhi: Penguin Books, 1992), 39.

43. Kangle, *The Kauṭīlya Arthaśāstra, Part II*, 4.7.14.

44. Rangarajan, *Kautilya*, 36.

45. Amartya Sen, personal communication with author, August 2003.

46. *Encyclopædia Britannica Online*, s.v. "Consequentialism," www.britannica.com/EBchecked/topic/1518627/consequentialism. Amartya Sen observes that classic utilitarianism is grounded not just on consequentialism, but also comprises "welfarism," which judges a consequent state of affairs also only by utility ("paying no direct attention to such things as the fulfilment or violation of rights, duties, and so on"), and "sum-ranking," which requires "that [in a consequent state of affairs] the utilities of different people be simply summed together," without attention to distributional issues or equity. See Amartya Sen, *Development as Freedom* (New York: Knopf, 1999), 58–59. In other words, classic utilitarianism can be viewed as a kind of hyperconsistent consequentialism, where, at each stage of the evaluation of the results of actions, only utilitarian consequences are evaluated.

47. Roger Boesche, *The First Great Political Realist: Kautilya and His Arthasastra* (Lanham, MD: Lexington Books, 2002).

48. As noted in the text, after Alexander's death, Seleucus Nikator founded a Hellenistic kingdom that included most of the Near East; his successors were known as the Seleucids.

49. Romila Thapar, *Aśoka and the Decline of the Mauryas, with a New Afterword, Bibliography and Index* (Delhi: Oxford University Press, 1997), 1–19.

50. Pali is a Sanskrit-derived language spoken in ancient Sri Lanka.

51. Thapar, *Aśoka and the Decline*, 9.

52. Ibid., 25.

53. Ibid., 22.

54. Vincent A. Smith, *The Oxford History of India*, 4th ed, ed. Percival Spear. (New Delhi: Oxford University Press, 1994), 118.

55. Stanley Wolpert, *A New History of India* (New York: Oxford University Press, 1997), 62.

56. Ibid., 46.

57. Romila Thapar, *A History of India*, vol. 1 (Harmondsworth, UK: Pelican Books, 1966), 46–47.

58. Wolpert, *New History*, 37.

59. Ibid., 50–51.

60. Armstrong, *Great Transformation*, 237.

61. McEvilley, *Shape of Ancient Thought*, 278–79.

62. Thapar, "Epigraphic Evidence and Some Indo-Hellenistic Contacts During the Mauryan Period," 460 (see chap. 1, n. 35).

63. Thapar, "Renunciation," 882.

64. Gail Omvedt, *Buddhism in India: Challenging Brahmanism and Caste* (New Delhi: Sage, 2003), 147.

65. Ibid., 148.

66. Ibid., 137.


Chapter 3: The Great Dilemma

1. Bill Joy, "Why the Future Doesn't Need Us," *Wired,* April 2000, 238–62.

2. George Soros, *George Soros on Globalization* (New York: Public Affairs, 2002), 165.

3. Committee of Government Oversight and Reform, *Testimony of Alan Greenspan at Hearing on the Role of Federal Regulators in the Financial Crisis,* U.S. House of Representatives, October 23, 2009, http://clipsandcomment.com/wp-content/uploads/2008/10/greenspan-testimony-20081023.pdf.

4. Robert D. Kaplan, *Warrior Politics: Why Leadership Demands a Pagan Ethos* (New York: Random House, 2002), 9.

5. Gabor Steingart, *The War for Wealth: The True Story of Globalization, or Why the Flat World Is Broken* (New York: McGraw Hill, 2008), 17.

6. Alex Perry, *Falling off the Edge: Travels through the Dark Heart of Globalization* (New York: Bloomsbury Press, 2008), 18, 27.

7. John Gray, *False Dawn: The Delusions of Global Capitalism* (New York: New Press, 1998), 17.

8. George Soros, *The Crisis of Global Capitalism: Open Society Endangered* (New York: Public Affairs, 1998), xxviii.

9. Ibid., 235.

10. Harvey Cox, "The Market as God: Living in the New Dispensation," *Atlantic Monthly,* March 18, 1999, 23.

11. Louis Dumont, *From Mandeville to Marx: The Genesis and Triumph of Economic Ideology* (Chicago: University of Chicago Press, 1977).

12. John Stuart Mill, *Autobiography,* ed. Jack Stillinger (Boston: Houghton Mifflin, 1969), 42.

13. Richard Bronk, *Progress and the Invisible Hand: The Philosophy and Economics of Human Advance* (London: Warner Books, 1999), 101.

14. Mill, *Autobiography,* 42.

15. Amartya Sen points out three deficiencies in the classic utilitarian perspective: "distributional indifference" (only the total happiness in society matters, not its distribution—a lesser aggregate "happiness" might be desirable if gross inequalities were also reduced); "neglect of rights, freedoms and other non-utility concerns... we do not necessarily want to be happy slaves or delirious vassals"; and "adaptation and mental conditioning"—the most oppressed in a society may mentally adjust their feelings and desires to be content with their lot. Sen, *Development as Freedom,* 62 (see chap. 2, n. 46).

16. John Stuart Mill, "Bentham," in *Utilitarianism and Other Essays,* ed. Alan Ryan (London: Penguin Books, 1987), 148–50.

17. Mill, *Autobiography,* 138.

18. Adam Smith, *The Theory of Moral Sentiments*, vol. 1 (1817; repr., Washington, DC: Regnery, 1997), 245.

19. Ibid., 247.

20. Smith studied at the University of Glasgow in the late 1730s, where he was influenced by Francis Hutcheson, father of the "Scottish Enlightenment." He attended Hutcheson's lectures on the Greek and Latin Stoic philosophers, which, according to biographer James Buchan, "influenced Smith in all his reasonings." James Buchan, *The Authentic Adam Smith: His Life and Ideas* (New York: W. W. Norton, 2006).

21. Smith, *Theory of Moral Sentiments*, vol. 1, 248.

22. Ibid., 249.

23. Ibid., 248.

24. Wen Jiabao, interview by Lionel Barber et al., "Message from Wen," *Financial Times,* February 2, 2009.

25. Sen, *On Ethics and Economics,* 2, 6 (see chap. 1, n. 17).

26. Smith, *Theory of Moral Sentiments*, vol. 1, 63–64.

27. Ibid., 115.

28. Omvedt, *Buddhism in India,* 29 (see chap. 2, n. 64).

29. Smith, *Theory of Moral Sentiments*, vol. 1, 255.

30. Ibid., 257.

31. Adam Smith, *The Theory of Moral Sentiments*, vol. 2 (1817; repr., Washington, DC: Regnery, 1997), 101–2.

32. From Bernard Mandeville, *The Fable of the Bees: Or, Private Vices, Publick Benefits* (1714). Numerous versions are available on the Web; here is the link I used: http://pedagogie.ac-toulouse.fr/philosophie/textes/mandevillethefableofthebees.htm.

33. Smith, *Theory of Moral Sentiments*, vol. 2, 165.

34. Margaret Thatcher, interview by Douglas Keay, "Aids, Education and the Year 2000," *Women's Own* (London), October 31, 1987, 8.

35. Smith, *Theory of Moral Sentiments*, vol. 2, 171.

36. Karl Polanyi, *The Great Transformation* (Boston: Beacon Press, 1957), 35.

37. J. Oloka-Onyango and Deepika Udagama, *The Realization of Economic, Social and Cultural Rights: Globalization and Its Impact on the Full Enjoyment of Human Rights,* report prepared for the Sub-Commission on the Promotion and Protection of Human Rights of the UN Economic and Social Council (Geneva, June 15, 2000), E/CN.4/Sub.2/2000/13.

38. Polanyi, *Great Transformation,* 46.

39. This fundamental cultural tension between the socially disintegrating effects of market capitalism and the society that supports it is another recurrent theme in contemporary social commentary. See, for example, Daniel Bell, *The Cultural Contradictions of Capitalism* (New York: Basic Books, 1976).

40. Polanyi, *Great Transformation,* 178.

41. Ibid., 29.

42. Ibid., 40.

43. Ibid., 237.

44. Manuel Castells, *The Information Age—Economy, Society and Culture*, vol. 1, *The Rise of the Network Society* (Oxford: Blackwell, 1996), 3.

45. G. Pascal Zachary, "A Philosopher of the Web Is a Hit in Silicon Valley," *Wall Street Journal* (eastern edition), October 1, 1998.

46. Castells, *Information Age*, vol. 1, 376–464.

47. Ibid., 462.

48. Pranay Gupta, "Questions and Answers: Klaus Schwab," *Earth Times*, February 15, 2000, 21.

49. Castells, *Information Age*, vol. 1, 412–23.

50. Manuel Castells, "An Introduction to the Information Age," City 7, May 1997, 11 (emphasis added).

51. There is a large and still-growing literature on this theme. See, for example, Moises Naim, *Illicit: How Smugglers, Traffickers, and Copycats Are Hijacking the Global Economy* (New York: Doubleday, 2005), and Raymond Baker, *Capitalism's Achilles Heel: Dirty Money and How to Renew the Free-Market System* (New York: John Wiley & Sons, 2005).

52. Castells, *Information Age*, vol. 1, 3.

53. The title of a book on globalization by Rutgers professor Benjamin Barber.

54. Castells, *Information Age*, vol. 1, 22–23; Manuel Castells, *The Information Age—Economy, Society and Culture*, vol. 2, *The Power of Identity* (Oxford: Blackwell), 123–34, 137.

55. Castells, *Information Age*, vol. 1, 477–78.

56. Ibid.

57. Guy Debord, *The Society of the Spectacle*, trans. Ken Knabb (Detroit: Black & Red, 1983), I.1, I.4, I.16, originally published as *La Société du Spectacle* (Paris: Buchet/Chastel, 1967). The work consists of 221 consecutively numbered paragraphs divided into nine chapters; the roman numerals refer to the chapter, the arabic number following the roman numeral is the number of the paragraph in the chapter.

58. Debord's thought anticipated by two decades one of Castells's main insights: "The new power lies in the codes of information and in the images of representation around which societies organize their institutions, and people build their lives, and decide their behavior." Castells, *Information Age*, vol. 1, 359.

59. Guy Debord, *Comments on the Society of the Spectacle*, trans. Malcolm Imrie (London: Verso, 1990), 27, originally published as *Commentaires Sur La Société du Spectacle* (Paris: G. Lebovici, 1988).

60. Debord, *Society of the Spectacle*, II.42.

61. Ibid., IX.218.

62. Daniel J. Boorstin, *The Image: A Guide to Pseudo-Events in America* (1961; repr., New York: Vintage Books, 1992).

63. Debord, *Comments on the Society*, 56.

64. Ibid., 15.

65. Thucydides, *The Complete Writings: The Peloponnesian War*, trans. John H. Finley Jr. (New York: Modern Library, 1951), 14–15.

66. Castells, *Information Age*, vol. 2, 127.

67. Robert Wright, "Will Globalization Make You Happy?" *Foreign Policy*, no. 120, September–October 2000, 60–61.

68. Czeslaw Milosz, "Recovering a Reverence for Being," *New Perspectives Quarterly* 16, no. 3 (Spring 1999): 6.

69. Ibid., 8.

70. Ibid.

71. Ibid., 9.

Chapter 4: The *Arthasastra*

1. Barry Bearak, "Many, Many in India Want to Be a Millionaire," *New York Times*, August 27, 2000.

2. Mary Catherine Bateson, "It's Just a Game, Really," *New York Times*, August 27, 2000, section 4.

3. R. P. Kangle, trans., *The Kauṭīlya Arthaśāstra, Part II*, 1.13.21 (see chap. 1, n. 9).

4. Ibid., 1.17.5.

5. We recall that the mythical accounts of Kautilya's life have him using this stratagem more than once!

6. Kangle, *The Kauṭīlya Arthaśāstra, Part II*, 1.13.21.

7. Ibid., 1.12.1.

8. Vincent A. Smith, *Oxford History*, 107 (see chap. 2, n. 54).

9. Lannoy, *Speaking Tree*, 314 (see chap. 1, n. 10).

10. C. Formichi, "Pensiero e azione nell' India antica," *Revista Italiana di Sociologica* (1914), quoted in Narasingha P. Sill, *Kautilya's Arthasastra: A Comparative Study* (New York: Peter Lang, 1989), 22.

11. See discussion in R. P. Kangle, trans., *The Kauṭīlya Arthaśāstra, Part III: A Study* (Delhi: Motilal Banarsidass, 1992), 59–115.

12. Ibid.

13. Kangle, *The Kauṭīlya Arthaśāstra, Part II*, 1.1.1.

14. Ibid., 15.1.1.

15. Ibid., 1.19.6–24; Mookerji, *Chandragupta Maurya and His Times,* 55–56 (see chap. 1, n. 22).

16. Kangle, *The Kauṭīlya Arthaśāstra, Part II*, 1.21.1.

17. Ibid., 1.19.34–35.

18. Ibid., 1.12.6, 1.12.17–20.

19. Lannoy, *Speaking Tree,* 320.

20. Ibid.

21. Kangle, *The Kauṭīlya Arthaśāstra, Part II*, 1.4.4.

22. Ibid., 1.4.8–10.

23. Ibid., 1.4.12.

24. Ibid., 1.4.13–14.

25. Smith, *Theory of Moral Sentiments*, vol. 1, 115 (see chap. 3, n. 18).

26. Kangle, *The Kauṭīlya Arthaśāstra, Part II*, 2.1.1–20.

27. Ibid., 2.16.11–13.

28. Ibid., 2.1.19.

29. Ibid., 2.12.23.

30. Ibid., 2.12.37.

31. Thapar, *History of India*, vol. 1, 89 (see chap. 2, n. 57).

32. See Marc Reisner, *Cadillac Desert: The American West and Its Disappearing Water* (New York: Penguin Books, 1987).

33. Kangle, *The Kauṭīlya Arthaśāstra, Part II*, 2.2.5.

34. Ibid., 2.17.4–12.

35. Ibid., 2.2.4.

36. Ibid., 2.26.1

37. Ibid., n. 1.

38. Ibid., 2.2.6–13.

39. Ibid., 2.26.5.

40. Ibid., 3.19.26–27, 28.

41. Rangarajan, *Kautilya,* 36 (see chap. 2, n. 42).

42. Stewart L. Udall, *The Quiet Crisis and the Next Generation* (Salt Lake City: Peregrine Smith Books, 1988), 106.

43. Ibid.

44. Kangle, *The Kauṭīlya Arthaśāstra, Part II*, 2.25.11.

45. Ibid., 2.25.16–24.

46. Ibid., 2.25.12–15.

47. Ibid., 2.27.30.

48. Ibid., 2.27.23.

49. Ibid., 4.2.18–19.

50. Ibid., 2.21.31.

51. Ibid., 4.1.56–57.

52. Ibid., 2.21.24–25.

53. Ibid., 4.13.9.

54. Ibid., 3.14.1–3.

55. Ibid., 3.13.31.

56. Ibid., 3.14.12–18.

57. Ibid., 5.3.3–17.; Mookerji, *Chandragupta Maurya and His Times*, 86–87.

58. Lawrence Mishel, "CEO Pay-to-Minimum Wage Ratio Soars," *Economic Snapshots*, Economic Policy Institute, June 27, 2006, www.epinet.org/content. cfm/webfeatures_snapshots_20060627.

59. This is a conservative estimate; at the end of 2005 the average wage of Mexican workers along the border in Juarez, Mexico, was $1.25 an hour, as compared to the then prevailing U.S. minimum wage of $5.15 an hour. Louie Gilot, "Minimum Wage to Rise in Mexico," *Bahia de Banderas News*, December 2005, www.banderasnews.com/0512/nz-mexwage.htm.

60. Arvind N. Das, *The State of Bihar: An Economic History without Footnotes* (Amsterdam: VU University Press, 1992).

61. Ibid., 9.

62. Ibid.

63. Harvey Wish, ed., *Antebellum: Writings of George Fitzhugh and Hinton Rowan Helper on Slavery* (New York: Capricorn Books, 1960), 41–157.

64. Kangle, *The Kauṭīlya Arthaśāstra, Part III*, 186–87 (see chap. 4, n. 11); Thapar, *Aśoka and the Decline of the Mauryas*, 89–91 (see chap. 2, n. 49).

65. Kangle, *The Kauṭīlya Arthaśāstra, Part II*, 3.13.1–23.

66. Thapar, *Aśoka and the Decline*, 92.

67. Mookerji, *Chandragupta Maurya and His Times*, 94.

68. Kangle, *The Kauṭīlya Arthaśāstra, Part II*, 2.6.11–28.

69. A. C. Sastri, *Studies in Kauṭilya Vocabulary* (Delhi: Parimal Publications, 1990), 55.

70. Kangle, *The Kauṭīlya Arthaśāstra, Part II*, 5.2.35–36.

71. Ibid., 2.7.1–9.

72. Ibid., 2.7.30–33.

73. Ibid., 4.9.2–11.

74. Ibid., 3.1.1.

75. Ibid., 4.9.21.

76. Ibid., 4.9.24.

77. Ibid., 2.5.5–6.

78. Ibid., 2.23.2, 2.24.2.

79. Ibid., 5.3.38.

80. R. Shamasastry, trans., *The Kauṭīlya's Arthaśāstra* (Mysore: Padam Printers, 1998), 220–21; *The Kauṭīlya Arthaśāstra, Part II*, 3.18.1–5.

81. Kangle, *The Kauṭīlya Arthaśāstra, Part II*, 4.11.21.

82. Ibid., 4.8.21–22.

83. Ibid., 4.8.14, 17–18, 27.

84. Ibid., 4.11.1, 17, 20.

85. Ibid., 4.11.6.

86. Ibid., 4.13.40–41.

87. Ibid., 4.13.33.

88. Hemangini Jai, "Lokasaṁgraha in Kauṭīlya," in *Perceptions on The Kauṭīlya Arthaśāstra*, ed. K. P. Jog (Mumbai: Popular Prakashan, 1999), 91.

89. Kangle, *The Kauṭīlya Arthaśāstra, Part II*, 6.1.1.

90. Ibid., 5.3.35–36.

91. Smith, *Oxford History*, 105–6 (see chap. 2, n. 54).

92. Zbigniew Brzezinski, *The Grand Chessboard: American Primacy and Its Geostrategic Imperatives* (New York: Basic Books, 1997), 10–11.

93. Kangle, *The Kauṭīlya Arthaśāstra, Part II*, 6.2.13–22.

94. Ibid., 6.2.5.

95. Ibid., 9.6.56–61.

96. Ibid., 7.16.3.

97. Ibid., 9.1.9.

98. Ibid., 9.1.15.

99. Ibid., 9.4.26.

100. Ibid., 9.4.27.

101. Samuel P. Huntington, *The Clash of Civilizations and the Remaking of World Order* (New York: Simon & Schuster, 1996).

102. See, for example, Amartya Sen, *Identity and Violence: The Illusion of Destiny* (New York: W. W. Norton, 2006), 46–49.

103. Brzezinski, *Grand Chessboard*, 39–40.
104. Kangle, *The Kauṭīlya Arthaśāstra, Part II*, 10.3.47.
105. Ibid., 13.4.52.
106. Ibid., 13.4.22–24.
107. Ibid., 13.4.5.
108. Ibid., 2.1.26.
109. Ibid., 2.1.26, 28.
110. Ibid., 2.28.18.
111. Sen, *Development as Freedom*, 237 (see chap. 2, n. 46).
112. Jean Dreze and Amartya Sen, *Hunger and Public Action* (Oxford: Oxford University Press), 4, quoting Shamasastry's translation of Kautilya's Arthasastra, 4.3 (see chap. 4, n. 80).
113. Kangle, *The Kauṭīlya Arthaśāstra, Part II*, 4.3.19–20.
114. Weber, "Politics as a Vocation," in *From Max Weber*, 79 (see chap. 1, n. 13).
115. Ibid., 123 (emphasis added).
116. Ibid., 120.
117. A classic analysis of the utopian and realist approaches is found in Carr, *Twenty Years' Crisis* (see chap. 1, n. 15).
118. Kangle, *The Kauṭīlya Arthaśāstra, Part II*, 1.3.4–12.
119. Ibid., 1.3.13.
120. Shubhada Joshi, "Exploring the Areas of Dandaṇḍīti and Dharma," in *Perceptions on The Kauṭīlya Arthaśāstra*, 65, 67 (see n. 88).
121. Ibid.
122. See discussion in Mookerji, *Chandragupta Maurya and His Times*, 50–51; M. V. Krishna Rao, *Studies in Kauṭilya* (New Delhi: Munshiram Manoharlal, 1979), 69–71, 81; Usha Thakkar, "Morality in Kauṭilya's Theory of Diplomacy," in *Perceptions on The Kauṭīlya Arthaśāstra*, 8–13 (see n. 88).
123. Weber, "Politics as a Vocation," in *From Max Weber*, 123.
124. Carr, *Twenty Years' Crisis*, vii, 32–36.
125. Ibid., 22–40.
126. Ibid., 27.
127. Kangle, *The Kauṭīlya Arthaśāstra, Part III*, 282.
128. Carr, *Twenty Years' Crisis*, 119.
129. Ibid., 93.
130. Ibid., 10.
131. Ibid., 96.
132. Weber, "Politics as a Vocation," in *From Max Weber*, 128.

Chapter 5: The Gift of Dirt
1. Mindy Aloff, "Together, as One, They Live, Work and Perform," *New York Times*, October 22, 2000.
2. H. A. Giles, trans., *The Travels of Fa-hsien (399–414 A.D.) or Record of the Buddhistic Kingdoms* (Cambridge: Cambridge University Press, 1923), 81.
3. Strong, *Legend of King Aśoka*, 6–7 (see chap. 1, n. 20).
4. Ibid., 19.

5. Ibid., 22.

6. Thapar, *Aśoka and the Decline of the Mauryas,* 24 (see chap. 2, n. 49).

7. Strong, *Legend of King Aśoka,* 22.

8. Ibid., 25.

9. Harvard anthropologist Stanley Tambiah has written extensively on the influence of the Ashoka legacy and myth on the contemporary political cultures of Sri Lanka and Thailand. See Stanley J. Tambiah, *World Conqueror and World Renouncer* (see chap. 1, n. 19); *The Buddha's Conception of Universal King and Its Manifestations in South and Southeast Asia* (Kuala Lumpur: University of Malaya, 1987); and *Buddhism Betrayed?* (Chicago: University of Chicago Press, 1992).

10. Strong, *Legend of King Aśoka,* 63.

11. Ibid., 65.

12. Ibid., 206.

13. Ibid., 211.

14. Giles, *Travels of Fa-hsien,* 57.

15. Strong, *Legend of King Aśoka,* 212.

16. Ibid., 206.

17. Ibid., 210.

18. Ibid., 210–11.

19. Ibid., 232–33.

20. We recall that Ashoka, according to the Pali chronicles, married Tissarakha after the death of his first main queen, Asanhimitta.

21. Strong, *Legend of King Aśoka,* 151.

22. Ibid., n. 32.

23. Ibid., 257–58.

24. Ibid., 224–25.

25. Ibid., 235–36.

26. The characterization is John Strong's (*Legend of King Aśoka,* 151).

27. Ibid., 236.

28. Ibid., 117.

29. Ibid.

30. Ibid., 221.

31. "2300-Year-Old Artefacts May Change Ashoka-Buddhist History," *The Organizer* (New Delhi) 57, no. 52 (July 9, 2006): 12, www.organiser.org/dynamic/modules.php?name=Content&pa=showpage&pid=138&page=12.

32. René Grousset, *In the Footsteps of the Buddha* (New York: Orion Press, 1971), 204–6, citing the biography of Hsuan Tsang (Xuanzang) compiled in the eighth century AD by the Chinese monks Huili and Shi Yangcong. For a more recent translation, see *A Biography of the Tripitaka Master of the Great Ci'en Monastary of the Great Tang Dynasty, translated from the Chinese of Sramana Huili and Shi Yangcong,* trans. Li Rongxi (Berkeley, CA: Numata Center for Buddhist Translation and Research, 1995), 150–53.

33. Grousset, *In the Footsteps,* 204.

34. Ibid.

35. Ibid., 204–5.

36. Ibid., 205–6.

37. Ibid., 206.

38. Ibid., 265–66.; see John S. Strong, "Rich Man, Poor Man, Bhikkhu, King: Quinquennial Festival and the Nature of Dana," in *Ethics, Wealth, and Salvation: A Study in Buddhist Social Ethics*, ed. Russell F. Sizemore and Donald K. Swearer (Columbia: University of South Carolina Press), 107–23.

39. Strong, *Legend of King Aśoka*, 266–68.

40. Here is Strong's summary of how the quinquennial festival (the *pancavarsika*) illuminates dana: "(1) The pancavarsika involves the lavish giving of material goods to the *sangha*. (2) The display and giving of all this wealth call to mind the glories of kings and deities, so that…the act of *dana* involves an experience of divinity or royalty…. (3) This experience appears to be transformative, for it stimulates in the donor a resolve for a new kind of *dana*,—a total dhammic gift of one's self to the *sangha*…. (4) Nonetheless, at the same time this dhammic gift of the self to the *sangha* occasions a restitution of the donor's previous status and wealth—a restitution that, moreover, involves a rebirth and renewal of the individual." Strong, "Rich Man, Poor Man," in *Ethics, Wealth, and Salvation*, 115 (see n. 38).

41. Strong, *Legend of King Aśoka*, 94.

42. Strong, "Rich Man, Poor Man," in *Ethics, Wealth, and Salvation*, 117.

43. Strong, *Legend of King Aśoka*, 95.

44. Smith, *Theory of Moral Sentiments*, vol. 1, 114 (see chap. 3, n. 18); and vol. 2, 101 (see chap. 3, n. 31).

45. Adam B. Seligman, *Modernity's Wager: Authority, the Self, and Transcendence* (Princeton, NJ: Princeton University Press, 2000).

46. Strong, *Legend of King Aśoka*, 291–92.

47. According to Strong, a koti was probably a crore, or 10 million (*Legend of King Aśoka*, 97).

48. Ibid., 288.

49. Myrobalan is an astringent, plumlike berry that was renowned in India for its medicinal qualities. A very small dose produced strong results.

50. Strong, "Rich Man, Poor Man," in *Ethics, Wealth, and Salvation*, 120 (see n. 38).

51. Strong, *Legend of King Aśoka*, 291.

52. Ibid., 291–92.

53. Ibid., 292.

54. Kangle, *The Kauṭīlya Arthaśāstra, Part II*, 5.3.35–36.

55. Mookerji, *Chandragupta Maurya and His Times*, 165–82 (see chap. 1, n. 22).

56. Historically, it is known that after Ashoka's death, the Mauryan Empire entered a decline. See Thapar, *Aśoka and the Decline*, 182–212. Historians concur that the last Maurya, Brhadratha, was probably murdered around the year 183 BC by his military chief of staff, Pushyamitra Sungha. See Keay, *India: A History*, 105 (see chap. 1, n. 27); and Smith, *Oxford History*, 138 (see chap. 2, n. 54). The seventh-century-AD account of the Sanskrit writer Bana sets the scene of the coup d'état during one of Brhadratha's morning reviews of the army.

57. Smith, *Oxford History*, 139.

58. Basham, *The Wonder That Was India* (Calcutta: Rupa, 1986), 58; Romila Thapar, *A History of India,* vol. 1 (Harmondsworth, UK: Pelican Books, 1966), 92; Keay, *India: A History,* 105.

59. Basham, *Wonder That Was India,* 43.

60. Strong, *Legend of King Aśoka,* 293.

61. Ibid., 293–94.

Chapter 6: The Greatest Conquest

1. John Keay, *India Discovered* (New York: HarperCollins, 1988), 58, citing Markham Kittoe's report to the Asiatic Society.

2. Keay, *India Discovered,* 46.

3. Ibid., 56.

4. An account of the deciphering of the Ashokan edicts, and of James Prinsep's heroic role, is found in John Keay's *India Discovered,* 39–63.

5. Stanley Wolpert, *A New History of India* (New York: Oxford University Press, 1997), 63.

6. Romila Thapar, *Aśoka and the Decline of the Mauryas, with a New Afterword, Bibliography and Index* (Delhi: Oxford University Press, 1997), 35; John Keay, *India: A History,* (New York: Atlantic Monthly Press, 2000), 91.

7. In this chapter, quoted text from the Ashokan edicts (major rock edicts, first and second separate rock edicts, and major pillar edicts) are all from Thapar, *Aśoka and the Decline,* app. 5, "A Translation of the Edicts of Ashoka," 250–66, unless otherwise specified.

8. T. W. Rhys Davids, *Buddhist India* (1903; repr., Delhi: Motilal Banarsidass, 1997), 297.

9. Vincent A. Smith, *Aśoka: The Buddhist Emperor of India* (Delhi: Low Price, 1990).

10. N. A. Nikam and Richard McKeown, *The Edicts of Asoka* (Chicago: University of Chicago Press, 1974).

11. Thapar, *Aśoka and the Decline,* 125, n. 4.

12. Keay, *India: A History,* 95–96.

13. Romila Thapar, "Aśoka and Buddhism as Reflected in the Aśokan Edicts," in *Cultural Pasts: Essays in Early Indian History* (New Delhi: Oxford University Press, 2000d), 435. Ashoka deals separately with his relation to Buddhism and the Buddhist community in four minor rock edicts (see chapter 7). In these minor inscriptions, when he mentions dhamma, he may be referring to its more narrow sense as the Buddha's teachings. (By convention, the Buddha's teachings are sometimes referred to as the Buddha's *dharma,* the Sanskrit term; some authorities use instead the Pali term *dhamma,* since the largest body of literature on the Buddha's life is in Pali.)

14. Thapar, *Aśoka and the Decline,* 165.

15. Ibid., 116–17, 166.

16. Ibid.

17. Woodcock, *Greeks in India,* 56 (see chap. 1, n. 32).

18. Here, an interesting dilemma is posed; namely, how absolute should toleration

be: Ashoka obviously thinks it stops when a belief involves sacrificing animals, and disparagement of other beliefs is quite in order when they entail "ceremonies which are trivial and useless" (ninth rock edict).

19. At least in the case of Ujjain, the reference is to an interval "not exceeding three years."

20. Robert Thurman, for example, in *Inner Revolution* (see chap. 1, n. 30), while acknowledging that Ashoka "remained quite hot tempered, [and] could react violently," claims that "universal democratism is the fifth operative principle in Ashoka's effort and is reflected in his edicts" (114, 129).

21. Smith, *Oxford History,* 134 (see chap. 2, n. 54).

22. Ibid.

23. Thapar, *Aśoka and the Decline,* 174–75.

24. Stanley J. Tambiah, for example, accepts this interpretation, calling Ashoka's proclamation of uniformity a "startling contrast to the notion of graduated punishment and graduated legal privileges according to varna status" promulgated in the ancient Indian legal Code of Manu. Tambiah, *World Conqueror and World Renouncer,* 58 (see chap. 1, n. 19).

25. Thapar, *Aśoka and the Decline,* 104.

26. Thapar, "Aśoka and Buddhism," 436 (see n. 13).

27. See, for example, Centre for Science and Environment (CSE), *The State of India's Environment 1984–85: The Second Citizens' Report* (New Delhi: Centre for Science and Environment, 1985), 70–71.

28. Hirakawa Akira, *A History of Indian Buddhism from Sakyamuni to Early Mahayana,* trans. and ed. Paul Groner (Honolulu: University of Hawaii Press, 1990), 98–99; Thurman, *Inner Revolution,* 126–27.

29. B. G. Gokhale, *Asoka Maurya* (New York: Twayne, 1966), 90–91, quoted in Tambiah, *World Conqueror,* 57.

30. Israel Selvanayagam, " Aśoka and Arjuna as Counterfigures Standing on the Field of Dharma: An Historical-Hermeneutical Perspective," *History of Religions* 32, no. 1 (August 1992): 64.

31. Thapar, *Aśoka and the Decline,* 144–45; Keay, *India: A History,* 97.

32. Mookerji, *Chandragupta Maurya and His Times,* 236–45 (see chap. 1, n. 22).

33. Or, if one prefers a technical philosophical terminology, here Ashoka's ethics are deontological, Kautilya's radically consequentialist. But as we shall see, there is much that is consequentialist, or Kautilyan, in Ashoka too.

34. Mookerji, *Chandragupta Maurya and His Times,* 238.

35. R. P. Kangle, trans., *The Kauṭīlya Arthaśāstra, Part II,* 2.36.44, 47 (see chap. 1, n. 9).

36. Ibid., 3.18.2–4.

37. Ibid., 1.3.13.

38. Kangle, *The Kauṭīlya Arthaśāstra, Part III,* 281 (see chap. 4, n. 11).

39. Given the much-publicized failures of much bilateral and multilateral aid, this is by no means an ironic proposal.

40. "Ashoka prohibited all animal sacrifices which constituted the very essence of Brahmanic religion. The Brahmins had not only lost state patronage but

they lost their occupation which mainly consisted in performing sacrifices for a fee which often times was very substantial and which constituted their chief source of living." See B.R. Ambedkar, "The Birth of a Counter-Revolution," in *Aśoka 2300 Jagajjyoti: Aśoka Commemoration Volume 1997 A.D./2541 B.E.*, ed. Hemendu Bikash Chowdhury (Calcutta: Bauddha, 1997), 39–43. But other authorities differ. See Hemchandra Raychaudhuri, *Political History of Ancient India* (Delhi: Oxford University Press, 1997), 314–17.

41. See discussion in Vidya Dhar Mahajan, *Ancient India* (New Delhi: S. Chand, 1974), 275–80; Thapar, *Aśoka and the Decline*, 197–212.

42. Thapar, *Aśoka and the Decline*, 310–21.

43. Mahajan, *Ancient India*, 277.

44. Lannoy, *The Speaking Tree*, 15–16 (see chap. 1, n. 10).

45. Wolpert, *New History*, 68 (see chap. 2, n. 55); Thapar, *Aśoka and the Decline*, 204.

46. Lannoy, *Speaking Tree*, 16.

47. Thapar, *Aśoka and the Decline*, 207.

48. Ibid., 207–12.

49. Wolpert, *New History*, 69.

50. Arnold J. Toynbee, *Mankind and Mother Earth: A Narrative History of the World* (New York: Oxford University Press, 1976), 229.

51. Giles, *The Travels of Fa-hsien*, 47–48 (see chap. 5, n. 2).

Chapter 7: Ashoka's Legacy

1. John S. Strong, "Images of Aśoka," in *King Aśoka and Buddhism: Historical and Literary Studies*, ed. Anuradha Seneviratna (Kandy, Sri Lanka: Buddhist Publication Society, 1994), 121.

2. Dipak Kumar Barua, "Emperor Aśoka and Human Rights," in *Aśoka 2300 Jagajjyoti: Aśoka Commemoration Volume 1997 A.D./2541 B.E.*, ed. Hemendu Bikash Chowdhury (Calcutta: Bauddha Dharmankur Sabha [The Bengal Buddhist Association], 1997), 117–24.

3. C. Pandering Bhatta, "The Environmental Context: Aśokan Approach," in *Aśoka 2300 Jagajjyoti*, 125–27 (see n. 2).

4. Gita Mehta, "Ashoka, Beloved of the Gods," *Tricycle: The Buddhist Review* (Winter 1998): 125–27.

5. Thapar, *Aśoka and the Decline of the Mauryas*, 125, n. 4 (see chap. 2, n. 49).

6. Mehta, "Ashoka, Beloved," 25.

7. Jawaharlal Nehru, "The Aśoka Chakra and the National Flag of India," in *Aśoka 2300 Jagajjyoti* (see note 2), 168.

8. Charles F. Keyes, "Buddhist Pilgrimage Centers and the Twelve Year Cycle: Northern Thai Moral Orders in Space and Time," *History of Religions* 15, no. 1 (1975): 78.

9. Richard Gombrich, "Aśoka: The Great Upāsaka," in *King Aśoka and Buddhism*, 6 (see n. 1).

10. Buyantyn Dashtseren, "Aśoka's Principle of Unity of State and Religion in Mongolia," in *Aśoka 2300 Jagajjyoti*, 159–61 (see n. 2).

11. Tambiah, *World Conqueror and World Renouncer*, 54 (see chap. 1, n. 19).

12. Thapar, *Aśoka and the Decline*, 42, 45.

13. Ibid., 45.

14. Strong, *The Legend of King Aśoka*, 24 (see chap. 1, n. 20).

15. Trevor Ling, *The Buddha: Buddhist Civilization in India and Ceylon* (New York: Charles Scribner's Sons, 1973), 200.

16. Keay, *India: A History*, 115–17 (see chap. 1, n. 27).

17. Ling, *Buddha*, 198.

18. Arnold J. Toynbee, *Civilization on Trial* (New York: Oxford University Press, 1948), 53.

19. Thapar, *Aśoka and the Decline*, 261 (translation of the Bhabra Minor Rock Inscription).

20. Wolpert, *New History*, 320 (see chap. 2, n. 55).

21. Sangharakshita, *Ambedkar and Buddhism* (Glasgow, UK: Windhorse, 1986), 10.

22. Ibid., 46.

23. Ibid., 48–49.

24. Ibid., 56.

25. Ibid., 111.

26. Ibid., 109, citing B. R. Ambedkar, *The Untouchables*, 3rd ed. (Balrampur, U.P., India: Bharatiya Bauddha Shiksha Prishad Shravastri, 1997), 101; India's constitution abolished untouchability, becoming law on January 26, 1950. In 1955 the Untouchability Act was passed, setting out various legal remedies and penalties for acts of discrimination against untouchables (now more commonly referred to as Dalits). The Indian government also established "affirmative action" quotas for employment of exuntouchables and reserved seats in state legislatures and universities. Wolpert, *New History*, 358, 365–66. The political power of untouchables also grew immensely in independent India, including the election of Dalits to head state governments. But in some rural areas, the brutal discrimination that Ambedkar experienced is virtually unchanged: "Still today in India," a 2007 account reports, "a Dalit…can be killed for accidentally brushing against a cast Hindu…In public schools, Dalit children may be allowed into class with caste children, but they often have to sit apart and are made to eat a distance from the other children." Mira Kamdar, *Planet India* (New York: Scribner, 2007), 165.

27. Sangharakshita, *Ambedkar and Buddhism*, 79.

28. Ibid., 127–28.

29. Ibid., 128.

30. H. L. Seneviratne, *The Work of Kings: The New Buddhism in Sri Lanka* (Chicago: University of Chicago Press, 1999), 22–23.

31. In Sri Lanka the Bodhi is also called the Bo tree.

32. Tambiah, *Buddhism Betrayed?*, 75 (see chap. 5, n. 9).

33. Ibid., 1, citing the *Mahavamsa*, chap. 25, vv. 101–11.

34. Seneviratne, *Work of Kings*, 21.

35. Tambiah, *Buddhism Betrayed?* 106.

36. Ibid., 60.

37. Ibid., 20.

38. B. G. Gokhale, *Ancient India History and Culture* (Calcutta: Asia, 1956), 47.

39. Israel Selvanayagam, "Aśoka and Arjuna as Counterfigures Standing on the Field of Dharma: An Historical-Hermeneutical Perspective," *History of Religions* 32, no. 1 (August 1992): 59–76, 61–65.

40. Ibid., 61–62.

41. Ibid., 61.

42. Ibid., 63.

43. Swami Paramananda, trans., "The Blessed Lord's Song, Sriman-Bhagavad-Gita," in *The Wisdom of India*, ed. Lin Yutang (London: Michael Joseph, 1949), ii, 31, 33, 58.

44. Ibid., iii, 35; xviii, 47, 64, 103.

45. G. C. Haughton, ed., *The Institutes of Manu* (New Delhi: Cosmo Publications, 1982), 10.97, quoted in Selvanayagam, "Aśoka and Arjuna," 66.

46. Selvanayagam, "Aśoka and Arjuna," 66.

47. Swami Paramananda, trans., *Bhagavad Gita*, xi, 32, 33; ii, 22; xviii, 6, 58, 86–89, 100.

48. Jacqueline Hirst, "Upholding the World: Dharma in the Bhagavadgita," in *The Fruits of Our Desiring: An Enquiry into the Ethics of the Bhagavadgita for Our Times*, ed. Julius Lipner (Calgary, Canada: Bayeux Arts, 1997), 48–66.

49. Paramananda, *Bhagavad Gita*, xi, 33, 87.

50. Tilak, quoted in Wolpert, *New History*, 261.

51. Wolpert, *New History*, 261.

52. Selvanayagam, "Aśoka and Arjuna," 74.

53. Ibid.

54. Ibid., 74–75.

55. Lannoy, *The Speaking Tree*, 296 (see chap. 1, n. 10).

56. Nick Sutton, "Aśoka and Yudhisthira: A Historical Setting for the Ideological Tension of the *Mahābhārata*?" *Religion* 27 (1997): 333–41.

57. J. A. B. van Buitenen, trans., *The Mahābhārata*, vol. 2, *The Book of the Assembly Hall* and *The Book of the Forest* (Chicago: University of Chicago Press, 1975), 3.31.1–46, 280–81.

58. Ibid., 3.34.55–60, 289.

59. R. C. Zaehner, *Hinduism* (Oxford: Oxford University Press, 1966), 118.

60. Kisari Mohan Ganguli, trans., *The Mahabharata of Krishna-Dwaipayana Vyasa*, 3rd ed., vol. 8, pt. 1 (Santi Parva, New Delhi: Munshiram Manoharial, 1973), 12.167, 366.

61. For an exposition of this analysis, see Zaehener, *Hinduism*, 114–24; Lannoy, *The Speaking Tree*, 302–6.

62. Ganguli, *Mahabharata*, 368.

63. Zaehner, *Hinduism*, 116.

64. Cambridge historian Percival Spear describes the Ashokan-Buddhist influence on Hinduism as follows: "To sum up, it may be said broadly that in India Buddhism acted as the reagent to Hinduism. It acted as the stimulus for the development of the parent cult and passed away when it had done its work.... It can also claim to have introduced a moral content into the concept of *dharma* or re-

ligious duty; and in particular the introduction of compassion to the list of the Hindu virtues.... It was Buddhist influence which ended the Vedic and post-Vedic phase of Hinduism, a religion of nature worship and sacrifice.... The Brahmins triumphed but only at the price of taking Buddhist ideas into partnership." Percival Spear, *India: A Modern History* (Ann Arbor: University of Michigan Press, 1961), 68.

Chapter 8: To Uphold the World

1. Michel de Montaigne, "On Cannibals," in *Essays,* trans. J. M. Cohen (London: Penguin Books, 1993), 118.
2. Ibid.
3. Ibid.
4. Soros, *Crisis of Global Capitalism,* 84 (see chap. 3, n. 8).
5. Michael Hardt and Antonio Negri, *Empire* (Cambridge, MA: Harvard University Press, 2000).
6. This is a blurb from the dust cover of Hardt and Negri's *Empire.* The attribution is listed as Slavoj Zizek (a famous Slovenian philosopher).
7. Hardt and Negri, *Empire,* xii (emphasis in original).
8. Ibid., 321, 346.
9. Ibid., xiv.
10. This perception of the tension between a globalized world of instrumental, economistic rationality and the exacerbated quest for an anchor of self-identity is increasingly common in many contemporary analyses. Alain Touraine, the French sociologist, for example, sees our dilemma as "a break between the instrumental world and the symbolic world, between technology and values." "What is emerging from the ruins of modern societies and their institutions," he observes, "is, on the one hand, global networks of production, consumption and communication and, on the other hand, a return to community...throughout the world there are more and more identity-based groupings and associations, sects, cults and nationalisms based on a common sense of belonging and they are becoming stronger." See Alain Touraine, *Can We Live Together: Equality and Difference,* trans. David Macey (Stanford, CA: Stanford University Press, 2000), 2, 5.
11. Arnold J. Toynbee, *Civilization on Trial* (New York: Oxford University Press, 1948), 7.
12. Thucydides, *Complete Writings,* 14–15 (see chap. 3, n. 65).
13. Seventh pillar edict, trans. Thapar, *Aśoka and the Decline of the Mauryas,* 266 (see chap. 2, n. 49).
14. Sen, *Development as Freedom,* 85 (see chap. 2, n. 46).
15. Martha C. Nussbaum, *Women and Human Development: The Capabilities Approach* (Cambridge: Cambridge University Press, 2000), 70.
16. Ibid., 5.
17. Ibid. (emphasis in original).
18. Ibid., 78–80.
19. Ibid., 195.

20. Ibid., 157.

21. Hardt and Negri, *Empire,* 413.

22. This reason is philosophically called transcendental reason, based on Immanuel Kant's terminology: "Modernity as a civilizational project is predicated on the wager that transcendence can be represented as no more than transcendental reason yet still maintain its authoritative nature and sacred aura: Immanuel Kant's 'starry heavens above and moral law within' or the 'self-evident' truths of the Declaration of Independence." See Seligman, *Modernity's Wager,* 29 (see chap. 5, n. 45).

23. Seligman, *Modernity's Wager,* 121–22.

24. J. A. B. van Buitenen, trans., *The Mahābhārata,* vols. 2, 3, *The Book of the Forest* (Chicago: University of Chicago Press, 1975), 3.31.46, 281.

25. Seligman, *Modernity's Wager,* 47–48, 54–55. Eric Voegelin (1901–85), whom Seligman cites several times, viewed the disintegration of a shared belief in a transcendental reality (a use of the word transcendental totally different from the Kantian sense discussed in n. 22) as the underlying political and cultural crisis of the West, spurring the creation of ersatz political religions, such as fascism, communism—and modern democratic liberalism. No modern thinker has engaged this theme more deeply than Voegelin, whose collected works, published by the University of Missouri Press, total thirty-four volumes. For an introduction to his thought, see Michael P. Federici, *Eric Voegelin: The Restoration of Order* (Wilmington, DE: ISI Books, 2002).

26. Vaclav Havel, "Faith in the World," *Civilization* (May 1998): 52.

27. Hans Küng, *Global Responsibility: In Search of a New World Ethic* (New York: Continuum, 1993), 29–30.

28. Havel, "Faith in the World," 50–53.

29. Küng, *Global Responsibility,* 53.

30. Castells, *Information Age,* vol. 1, 477–78 (see chap. 3, n. 44).

31. Salvatore Frigerio, *Camaldoli: Historical, Spiritual, and Artistic Notes* (1991; repr., Verucchio, Italy: Pazzini Editore, 1997).

32. Clarence J. Glacken, *Traces on the Rhodian Shore: Nature and Culture in Western Thought from Ancient Times to the End of the Eighteenth Century* (Berkeley: University of California Press, 1967), 339, cited in Larry L. Rasmussen, *Earth Community, Earth Ethics* (Maryknoll, NY: Orbis Books, 1996), 270.

33. The Jubilee 2000 campaign for debt relief has continued in the United Kingdom as the Jubilee Debt Campaign and in the United States as the Jubilee USA Network.

34. I owe much of this analysis to two works: M. Douglas Meeks, *God the Economist: The Doctrine of God and Political Economy* (Minneapolis: Fortress Press, 1989), and Rasmussen, *Earth Community.*

35. Aristotle, *The Politics,* I viii 1256b26, I ix, 79–82 (see chap. 1, n. 8).

36. Bell, *Cultural Contradictions of Capitalism,* 223 (see chap. 3, n. 39).

37. Ibid., 281–82.

38. Rasmussen, *Earth Community,* 94.

39. Ibid.

40. Meeks, *God the Economist,* 171.

41. Exodus 23:11.

42. Deuteronomy 24:19–21.

43. Leviticus 25:10.

44. Meeks, *God the Economist,* 89.

45. Ibid., 76; Rasmussen, *Earth Community,* 92. But *the Oxford English Dictionary* states that "there is no ground for the assumption that *stigweard* originally meant 'keeper of the pig-sties.'"

46. Rasmussen, *Earth Community,* 92. See further Rasmussen's discussion of stewardship, 23–36.

47. Adam B. Seligman, in *Modernity's Wager,* argues that the U.S. political system is not simply grounded in enlightenment, reason, or positive law; it is rooted in a sense of transcendent grace, in individual rights perceived as being grounded in God and nature. This line of reasoning is particularly interesting, since while espoused by a liberal social thinker, it repeats certain arguments of the American religious Right. Certainly, at moments of great historical crisis—Lincoln's addresses in the Civil War, for example—the appeal to the transcendent grounding of the past and future of the American Republic has been a defining characteristic.

48. Vaclav Havel, "The Need for Transcendence in the Postmodern World" (address, Independence Hall, Philadelphia, July 4, 1994), www.worldtrans.org/whole/havelspeech.html.

49. Albert O. Hirschman, "The Search for Paradigms as a Hindrance to Understanding," *World Politics* 22 (April 1970): 329–43.

50. Ibid., 329.

51. Ibid., 335.

52. Ibid., 340. For an entertaining and provocative essay on this theme, see Nassim Nicholas Taleb, *The Black Swan: The Impact of the Highly Improbable* (New York: Random House, 2007).

53. James C. Scott, *Seeing Like a State: How Certain Schemes to Improve the Human Condition Have Failed* (New Haven, CT: Yale University Press, 1998), 4–5.

54. Ibid., 342.

55. Ibid., 345.

56. Hirschman, "Search for Paradigms," 338, 342.

57. Stephen Toulmin, *Cosmopolis: The Hidden Agenda of Modernity* (Chicago: University of Chicago Press, 1990), 69–71.

58. Ibid., 30–35.

59. Seligman, *Modernity's Wager,* 128.

60. He speaks of the "totalizing Jacobean project, one which has all too often conflated a substantive rationality with an instrumental one and has sought to promulgate an overarching…all-encompassing ideology (whether of the right or left)." What is needed is "a midpoint between nihilism and postmodern relativism, on the one hand, and absolutist claims of both faith and reason, on the other." Seligman, *Modernity's Wager,* 128, 138.

61. Milosz, "Recovering a Reverence for Being," 4–9, 8 (see chap. 3, n. 68).

62. Brand, *Clock of the Long Now* (see chap. 1, n. 25).

63. Ibid., 8–9.

64. Vaclav Havel, "The Spiritual Roots of Democracy," *Lapis* no. 1 (Spring 1997): 30 (emphasis added).

65. Ibid. (emphasis added).

66. Erik H. Erikson, *Gandhi's Truth: On the Origins of Militant Nonviolence* (New York: W. W. Norton, 1969), 156–57, 200, 217, 385.

67. Toynbee, *Civilization on Trial,* 80–81.

68. Octavio Paz, *Itinerary: An Intellectual Journey,* trans. Jason Wilson (New York: Harcourt, 1999).

69. Ibid., 92–93.

70. Ibid., 95.

71. Ibid.

72. Ibid., 96.

73. Ibid., 96–97.

74. Albert Schweitzer, *Out of My Life and Thought: An Autobiography* (New York: Mentor Books, 1960), 126.

75. Ibid., 110.

76. Ibid.

77. Ibid., 124.

78. Ibid., 126–27.

79. Paul Johnson, *The Civilization of Ancient Egypt* (New York: HarperCollins, 1999), 50.

80. Ibid., 136.

81. Weber, "Politics as a Vocation," 123 (see chap. 1, n. 13).

82. Reinhold Niebuhr to James B. Conant, March 6, 1946, quoted in Richard Fox, *Reinhold Niebuhr: A Biography* (New York: Pantheon, 1985), 225.

83. To cite one example among many, "It is essential to arrange for a regulatory framework whose task would be to bring moral norms and economic norms into coherence. If the world's problem is that today global consciousness is ahead of political reality, as debates concerning medicine and debt have demonstrated, it cannot be deprived of a practical outlet for long." See Daniel Cohen, *Globalization and Its Enemies* (Cambridge, MA: MIT Press, 2006), 160–61

84. Rabindramath Tagore, "Aśoka: The Great Emperor," in *Aśoka 2300 Jagajjyoti*, 9 (see chap. 7, n.2).

criminal law, 29–30, 76, 82–84, 131;
on *danda,* 70–71, 84, 87; on development, 71–75; on *dharma,* 28–29; on
diplomacy, 66–67, 85–90; discovery
of, 9, 10, 67–68; on economy, 6–7,
35, 71–82; edicts of Ashoka and,
130; on environment, 72–75, 130;
on espionage, 28–29, 30, 67, 68–71,
75–76, 81, 82, 87–88, 131; on ethics,
xiv, 90–93, 131; on force, 70–71,
72, 84, 87, 131–32; on government,
28–29, 135, 148; on housing, 30; on
justice, 71; Kautilya in, 26; on kingship, 68–71, 86, 131; on labor, 30,
77–80; on law, 82–84; market fundamentalism and, 42; on military,
72, 85; on nonviolence, 92; origins
of, 67–68; on politics, 68, 90–93; on
prison administration, 131; on realpolitik, 18, 28–29, 66–67; on regulation, 75–82; on religion, 29, 131; on
security, 67, 68–71; on taxation, 90;
on trade, 14–15, 30, 72, 76–77, 134;
on treasury, 72, 80–82; on war, 33,
86–87, 89–90; on wealth, xiv, 28–29,
35, 42, 68, 72, 86–88, 131–32, 155;
on welfare, 30, 69, 70, 90, 131; on
women, 30
Aryas, 80
Asanhimitta, 34
Ashoka: accomplishments of generally, ix–x, xiii–xiv; ancestry of, 14;
appearance of, 9, 98–99, 100; as
archetype, 7; Buddhism, conversion to, 33–34, 96, 99–100, 143,
180, 183–84; Buddhism, mythology
of, 9–10, 32–36, 97–99; Buddhism,
spread of, ix, 17–18, 34, 101–4, 138,
139–40, 141, 183; as *chakravartin,*
17–18, 98, 99; children fathered by,
33, 34, 35, 98, 100–101, 106, 109,
123, 140, 144; daily schedule of, 69;
death of, 108–9; decline of, 133–35;
as deontologist, 31, 37; *dharma* and,
101–4, 109; diplomacy of, 33, 34, 35,

123; economy of, 71; as fierce, xi,
100–101, 109, 122, 180–82; gifts and,
98–99, 104–9, 110–11; globalization
and, xiii–xiv, 111; government of,
xiv, 6, 7; in history, 8–11, 19, 32–38,
112–35, 141; instruction tours by,
118, 122, 130; in Jainism, 10, 32; as
Jaya, 98–99, 109; justice and, 49;
Kautilya complements, 18, 128–33,
148, 182; legacy of, 135, 136–55,
180–82; myth of, 8–11, 32–38,
96–111, 119, 123, 141, 180; names
of, 3, 100, 104, 109, 114, 122, 180;
pillar capital of, 16–18; as righteous,
103–4; succession by, 32; symbols
of, 137–38; torture by, 9–10, 33, 96,
99–100; tragedy of, 180–82; wives
of, 33, 34–35, 100–101, 109. *See also*
edicts of Ashoka
Ashoka's Hell, 9–10, 33, 96, 99–100
*Ashokavadana:* Ashoka's Hell in,
99–100; behavior in, 119; *dharma* in,
102–3; diplomacy in, 123; festivals
in, 105–6; gift of dirt in, 98–99;
legacy of, 139; origins of, 32, 97–98;
Pushyamitra Sungha in, 110; Tissarakha and Kunala in, 100–101
Asia Minor, 22
*asramas,* 92
*astika* sects, 23–24
astrology, 88
Augustine, Saint, 121
Aurelius, Marcus, 47
authority, 163–65, 169
*Autobiography* (Mill), 44–45
*avadana,* 97–98
Axial Age, 15–18, 97, 163, 173, 181

Babylon, 21, 119
Bacon, 171
Bamberg, Bishop of, 165
Bana, 67
behavior: in *Ashokavadana,* 119; *dharma*
and, 119, 129; edicts of Ashoka on,
x, xi, 2, 116–17, 118–19, 119–20,